*The Future of the
Christian Sunday*

The FUTURE of the
CHRISTIAN SUNDAY

by CHRISTOPHER KIESLING, O.P.

SHEED & WARD   NEW YORK

© Sheed and Ward, Inc. 1970
Library of Congress Catalog Card Number: 71-106155
Standard Book Number: 8362-1229-0

Manufactured in the United States of America

To Marjorie Anne

ACKNOWLEDGMENTS

Portions of this book are revised versions of articles or parts of articles which were previously published in periodicals and to which various publishers hold the copyrights. Acknowledgement is made to B. Herder Book Company, St. Louis, Mo., for permission to use in Chapter I material which originally appeared in *Cross and Crown* 19 (1967), pp. 133-45, under the title "The Threat to the Christian Sunday"; to *Review for Religious*, St. Louis, Mo., for permission to use in the first part of Chapter IV material which originally appeared in that journal, Vol. 27 (1968), pp. 281-88, under the title "Celebration of the Paschal Mystery: the Eucharist"; to Joseph F. Wagner, Inc., New York, for permission to use in the latter part of Chapter VII and in Chapter VIII material which originally appeared in *The Homiletic and Pastoral Review* 68 (1967), pp. 23-29; 113-21, under the title "Sunday Rest: A New Approach."

Acknowledgment is also made to the Westminster Press, Philadelphia, Pa., and to SCM Press, Ltd., London, England, for permission to quote in Chapter II from Willy Rordorf, *Sunday: The History of the Day of Rest and Worship in the Earliest Centuries of the Christian Church* (1968); to the McGraw-Hill Book Company, New York, for permission to quote in Chapter III from Louis F. Hartman, *Encyclopedic Dictionary of the Bible* (1963); to Viktor E. Frankl for permission to quote in Chapter V from his book *Man's Search for Meaning* (New York: Washington Square Press, Inc., 1963), and to the America Press, New York, for permission to quote in Chapter VI from *The Documents of Vatican II,* Walter M. Abbott, ed. (1966).

Scriptural quotations are from *The Jerusalem Bible,* except where it is noted that the Confraternity of Christian Doctrine translation has been used. Acknowledgment is made to Doubleday & Company, Inc., Garden City, New York, and Dartow, Longman & Todd, Ltd., London, England, for permission to quote from *The Jersualem Bible* (copyright © 1966 by Darton, Longman & Todd, Ltd. and Doubleday & Company, Inc. Reprinted by permission of the publisher), and to the Confraternity of Christian Doctrine, Washington, D.C., for permission to quote from its edition of the Bible.

FOREWORD

This book is about much more than the Christian Sunday. The future of the Christian Sunday involves several problems currently plaguing Christians and the Church, including the proper Christian attitude toward the world and hence the very meaning of the Gospel. It raises questions about the style of Christian life appropriate in a technological culture, the territorial parish system, and the role of priests and ministers in the life and mission of the Christian people. In view of the intimate connection between the Christian Sunday and so many other aspects of Christian life, it is surprising that in this era of challenge to almost every element of traditional Christianity, the Christian Sunday has escaped widespread radical questioning.

This relative silence about the Christian Sunday may be a sign that for very many people it is already dead, an institution of the past that is now simply a subject for historical research and irrelevant sermons. Or the silence may be a sign of blindness to the actual situation. Enough traces of the Christian Sunday yet exist to give the impression that it is still a living if not robustly healthy institution, whereas it is, in fact, very sick. In any case, the Christian people—Catholic, Orthodox, and Protestant—ought to face the plight of the Christian Sunday and evolve some strategy to cope with the pastoral problems implied in it. This book is meant to contribute to this confrontation and pastoral planning.

The problem of the Christian Sunday's future is addressed here as it emerges in the United States, even though it is a problem confronting the universal Church. It is approached in a way which will be meaningful to Catholics, Protestants, and Orthodox insofar as this is possible given the diverse origins of the problem in the different traditions, the diversity of language and theology in which each naturally discusses the problem, and the differences of ecclesial organization and life in each of the Churches. No claim is made that this book presents a strictly ecumenical theology and pastoral program by drawing equally from all the traditions; but it is hoped that what is proposed here will be helpful not only to Catholics but to all Christians and all the Churches in today's secular, technological culture, which is so different from any of the cultures encountered by Christianity in the past.

I wish to thank the following people for reading an early draft of this book and offering their suggestions:

Rev. Richard J. Anderson, former pastor of St. John's Episcopal Church, Dubuque, Iowa, and now pastor of Grace Episcopal Church in Buffalo, New York; Rev. Angelo Kasemeotis, pastor of St. Elias the Prophet Greek Orthodox Church, Dubuque, Iowa; Mrs. Margarethe B. J. Brown, Secretary of Studies, Commission on Ecumenical Mission and Relations of the United Presbyterian Church in the United States of America, New York City; Rev. Carl Trutter, O.P., Director of Apostolic Works at the Aquinas Institute of Theology, Dubuque, Iowa, and Mr. Leonard F. X. Mayhew, editor of Sheed and Ward, New York. Any deficiencies in this book, however, must be attributed to me.

I thank also the typists, especially Brother Joachim M. Thiel, O.P., Mrs. Ursula Neyens, and others who worked to prepare the manuscript and see it through to publication. A debt of gratitude is also owed to my colleagues at the Aquinas Institute of Theology for both their encouragement and their assuming of tasks that otherwise would have fallen to me and prevented me from completing this work.

CHRISTOPHER KIESLING, O.P.
Dubuque, Iowa

Contents

The Future of the Christian Sunday

1

THREATS TO
THE CHRISTIAN SUNDAY

Christians have observed Sunday in various ways during the course of history. The oldest observance is worship. In the early Church this consisted of a service of the Word and a celebration of the Eucharist, and these remained the constituents of Sunday worship until the Reformation, although during the Middle Ages reception of the Eucharist by the laity was rare. Since the Reformation, Sunday worship for Protestants has generally been a service of the Word with the reading of Scripture, sermon, hymns, and prayers; the Eucharist has been celebrated only three or four times a year, although today Protestantism is gradually restoring the weekly celebration. Roman Catholics have had the Mass, which, although essentially a liturgy of the Word and of the Eucharist, was until recently shrouded in the obscurity of Latin and obsolete ritual. By custom at various times and places Sunday worship also included Matins or Vespers or, for Roman Catholics, Benediction of the Blessed Sacrament.

Since the fourth century rest from work has also been a way in which Christians have observed Sunday. Here too there has been variety. Christians have abstained from different kinds of activities from century to century and from country to country. In the Protestant Churches the observance of rest has been generally more austere than in the Roman Catholic Church and at times has overshadowed worship in importance.

More significant than the particular forms of worship in which Christians have engaged and the particular kinds of activities from which they have abstained has been the understanding that they have had about Sunday and the conviction of faith that they have poured into its observance. The day was invested with the sacredness of divine sanction by applying to it the commandment, "Keep holy the Sabbath." It was a day of freedom from a miserable world of work for the joys of nature, family, and the worship of God. Yet because it was not occupied with work, it was a day fraught with moral danger, and many pleasures which at present are regarded as innocent were then proscribed.

Today forces in American culture and in the Christian community are menacing the institution of the Christian Sunday. An obvious threat is business. A few decades ago in the United States stores were rarely open on Sunday, except some corner groceries, a few drug stores, some filling stations, and places of entertainment. Now, however, shopping can be done seven days a week. No one needs to plan ahead because stores supplying an incredible variety of goods for an almost inconceivable number of needs are open throughout the day and night. A familiar advertisement is "Open All Day Sunday," and on this day it is a common sight to see shopping center parking lots packed with the cars of customers.

The traditional Christian Sunday is also menaced by contemporary forms of recreation, which are becoming increasingly sophisticated and require large investments of time, attention, and energy. Assisted by high wages, credit cards, short working weeks, and fast transportation, recreational activities become weekend excursions. Skiing is a good example. One does not ski in one's backyard or in the local community's park for a few hours on a Sunday afternoon. One usually has to travel some distance to a ski resort, and upon arrival, make the most of every minute, either on the slopes or in the pleasant surroundings of "aprés-ski" conviviality. The mind may be swept clear of the cobwebs of business concerns when Monday morning comes, but God may have been completely forgotten.

Because skiing, boating, mountain climbing, hunting, spelunking, and touring are "recreation" and not "work," they have been accepted as quite in harmony with the Christian Sunday. But our Puritan forefathers would not have thought the same of activities which absorb so much attention and energy, and which focus for so long on human actions, skills, and arts.

The frequent necessity of contemporary forms of recreation make them an especially serious though subtle
threat to the Christian Sunday. Many business and
professional men can get necessary relaxation from
their work and time for their families only if they can
escape from telephones. They must leave home and the
city for a cabin on the lake, a boat on the river, or a
camping site in the woods. They begin their period of
rest Friday evening or Saturday morning and cannot
reasonably be expected to return from their hideaway
until Sunday evening or, if it is a long holiday weekend,
until Monday evening. Wherever they may be, they
may find it impossible or very inconvenient to attend
church on Sunday, certainly in their own parish. This
situation could be dismissed as no serious problem if it
were a matter of only a few people and a couple of
Sundays a year, but it increasingly involves more and
more people and several or even most Sundays a year.

A third threat to the familiar Christian Sunday is the
hectic activism of contemporary American life. Life
moves at a rapid pace today. Cities are in the throes of
renewal, rebuilding, and redevelopment. Telephones,
teletype, and television link metropolitan centers with
one another so that business, abetted by computers and
business machines of every sort, can be carried on at a
breakneck speed. A highly competitive economy, con-
centrated on producing and selling consumer goods,
continuously demands new markets and new products.
Advertising must be fresh and imaginative. Selling and
buying must increase in volume and tempo. Carried

forward by the current, political and social activities are speeded up to keep pace with the economic activity with which they are intricately bound. Whether it be in international affairs, state or city government, local community projects for better schools, or neighborhood renewal, there is a mounting daily demand for meetings of bureaus, boards, and committees to deal with an increasing number of problems.

In such an atmosphere, Sunday as a day of rest is almost a traumatic experience for many people. With jangled nerves and excited imaginations, the only form rest can take is diversion—activity which is different in kind from what is done all week long but which moves at the same rapid pace. The idea that time should be given on Sunday to a slow-moving service of worship, to reading the Bible and Christian literature, and to contemplating the wonders of God's creation is nearly unthinkable for most Americans. They need some kind of activity which can utilize their agitated energies. They find in the traditional Christian Sunday only boredom and restlessness which are psychologically more fatiguing than refreshing.

When the forces of life clash with social structures, the forces of life eventually conquer. American society will form the personalities of its members to fit its activist culture so that the hectic activism of American life will eventually swamp the traditional Christian Sunday.

A fourth threat to the centuries-old Christian Sunday is the disintegration of social life. In their book, *The Split-Level Trap,*[1] Richard and Katherine Gordon, and

Max Gunther, contrast life in the modern suburban town with life in an idealized rural community or industrial-town neighborhood, the community that once was typical of America. In this typical community people knew each other well. Most were old residents and many had been born and reared in the community. Families—grandparents, parents, children, uncles, cousins—all lived together. They had similar tastes, values, and understandings because they had been near each other for so long and had shared the same experiences. They talked the same language, enjoyed the same games, aided each other in carrying out life's chores and in suffering through its crises.

The mobile suburb is quite different. It is a place of perpetual coming and going, and only a few families have roots in the community. As a result there is a lack of loving interest in the town as well as a lack of social machinery by which people can become easily acquainted. The suburb, in fact, is not populated by families but by the spun-off nuclei of families. With relatives left behind, husband, wife, and children have come here to live by themselves and to face life alone.

What is true of the suburban civil community is true also of the suburban Christian parish community. Only a relatively small percentage of the parishioners know one another well. Their strongest social ties—with relatives or long-standing friends—bind them to people outside the parish. They do not regard their Sunday worship in the parish church as a gathering in which they will share with others the joy and consolation of their common faith and experiences. Sunday worship is their individual fulfillment of their duty toward God, their own expression of their private religious commitment. The fact that they discharge their duty and profess their faith with the particular people who live in the same territory is circumstantial. They could just as well, and perhaps more enjoyably, fulfill their obligation and acknowledge their faith elsewhere.

Similar disintegration affects city neighborhoods, both the older ones and those which have been renewed. Even the family has disintegrated. Once the children reach adolescence, its members are drawn away from each other in different directions by diverse interests, values, and friends. The generation gap, which is so deep and obvious in contemporary society in comparison with past ages, separates parents from children more powerfully than walls or distance. Geographically also the family is split up: one member is away at college; another has driven to a nearby town for a weekend with a friend made at summer camp; a third is married and living in another city. Except for the young children and their parents, the family does not go to church together on Sunday or spend the day together in recreation. This social disintegration threatens the Christian Sunday both as the traditional day of the Christian community's corporate worship and as the traditional day of family sharing.

A fifth threat to the Christian Sunday is the increasing secularization of American culture. Secularization is the historical development wherein men cease to be inspired with awe, fear, fascination, reverence, and a sense of dependence before nature; they cease to regard nature as the revealer of the holy, the sacred, the divine, a dimension of reality beyond empirical experience which ultimately controls the events of nature, human life, and history. The rise of pluralism—a concomitant of complex industrial society—and the adoption of the scientific method in all disciplines seeking to understand the universe and man are responsible for this trend. Man no longer stands awestruck before nature and his own existence; he can control them, or if he cannot yet do so, he believes that he will either control them some day or, at least, be able to provide for what he cannot control. In any case, he must learn to accept his limitations. Belief in an eternal world—a realm of the divine beyond this age, this time, this *saeculum* of the natural and the human—is gone. There is no sacred beyond the secular; the sacred does not invade the secular.

Even when men still believe in a transcendent God, they are aware that he acts through the creatures he has created, especially through human intelligence and will. Thus, even the believer in God does not stand paralyzed and passive in awe before nature and human life and the puzzles and threats which they present to understanding and survival. Rather, he does something to unravel nature's and life's mysteries, and to improve the human condition in the face of threats. He does not wait for miracles—intrusions of the sacred into the secular sphere—to explain experience and to rescue him from suffering and death.

In life and culture undergoing secularization, the Christian Sunday is obviously threatened by replacement by the secular Sunday. The secular Sunday is a day of freedom from the demands imposed by the struggle for survival and a better life, and enables men to experience together the pleasures and joys created by their skills, artistry, technology, science, and wisdom. The Christian Sunday can embrace all this— though very often in the past it has not—but it adds time for worship of God and injects into all the day's activities the spirit of worship. In view of what has been said about the influence of secularization upon the practical conduct of life of even believers in God, it is likely that Sunday is predominantly secular even for many Christians today. They devote some time to worship of God, but their activity during the day is not suffused with a spirit of worship. Therefore, the threats to the Christian Sunday also come from within the Christian community itself.

The Christian Sunday has been handed down from generation to generation through the complex process of socialization by which societies pass on their heritages. In this process children accept as unquestionable reality whatever they are told about the way things are and about the properly human way of acting. In time, of course, their own intelligence awakens. They learn about other ways in which things are, and they meet people who think and act differently. They then begin to question what they have been told about reality, truth, and correct conduct. This is a critical stage for individuals and society, for the young will then either accept and internalize, i.e., make their own, what they have been taught, and thus continue society's heritage for another generation; or they will abandon what they have been taught and adopt ideas, values, and behavior which make more sense to them in the total situation in which they find themselves. Youth's revolt from parental views, ideals, and conduct is as old as mankind, though the degree of revolt, the extent of its expression, and its outcome depend upon the provisions which a society makes for this stage of youth's development.

This questioning and subsequent acceptance or abandonment of a society's heritage is not restricted to youth, although it is especially characteristic of that period of life and most evident then. Questioning and especially rejection of society's heritage by older people is less frequent but often more decisive for the course a society will take. Pope John XXIII's call for a reexamination of the life of the Catholic Church and his own breaks with centuries-old customs is a good example of how decisive can be the rejection of social heritage by older people: Pope John initiated a veritable upheaval in the Catholic Church.

In the past, when Christians, young or old, questioned the Sunday observance which they were taught as children, many factors operated to lead them to continue to accept it, though slight modifications were made to suit new circumstances. On the side of reaffirmation was the firm custom of the Christian community, backed by the American way of life and often by civil legislation. Strong family unity also exerted pressure which prevented external revolt if not interior questioning. The predominant Christian understanding of life provided a rationale that justified what society and the family said was the right thing to do: human destiny lay in future bliss with God in heaven or in future misery in hell; this world was badly tainted with sin, and life through this sinful world was a perilous journey; God was a loving but stern Father who commanded many actions for man's salvation, among them keeping holy the Sabbath; only at the risk of divine punishment in hell for eternity did a man dare disobey God's command. Such an understanding of life, together with the sense of values and the feelings that accompanied it, facilitated the acceptance by successive generations of the traditional Christian Sunday which family and society practiced.

This understanding of life no longer has a monopoly in the Christian community, which today harbors even Christian secularists and atheists. They are few and in the long run probably insignificant. But not insignificant are the many more Christians who, although they still hold for eternal life and for the pilgrim quality of human life in this world, no longer see the world as a sinful territory through which they are making a passage fraught with peril. Nor do they see God as a stern Father exacting the fulfillment of duties toward him under the threat of eternal punishment. Evil and sin they admit; ample evidence of their existence is seen in poverty, hunger, discrimination, mental illness, crime, riots, and wars. But the world is God's creation, basically good, and man is called by God to work with him in developing the surprising and seemingly inexhaustible potentialities of nature and man for God's ultimate glory and man's happiness. The good Christian life does not consist in obeying externally imposed laws, whether they are God's command to keep holy the Sabbath or the Catholic Church's Canon 1248 concerning Sunday observance. The good Christian life consists in wholeheartedly entering into the execution of God's plan for the development of creation, and, especially, man. The Word of God became man. He said that the Sabbath was made for man, not man for the Sabbath (Mark 2:27).

In such a view of life questions about the value of Sunday observance do not find answers which satisfactorily confirm the practices derived from previous generations. In this view Christian life does not consist in keeping a particular day "holy" but in making all days what God intended them to be for man. The traditional Christian Sunday is irrelevant to authentic Christian life. When and where men worship, when and where they leisurely enjoy God's and man's handiwork, do not depend upon a cycle of time and positive laws of God or Church, but upon the needs and opportunities presented by human life anywhere at any time. Worship of God and the celebration of creation, moreover, occur in the interaction of persons who open for one another the ways to God and the marvels of creation. Worship and celebration are free from dependence upon sacred objects, places, and times; they depend rather on community and personal encounter.

Internal rejection of the long-standing Christian Sunday based on this new Christian view of life can express itself today in external revolt more easily than it could in the past, for the barriers to external rejection have been lowered. American culture has become secularized to a great extent. Many non-Christians and new-thinking Christians in pluralistic American society do not follow the centuries-old Christian Sunday. Consequently anyone who wishes to abandon observance of the Christian Sunday does not need the daring that was required in the past to run counter to the accepted social custom. The pressure of the family has also been reduced; youth are scattered over the nation and the world in schools, jobs, and military service so that parents may not even know how their children observe Sunday. It is easier today, therefore, for young Christians or for those with a new understanding of Christian life simply to abandon the traditional Christian Sunday instead of accepting and continuing it with modifications, as past generations have done. Some young people and post-Vatican II Christians are, in fact, doing just that—abandoning the Christian Sunday.

In many ways, then, the traditional Christian Sunday is being threatened. How the Christian people should respond to this situation is the next consideration.

Notes

[1] (New York: Dell Publishing Co., 1964), pp. 43-47.

II

RESPONSE

Abandonment of the Christian Sunday appears to be a sensible response to the threats against it. Rest from work on Sunday cannot possibly be maintained in the future against the onslaught of business. More and more Christians will find it impossible to participate normally in American life and at the same time observe rest from work on Sunday. Moreover, there is no need today for Christians to abstain from work on Sunday.

Sunday rest for Christians began only in the fourth century and was originally a humanitarian social institution established by civil authority to regulate the cycle of work and leisure; only subsequently was the rest of Sunday invested with religious significance.[1] The humanization which the Christian Sunday, the Jewish Sabbath, and the Moslem Friday promoted in the harsh world of past centuries no longer needs religious reinforcement. In the United States today, the five-day work week is the rule, and a four- or even three-day week is being discussed. Workers enjoy vacations of two, three, or four weeks, plus holidays. Both management and labor are concerned about ensuring ample leisure for workers. Indeed, one of the most urgent problems at present is the use of the abundant leisure which men already have as a result of our modern technological society. It would be well to recognize these facts and to drop Sunday rest as a Christian practice.

As for Sunday worship, many Christians have already abandoned it. The 1968 Gallup Poll on church attendance reported that only 65 percent of Catholics and 38 percent of Protestants queried in seven selected weeks during the year had attended church in that week.[2] These figures, low as they are compared with the ideal and practice of the past, are still higher than those of ten other nations in the Western world. However, since half of the Christian people are not being reached by Sunday worship (and its lack of attraction for young people is common knowledge), it should be abandoned and energies devoted to some other means of worshiping God and developing Christian community.

Sunday worship originated in a deep awareness of the need to build up the body of the Risen Christ,[3] and for the early Christians it was extremely important that the whole community assemble. Indeed, this corporate worship was so important to them that during persecutions they risked their lives to meet for it.

The large congregations in today's urban and sub-

and day, weather, and geography, for the technology which provides central heating and cooling, electric light, irrigation, and automobiles enables men to bypass many of the rhythms and restrictions of nature. Their activities are instead determined by their needs in the various spheres of life—biological, psychic, social—whenever and wherever these needs are felt. The activities of clergy and laity in fulfillment of their responsibilities to God and their mission to the world must also be governed, not by sacred times and places like Sunday morning and the church building, but by the needs of men and the opportunities to satisfy these needs whenever and wherever these opportunities occur.

All this implies the need for new styles of Christian life, community, witness, and service for clergy, laity, and religious. But maintenance of the traditional Christian Sunday is a ball and chain on the development of such new styles. Retention of Sunday corporate worship means large churches to provide space and opportunities for participation for all the members of each parish. It means staffing churches with clergy to preside over this Sunday worship, even though during the week some of this clergy is occupied only with busy-work. Respectable Sunday worship requires preparation during the week: a homily or sermon relating the liturgy to the daily news and the questions people are asking (inevitably controversial ones); account taken of the commentary to be given so that it ties in with the theme of the liturgy and the sermon; similar preparation of the Prayer of the Faithful; training of and practice by lectors and commentators so that they read not only clearly and loudly but also with understanding and feeling; selection of music which is simple enough for the people and yet in its texts and spirit appropriate to the theme of the liturgy; determination of the point in the worship where the music is to be sung, and the rhythm of the rite from beginning to climax to conclusion.

Even more preparation is required for outstanding Sunday worship. A thorough knowledge of liturgical legislation is required so that one is aware of all the options and opportunities inherent in the law and is not, therefore, restricted to a rigid and narrow format. Sunday worship will be alive to the extent that the celebrant and participants know what they are doing; this requires some biblical and theological education. More people must be involved in the planning of Sunday worship—not only the priest, organist, choirmaster, lector, and commentator, but also the people in the pews. Creative imagination must be used to provide variety in the pattern of Sunday worship and to incorporate into it elements of contemporary culture. Artistically talented people must be encouraged to perform for or in Sunday worship.

It is easy for Sunday worship and the buildings which house it to become the focal point of thought and energy for clergy and people, who then tend to think of the Christian life in terms of what they do in church on Sunday. They are not compelled to think of their Christian lives in terms of the world every day of the week.

The parish church, prompted by the need to provide

Sunday worship, gives rise to parish organizations, so-cials, fund-raising events, and the establishment of a Sunday school or a full-time parochial school. The clergy and the people must then be concerned not only with maintaining a church and providing Sunday wor-ship, but also with keeping a school building, recruiting competent teachers, and developing or finding an edu-cational program, at least a religious one for Sunday school. The laity become engrossed in the school, con-cerned about the quality of the religious education in the Sunday school and even the secular education in the parochial school. In Catholic parishes, religious are invited to staff the school and to devote themselves not to much-needed adult education, but to the education of children. The Christian people as a consequence be-come child-centered and turned in on themselves, rather than turned out to the world in the mission of the people of God.

If the Sunday observance of corporate worship were abandoned, new styles of Christian life, community, witness, and service could then be developed, at least in newly settled areas. A large building would not be needed for Sunday worship and, if the temptation to erect a school were resisted, the people would not fall so easily into an introverted Christian life, a poor sense of Christian community, and obsolete forms of service to the world. If new parishes could develop new styles, there would be some hope of reforming the old parishes. But if new parishes are forced into the pattern of the old, then there is little hope for either the old or the new. An effective way to free new parishes for new styles of Christian life would be to drop the observance of Sunday worship. Such a drastic move might give rise to an entirely new form of parish organization since Christians, deprived of the traditional Sunday worship, would seek to worship at another time, or even on Sunday, but under different conditions than prevail at present.

The routine and largely secularized manner in which rest on Sunday is now observed by many Christians prevents whatever religious meaning and value it does have from exercising any influence on people's lives. The Sunday observance of rest, moreover, has been one of the principal carriers of a somber, severe, and excessively otherworldly interpretation of Christianity. Abandonment of rest on Sunday as a Christian practice would offer the opportunity to develop new styles of Christian life which would express the joy, optimism, and acceptance of creation which are characteristic of Christian faith, hope, and love.

Abandonment of the Christian Sunday at this time, however, would be theologically and pastorally unsound. It would be theologically unsound because Christian life is life in community in the Risen Lord; if the Christian people are to celebrate this life, it is most appropriate that they celebrate it on the day of the Lord's resurrection, when his first disciples became aware of their new life with one another in the Risen Lord.

Moreover, Jesus himself commanded his disciples to

celebrate the Eucharist in memory of him: "Do this in memory of me." The celebration of the Lord's Supper is therefore most appropriately held on the day on which his life and mission reached their pivotal point, that is, on the day of his resurrection, which crowned his previous life, suffering, and death, and initiated his future actual lordship over all creation.

Furthermore, it can be argued that the observance of Sunday by worship is indirectly, at least, willed by Christ. The Protestant historian Willy Rordorf argues that the early Christians chose Sunday as the day to gather for worship—specifically, to celebrate the Eucharist—because when Christ broke bread with the disciples at "the Lord's Supper" on the evening of the day of his resurrection, Sunday, he instituted for a second time, as it were, the Eucharist,[4] and thus made Sunday "the Lord's Day."[5] Sunday worship, therefore, if not Sunday rest, is an essential ingredient of the Christian heritage; there is no choice as to whether it should or should not be kept. "If there is a problem about Sunday, it can be stated in this question: Are we willing to stand up for Sunday as the day for worship?"[6] Protestant theologians concerned with liturgical renewal tend to see such an intimate connection between the Eucharist and Sunday that they insist on no Sunday without the Eucharist and no Eucharist except on Sunday.[7]

Finally, as an historical religion, the maintenance of tradition is extremely important for Christianity. By tradition the Good News of salvation in Jesus Christ is handed down through the ages in confessions of faith,

Church teaching, discipline, customs, and liturgy. Before abandoning any formula or practice for a new one, extreme care must be taken to see that in doing so no essential part of the Good News is lost. The Christian Sunday has been one of the chief vehicles of tradition, and the Christian people must be certain of its meaning in terms of the Good News and certain that its meaning is or can be embodied in other practices which will serve as new vehicles of tradition. By choosing Sunday instead of some other day of the week to worship by celebrating the Eucharist, the apostles and early Christians told subsequent generations something about the significance of Christ and Christian life. Therefore, before the Christian people today abandon the Christian Sunday, they must be sure that they do not lose whatever it was the apostles and early Christians intended to convey.

These arguments do not rule out absolutely the abandonment of the Christian Sunday as it has been observed in the past. But they do rule out its abandonment without further theological investigation and especially without serious consideration of what would replace the traditional observance.

If the Christian Sunday were abandoned now, the Christian people would be left without a common symbol that expresses their faith and religion. To tell them that there is no need for a special day with special activities in special places, and to ask that they make every day Christian, carry out all their activities in every place in a spirit of worship, and fill their lives with the joy befitting the new creation in Christ, would be asking the psychologically impossible. Men need familiar, frequent, concrete, dynamic, temporal, and spatial symbols to preserve, nourish, and intensify their faith; this faith can then guide and inspire them in their daily living everywhere. Other observances could supply this need, of course, but at the present time it is not obvious to everybody what these other observances are.

Abandonment of the Christian Sunday would deprive the Christian people of a paradigm of Christian secularity or, in more prosaic terms, of a model of what Christian life in the world should be. Sunday rest from work instructs the faithful that they are to live in joyful freedom from sin and all the destructive forces which permeate the world. (It is not the intention of this teaching to imply that work itself is evil or sinful but that necessary work, which is often difficult or unpleasant, can symbolize sin and the destructive forces which hold men in bondage and anxiety.) Sunday rest teaches that the world and human life are essentially good, that they are God's creation, created anew in the Risen Christ, and men are called to have dominion over this creation for their use and enjoyment.

Sunday's corporate worship instructs the faithful that to be truly and fully human, one must be conscious of the fact that one owes all that one is and all that one possesses to God, and for this reason one should use, develop, and enjoy life in the world in a spirit of thanksgiving. Sunday worship also teaches the faithful to follow the example of Jesus Christ by accepting human life—both individual and social, with all its joys, sorrows, and even its suffering and death—with enthusiasm, hope, and joy. The corporate worship of Sunday is an exercise in fraternal charity: cooperation with fellowmen in proclaiming the kingdom of God and in breaking bread together in brotherhood.

The traditional Christian Sunday thus symbolizes the understanding and attitude which Christians should have toward life in this world. It teaches Christians how to live by actually living that way for a day. This is a far more effective method of teaching than abstract lessons or sermons. Instead of abandoning the Christian Sunday, therefore, its meaning and value should be made clearer to the Christian people so that they may extend its spirit into the other days of the week.

It is true that approximately one-third of the Catholics and two-thirds of the Protestants in the United States do not attend church on Sunday, either because they cannot or do not care to do so. It is probably true also that there is very little religious motivation for whatever Sunday rest they do observe. Nevertheless, abandonment of the Christian Sunday would deprive people of a concrete ideal toward which to strive. The tension created by this striving can serve as the force which impels Christians to organize and direct their lives in a way that will nourish their faith and make it active in the world.

Corporate worship in a community made up of men of every sort, and not merely men of one's own choosing, is a Christian ideal. Living freely, joyfully, and creatively in the world as God's sons in a new creation is also a Christian ideal. The Christian Sunday, as a concrete embodiment of these ideals, can draw Christians out of their narrow circles of family and intimate friends to mingle with all mankind; it can stimulate them to bear witness in the world to the joy, freedom, and creativity which belong to the new creation. To do away with the traditional Christian Sunday, therefore, would be to do away with a concrete ideal; and to do away with an ideal can be a most impractical move since it can mean the death of motivation and moral effort.

Abandonment of the Christian Sunday would also deprive the Christian people of a temporal and spatial articulation of Christian life that provides the opportunity for necessary reflection. Psychologists and psychiatrists point out that it is important for a person to divide his days, weeks, years, and his lifetime so that there is time for learning, for work, for relaxation, for privacy, for friends, and for any other element necessary for a full and balanced life. Space, too, must be articulated; in different places a person interacts differently with people, bears different responsibilities and authority, and does different things. By adequate articulation of time and space he is assured of a rhythm of life and a working together of life's components in such a way that living becomes full and rich, without strains and pressures beyond his strength.[8]

A fundamental need of Christian life, even as it is of human life, is reflection. Gabriel Marcel has pointed to the lack of reflection as a cause of today's "broken world," with its dehumanizing technology, massive state control, and powers of destruction.[9] Martin Heidegger depicts men as generally living "inauthentic" lives. Time-bound mortals thrown into existence and on their way to death, they do not confront their true selves but lose themselves in the common "they" of the masses and their superficial culture.[10]

Since reflection and confrontation of one's true being are as necessary for truly Christian life as for truly human life, time and place must be set aside for them in order to satisfy men's need for temporal and spatial articulation. The traditional Christian Sunday is precisely this: a time and place set aside for the purpose of reflecting on and responding to life in relation to self, fellowmen, nature, human culture, and ultimately God, the source of all being, power, and activity.[11]

Again, some other articulation of life could ensure this reflection, but up to now none has emerged clearly from the American culture. Sunday, then, will most likely continue to be available as a day that provides the temporal and spatial articulation necessary for reflection in Christian life, and that serves as a concrete symbol to express Christian faith, instruct in Christian secularity, and embody Christian ideals.

At present the economic, political, and religious life of the nations of the world follows the rhythm of the seven-day week, with Sunday, Saturday, or Friday a national holiday for all or some of their citizens. This rhythm of work and rest is deeply ingrained in men as a religious and social heritage which has become second nature to them. It does not seem likely that any major nation would or could successfully establish, let us say, a ten-day week. Such a step would cause a furor among religious people, but a more effective deterrent would probably be the snarl it would create in economic and political areas. Moreover, with the development of technology, the increase in the working population, and shorter work hours, it is more likely that instead of work taking over Sunday, leisure will take over the other days of the week. In a pluralistic society, furthermore, it should be possible for Christians to be free to observe Sunday by worship and rest, for Jews to have their Sabbath and Moslems their Friday. This could be accomplished by legislation if necessary. If people like Madalyn Murray can campaign, lobby, and file suits to protect the freedom of atheists not to pray, the Christian people can also exercise political action to protect their freedom not to work on a certain day or at a certain time if their conscience dictates that they must not. Government and society must guarantee the religious freedom of individuals in both the choice of their religious stance (even if it is against religion) and in its private and communal expression.

It has not been conclusively demonstrated that Sunday worship is totally incapable of achieving, to some degree at least, its original purpose of building Christian community.[12] Not every community is an intimate one made up of people who are very familiar with one another, bound by ties of affection and concerned primarily about the individual's and the community's total welfare. In some communities the members are only slightly acquainted and, lacking strong feelings toward their neighbors, are concerned about each other mainly in terms of the achievement of the community's common purpose. Sociologists distinguish societies into primary and secondary types, or *Gemeindschaft* and *Gesellschaft*. They also note that modern man belongs to and experiences many different communities. Moreover, no existing society is a "pure" type, but includes the characteristics of various communities, though the characteristics of one type may be more dominant or obvious in it. Sunday worship may not achieve the intimate type of community, but perhaps it is not meant to do so, for that type of community may not be the only ideal representation of all that comprises the reality of the body of Christ, the Church. Disillusionment and disappointment over the community-building power of Sunday worship are bound to occur if false expectations are nourished. Sunday worship may achieve or, with reform, be able to achieve some type of community whose importance to the body of Christ is not sufficiently appreciated today because of special contemporary needs and prejudices.

Although the traditional Christian Sunday involves a style of ecclesial organization, community, and ministry that impedes the development of new styles which would be more suitable to the needs of men in the contemporary world, the ecclesial structures and functions can nevertheless serve as scaffolding for new forms of Christian life. As the new forms are tested and

proved in regard to their viability and vigor, the scaffolding can be discarded. The purpose of this argument
is not to show that the *status quo* should be preserved,
but to indicate that positive efforts to develop ne
styles of life, ministry, community, and witness nee
not wait until after the present structures have beer.
dismantled. *Aggiornamento* must begin to work with
the existing structures, putting them to new uses insofar
as possible and supplementing them with new structures which will more adequately meet the needs of the
time and eventually replace the old forms.

Theological and pastoral reasons argue, therefore, for
the retention of the Christian Sunday at this time.
These arguments, however, do not resolve the many
difficulties which its observance presents or lessen the
serious threats to its continued existence. Already Sunday rest as a Christian reality is nearly dead, and Sunday worship is rapidly losing its grip on life. If the
Christian Sunday is to be preserved, even for a time, to
allow a transition to some other style of Christian life,
some immediate action must be taken to solve the problems which now plague it.

Catholics must be wary of attempting to solve the
problems by legal means. Some suggest that Canon 1248
of the Code of Canon Law, which obliges Catholics to
observe Sunday worship and rest, should be changed so
that the obligation of weekly worship could be fulfilled
on some other day of the week. This solution, however,
is based on a very individualistic understanding of Sunday worship. It implies that what is important on Sunday is that the individual Christian pay homage to God,

whereas what is really important is that the Christian community celebrate its origin, existence, and destiny and thereby build itself up. In other words it is not primarily the individual Christian's fulfillment of his personal responsibility to worship God that is at stake in regard to Sunday worship, but the responsibility of the Christian community to grow. To alter the Code of Canon Law so that it obliges Catholics to worship any day of the week at their personal convenience would reinforce this individualistic notion of Sunday worship and destroy rather than restore its original significance and purpose.

Some suggest that canon law should not impose any obligation at all on Catholics to worship on any day. This is an acceptable suggestion in view of the fact that the law is obviously ineffective. In the so-called Catholic countries of Europe and Latin America, only an extremely low percentage of Catholics obey it, and in the United States more and more Catholics are ignoring it. Restatement, increased emphasis, or reform of the law will gain no more obedience in the future than it does now.

On the other hand, canon law should not ignore Sunday altogether, particularly its worship. The obligation, however, should be placed on pastors to provide worship every Sunday for the Christian people, and to employ all possible means to make it attractive and meaningful. Those who interpret the law should refrain from perverting it into a legal obligation binding on individual Christians. This does not mean that a Christian would never seriously sin against his duty to God and to the Christian community by absence from Sunday worship. Deliberate refusal or habitual neglect to participate regularly in Sunday worship would surely be serious sin—not because of the law, but because of the intrinsic value and importance of the Christian community's worship for both itself and the individual. Neglect to participate out of sheer laziness would, in conjunction with other failures to respond to God's love in Jesus Christ and the needs of the Christian community, also constitute a serious offense.

The problem of the Christian Sunday can be solved only theologically and pastorally. There must be an understanding of the mystery of Christ, the Christian life, the Church, and the Christian Sunday in relation to these. Any decision about the future of the Christian Sunday must be implemented by appropriate pastoral action: education, reorganization of structures and ministries, new styles of community, and so forth. This book proposes that the Christian people should strive to preserve the Christian Sunday at this time with a new understanding of and a new attitude towards the activities of the day. Simultaneously, they should develop a style of Christian life, community, ministry, and witness which will not only support the Christian Sunday against threats to it, but will at the same time make Christian life less dependent upon it; consequently if the Christian Sunday is overwhelmed in the culture of the future, there will be something to take its place. This proposal recognizes the claims of the past, the threats of the present, and the possibilities of the future that have been considered in these first two chapters. The next three chapters will explore the theological principles which will underlie the pastoral strategy to be recommended in the last three chapters.

Notes

[1] For details of this development, see Willy Rordorf, *Sunday: The History of the Day of Rest and Worship in the Earliest Centuries of the Christian Church,* trans. A. A. K. Graham (Philadelphia: Westminster Press, 1968), pp. 154-73 © SCM Press, Ltd., 1968. Used by permission.

[2] *The Des Moines Register,* Dec. 22, 1968.

[3] Rordorf, *op. cit.,* pp. 244-45; also see pp. 226-27, 303.

[4] *Ibid.,* p. 233.

[5] *Ibid.,* p. 303; see also p. 221.

[6] *Ibid.,* p. 304.

[7] *Ibid.,* p. 303; J. J. von Allmen, *Worship: Its Theology and Practice* (New York: Oxford University Press, 1965), pp. 238-39.

[8] These ideas are developed in regard to another problem by Henri Nouwen in "A Psychologist on Priests' Identity Crisis," *The National Catholic Reporter,* May 17, 1967.

[9] *The Mystery of Being,* vol. I, *Reflection and Mystery* (Chicago: Henry Regnery Co., 1960), pp. 44-47.

[10] *Being and Time,* trans. John Macquarrie and Edward Robinson (New York: Harper & Row, 1962), pp. 163-68, 296-311.

[11] For an excellent analysis of Christian worship as reflection or reconsideration and response, see James F. White, *The Worldliness of Worship* (New York: Oxford University Press, 1967), pp. 20-31, 48-78.

[12] Cf. Raymond H. Potovin, "The Liturgy and Community: A Sociological Appraisal, *"Proceedings of the Twenty-Eighth North American Liturgical Week,* 28 (1967), pp. 76-87.

III

THE PASCHAL MYSTERY

The Christian Sunday is essentially a celebration of the paschal mystery. This may not be a very enlightening statement at this point, for people's idea of celebration is vague, however much experiential knowledge of it they may have. The phrase "paschal mystery" is unfamiliar to Protestants and most Catholics; only since Vatican II has it become part of the ordinary vocabulary of some more educated Catholics. But "celebration of the paschal mystery" does capture the essence of the Christian Sunday and thus provides a theological basis for meeting the problems which confront it.

The word "mystery" can be an obstacle to a correct understanding of the paschal mystery. It may be taken to mean simply "the inexplicable," or it may be interpreted as meaning "the holy," "the sacred," "the wholly other," which Rudolf Otto defined in his classic

work, *The Idea of the Holy,* as "fearsome and fascinat-
ing mystery" *(mysterium tremendum et fascinans).*[1] But
such meanings convey only what *kind* of thing the paschal mystery is; they do not explain *what* it is. For that
the biblical notion of mystery must be ferreted out.

"Mystery" is prominent in St. Paul's letters: 1 Cor.
2:6-16; Rom. 11:25-27; Eph. 1:4-12; 3:3-11; Col. 1:25-2:3; 1
Tim. 3:16. Reputable scholars no longer hold that St.
Paul borrowed the terminology and ideas of the Greek
mystery-religions and applied them to the events of
Jesus' life, death, and resurrection. St. Paul's notion of
mystery is rooted in the Old Testament, especially the
Wisdom literature, the Book of Daniel, and the apoca-
lyptic writings of later Judaism.[2]

In his first letter to the Corinthians, Paul writes:

.... we speak the wisdom of God, mysterious [literally: in
mystery], hidden, which God foreordained before the world
unto our glory, a wisdom which none of the rulers of this
world has known; for had they known it, they would never
have crucified the Lord of glory. But, as it is written, 'Eye has
not seen nor ear heard, nor has it entered into the heart of
man, what things God has prepared for those who love him.'
But to us God has revealed them through his Spirit. For the
Spirit searches all things, even the deep things of God (2:
7-10).[3]

What is called "mysterious" here is God's wisdom
which is hidden deep within the Divine Being, and
which has been revealed to men through the Spirit who
knows the depths of the Divine Being.

Wisdom in the ancient Near East did not mean the speculative philosophy of ancient Greece, of Plato and Aristotle.[4] It meant the practical arts of craftsmanship, scholarship, administration, upright living, and governing. Kings, naturally, were considered to possess wisdom above all others, for they governed the life of the nation and hence the activities of its members. Israel assimilated these ideas of wisdom, including the superior wisdom of the kings, when Israel became a kingdom. Israel's most illustrious king, Solomon, was famed above all else for his wisdom, which surpassed that of all the wise men of the Near East (1 Kgs. 5:9-14). The first gift which Solomon asked of God at the beginning of his reign was wisdom (*ibid.,* 3:7-9).

In common with Near Eastern thought, Israel regarded wisdom as proper to God. Indeed, God's wisdom is the root of creation: the phenomena of nature, the distinction between good and evil, the good life, the destiny of men and nations. God's wisdom is inscrutable, unfathomable, mysterious, but he freely bestows it upon men: artisans, privileged people like Joseph and Daniel, leaders like Moses, the kings, and their advisers. In other words, the mysterious wisdom of God is the radical plan governing all being and activity whether of nature or of man; and the various kinds of wisdom enjoyed by men are derived from God's wisdom, either by discernment of it through study of what it causes in the world, or by direct divine enlightenment through God's spirit.

The mysterious wisdom of God ordering all things is

devised in the heavenly council of God and his angels, with God giving the orders, and the angels suggesting and carrying them out. The prophet is the one who is admitted to the secrets of the decrees of this heavenly council. These pre-exilic ideas are carried over into post-exilic literature, where God's decrees for the order of the cosmos or for the destiny of men and nations are called "mysteries." This development is especially clear in the Book of Daniel, the pseudoepigraphical books of Enoch and Baruch, and the Qumran litera-ture.[5]

In the Book of Daniel, before he interprets the Babylonian king's dream, Daniel says:

May the name of God be blessed for ever and ever, since wisdom and power are his alone. His, to control the proces-sion of times and seasons, to make and unmake kings, to confer wisdom on the wise, and knowledge on those with wit to discern; his to uncover depths and mysteries, to know what lies in darkness; and light dwells in him (2:20-23).

And further: "O king, on your bed your thoughts turned to what would happen in the future, and the Revealer of Mysteries disclosed to you what is to take place. This mystery has been revealed to me. ..." (2:-29-30).

As Louis Bouyer notes, in this passage from the Book of Daniel are found the vocabulary and the association of ideas which are in St. Paul's letter to the Corinthians quoted previously: wisdom, mystery, revelation.[6] In both cases, moreover, this wisdom, this mystery, concerns the conduct of history. It must be concluded that in the biblical sense the paschal mystery *as mystery* is the humanly incomprehensible plan of God guiding creation, the course of history, and the destiny of men.

For Paul, this mystery of divine wisdom is summed up and revealed in Jesus Christ, crucified, risen, and made Lord. In the letter to the Colossians, Paul writes of "the mystery of God the Father of Christ Jesus, in whom are hidden all the treasures of wisdom and knowledge" (2:3-4).[7] The relative clause here does not mean that Jesus possesses great knowledge; it means, rather, that he is the realization, the embodiment, the incarnation, and hence the revelation of that wisdom and knowledge which is formulated in the depths of the Divine Being and which is the plan, the mystery, whereby the destiny of men and creation is guided. In his letter to the Ephesians, Paul writes of his call

to announce among the Gentiles the good tidings of the unfathomable riches of Christ, and to enlighten all men as to what is the dispensation [*economia*] of the mystery which has been hidden from eternity in God, who created all things; in order that through the Church there be made known. . . . the manifold wisdom of God according to the eternal purpose which he accomplished in Christ Jesus our Lord (3:8-11).[8]

The mystery, or plan, of God for creation and mankind is not completed, revealed, and accomplished in the death, resurrection, and exaltation of Jesus Christ. Jesus is only "the eldest of many brothers (Rom. 8:29), the "first to be born from the dead" (Col. 1:18). "Just as all men die in Adam, so all men will be brought to life in Christ; but all of them in their proper order: Christ as the first-fruits and then, after the coming of Christ, those who belong to him. After that will come the end, when he hands over the kingdom to God the Father, having done away with every sovereignty, authority, and power" (1 Cor. 15:22-24). In other words, the mystery, or plan, of God embraces not only the passage of Jesus through life and death under the conditions of sin to new life in God, but also the passage of men, as well as the fulfillment of the material universe, whatever that fulfillment may be.[9] The paschal mystery extends forward into the future to the parousia, the final coming of Christ, when God's creative project will be consummated.

In Paul's words, "the mystery is Christ among you" (Col. 1:27). The mystery is Christ as head, living through his spirit and his gifts in his members who constitute his body, the Church, and who through service, truth, and love grow to become "the perfect Man, fully mature with the fullness of Christ himself" (Eph. 4:13; cf. vss. 10-16). Hence the mystery includes the life of the Church and its members, explicit or anonymous (latent). The Christian life, communal and individual, explicit or anonymous, insofar as it is a following of Christ through suffering and death to new life in God, is included in the paschal mystery, as are all those activities within creation which, in virtue of the plan, the mystery, hidden from all ages in the depths of God, contribute to the attainment of God's purpose: the reconciliation of all

things in Christ, a new heaven and a new earth. Even
if some activities do not go by the name Christian, or
are not recognized as Christian, they are nevertheless
part of the paschal mystery. God wills the salvation of
all men, and there is only one mediator between God
and man—Jesus Christ (1 Tim. 2:5). Whatever has salvific
value is included in the mystery of Christ, the paschal
mystery.

Three senses of "mystery" have been noted in St.
Paul's writings, and it is helpful to keep them clearly in
mind: (1) the *plan* for creation and mankind engen-
dered in love within the depths of God's own being; (2)
the *anticipated partial realization* of this plan *in Jesus
Christ*, raised from the dead and made Lord over creation and mankind, and (3) *the ongoing realization* of the
plan *in creation* (cf. Rom. 8:19-23), *in men* (cf. Eph. 2:-
3-22), and *in the Risen Christ*, who strains forward toward the full realization of his lordship at his final
coming in the plenitude of his power and glory.

The mystery of which Paul writes has been subsequently qualified as "paschal." It could be qualified as
the mystery of Christ, the Christian mystery, the
parousial mystery, or the mystery of redemption. There
are still other possibilities. Any qualifier simply indicates the particular moment, characteristic, or compo-
nent of the mystery by which one first knows it and the
view of the one who explores and interprets it. The
qualifier "paschal" indicates that the mystery is known
initially in the event of Jesus' death and resurrection
which attracted to itself the language of the Jewish
Pasch (Passover) since it occurred at that time and was

understood by Jesus' disciples as fulfilling all that the Jewish Pasch commemorated and anticipated.[10] As early as 1 Corinthians, Paul wrote: "Christ, our passover, has been sacrificed" (5:7). Thus the paschal mystery is the divine plan for creation and mankind and that plan's realization as revealed in Jesus' death and resurrection.

Today, however, many assail the idea that there can be any such thing as a divine plan for the world, man, and their development and history. A divine plan for all this suggests a playwright's script with its directions for the scenery and props, its already determined characters, its plot, its precise sequence of words and events. All that remains is for the director, actors, and stage crew to follow the directions. They contribute, at most, interpretation, which in the final analysis is judged by how well it fulfills the intent of the playwright's script. So also God's plan predetermines not only the nature of the universe and man but also all the details of their development, all their activities, and all the turns of events in nature and history. Spontaneous changes in nature and free choices by men are illusions; they appear spontaneous and free, but in fact have long since, in eternity, been determined by the Master Playwright of creation.

That such an idea of God's plan for creation is far too naive to account for the facts is testified to by the controversies generated by Christian thinking on the relationship between God's grace and man's free will. No one has ever come forth with a universally accepted explanation. The Catholic Church's most heated debate over the problem, between Jesuits and Dominicans of the sixteenth century, ended in a draw.

Today there are even more facts, or at least more commonly held views, which render a simplistic idea of a divine plan unacceptable. The modern physicist sees the subatomic realm (and hence indirectly the whole of the universe composed of these particles) as ruled by Heisenberg's principle of uncertainty, or indeterminacy, and functioning according to laws of statistical probability. The physical universe is not a grand machine which always works in exactly the same way according to a predetermined design. A theory of biological evolution that involves chance mutation of genes giving rise to new species would not appear compatible with a predetermined plan for the evolution of life.

Raymond Nogar, a longtime student of evolution, in his book, *The Lord of The Absurd,* argues that there is no evidence for the order in nature which such scientists as Teilhard de Chardin, George G. Simpson, and Sir Julian Huxley claim to see.[11] If there were a divine plan, such an order should be discernible. Any attempt to explain history in terms of the simple unfolding or execution of a preconceived and willed plan of God would destroy history, for by its very nature history must be the result of men's free, unpredictable choices. It is taken for granted today that there is no such thing as a fixed human nature: man makes his own nature by his decisions and his culture. This determination of his own nature by his free choice is precisely what distinguishes man from animals, which are bound to be what they are and cannot make themselves to be what they wish. Whatever one may think about the ultimate truth of these views of the physical universe, life, history, and human nature, they are widely held opinions, and any concept of a divine plan must make sense within their frame of reference if it is to be credible to those who hold these views.

Faith in the sovereignty and fatherhood of God in view of the testimony of Scripture calls for acknowledgment of a divine plan in some sense of the word for nature, mankind, and their histories. But in these pages, at least, this plan includes only two items: a purpose, and the manner of achieving this purpose. A father may be said to have a plan for his son in the sense that he intends the son to reach maturity and determines to achieve this goal by a particular manner of child-rearing. He may, for example, raise the child in an atmosphere of general permissiveness, with a constant calling to account for the consequences of choices. Conversely, he may demand obedience to parental norms in everything; or demand obedience in some areas and allow permissiveness in others. On the basis of this purpose and this manner of proceeding, the father then deals with whatever choices the child makes and whatever turns in events result from these choices.[12]

The purpose of God's plan is the establishment of his reign, his kingdom, which Jesus preached. God's kingdom means for man *shalom,* a Hebrew word "so rich in meaning that there is hardly a single word in our modern language which can render adequately all its nuances."[13] The root *slm* means to be complete, whole,

sound, to live well. Absolutely it means welfare, prosperity, good health, etc., materially and spiritually, individually and socially. Relatively it means good
relationships between persons, families, nations, husband and wife, man and God. It is simultaneously
peace, integrity, justice, harmony, community. The
Messiah is the prince of *shalom* (Isaiah 9:6); Jeremiah
identifies Yahweh's plan as a plan for *shalom* (29:11); the
risen Jesus' greeting to his disciples when he appeared
to them Easter evening was: *"Shalom* be with you"
(John 20:20).

The manner in which God achieves his reign over
men and creation and bestows on them his *shalom* is
through the emergence of being and life from the possibilities inherent in what he has created and also
through his own power which calls into being and life
that which is not even within the possibilities of creation. That God brings about the emergence of being
and life from the possibilities inherent in what he has
created is affirmed notably in St. Thomas' theology that
secondary causes, that is, created agents, are truly
causes and not only apparently so. It is a constant temptation in religious thought to exalt God by demeaning
creatures, sometimes by regarding them as essentially
evil, sometimes by denying that they are really the
source of their activities, especially their good activities. St. Thomas consistently argues against depriving
creatures of their intrinsic potentialities, powers of action, and actual activity, while at the same time providing for God's role in the activity of creatures.[14]

That God brings about the emergence of being and

life from the possibilities inherent in creatures is also consonant with contemporary theories about the dynamic nature of the universe, biological evolution, and cultural development. ("Evolution" and "development" do not necessarily mean "progress" but simply "change.") That God brings about the emergence of being and life from the resources of his own power, quite apart from the possibilities inherent in creation, is affirmed in the doctrine of creation *ex nihilo* and the resurrection of Jesus from the dead; God is he "who brings the dead to life and calls into being what does not exist" (Rom. 4:17).

The concrete details of the goal of the divine plan, that is, the new creation in Jesus Christ, and the realization of that goal through events in natural and human history are hidden from human apprehension, despite God's revelation in Jesus Christ of his purpose and manner of achieving it. Quite rightly, therefore, the divine plan in itself, in its revelation, and in its realization is called "mystery," in the sense of "the obscure," "the unfathomable."

The logical conclusion of this interpretation of the paschal mystery as a divine plan is that men must orient their lives in such a way as to cooperate with God in the unfolding of the universe, life, history, and culture. God brings the new out of the potentialities inherent in creation through the instrumentality of men who must be ever alert and open to the new and the different. They must be especially receptive to the new and the different that God, by his own power, may unpredictably and unexpectedly bring about. And since men know that God's purpose is *shalom*—a fullness of being and life beyond description—they must, with courage born of the confidence that this is God's will, seize every opportunity to realize the possibilities for *shalom* which lie within reach, and pray and dispose themselves for the possibilities for *shalom* which lie within the infinite power of God.

The paschal mystery, therefore, embraces far more than the death and resurrection of Jesus. It signifies the plan and realization of the entire saving action of God in history. It reaches backward from Jesus' Pasch in his resurrection to the pasch of the Exodus, back, indeed, to the formation of the people who were led out of Egypt, and back to the foundation of the world. It reaches forward from the pasch of Jesus to our own Christian life, which is death with Jesus and rising to new life with him, and still further forward to his parousia, the final judgment, the resurrection of the body, and the new heaven and earth.

As a plan in the process of realization by God in cooperation with men, the paschal mystery invites men to action and to celebration.

Notes

[1]Trans. John W. Harvey (New York: Oxford University Press, Galaxy Books, 1958), pp. 12, 31.

[2]Among the many sources, see A. H. Armstrong, "Mystery and Mysteries, B. The Christian Mystery and the Mystery-Religions," *Downside Review* 80 (1962), pp. 214-25; Louis Bouyer, *The Paschal Mystery,* trans. Mary Benoit (Chicago: Henry Regnery Co. 1950), pp.

xvii-xx; 321-25; *idem, Liturgical Piety* (Notre Dame, Ind.: University of Notre Dame Press, 1955), pp. 86-98; Louis F. Hartman and P. van Imschoot, "Mystery," *Encyclopedic Dictionary of the Bible* (New York: McGraw-Hill Book Company, 1963), cols. 1581-84.

[3] Confraternity of Christian Doctrine translation.

[4] For this and the following paragraph, see Bouyer, *Liturgical Piety*, p. 94; Louis F. Hartman and P. van Imschoot, "Wisdom," *Encyclopedic Dictionary of the Bible*, cols. 2583-88; Walter Eichrodt, *Theology of the Old Testament* II, trans. J. A. Baker (Philadelphia: Westminster Press, 1967), pp. 80-92; A. Hulsbosch, *God in Creation and Evolution*, trans. Martin Versfeld (New York: Sheed and Ward, 1965), pp. 69-87.

[5] Details of this paragraph can be found elaborated upon in Raymond Brown, "The Pre-Christian Semitic Concept of Mystery," *The Catholic Biblical Quarterly* 20 (1958), pp. 417-43.

[6] *Liturgical Piety*, p. 95.

[7] Confraternity of Christian Doctrine translation.

[8] Confraternity of Christian Doctrine translation.

[9] Cf. Bouyer, *Liturgical Piety*, pp. 127-28, 173-84. The fulfillment of the material universe is implied in the resurrection of the body of Christ, for the body is part of the material universe (see Jürgen Moltmann, *The Theology of Hope*, trans. James W. Leitch (New York: Harper & Row, 1968), pp. 213-15); it is also implied in the recapitulation of *all* things in Christ (Eph. 1:10; Col. 1:20).

[10] Jean Daniélou, *The Bible and the Liturgy* (Notre Dame, Ind.: University of Notre Dame Press, 1956), pp. 87, 287.

[11] (New York: Herder & Herder, Inc., 1966), pp. 68-81, 118-19, 142-52.

[12] For some rethinking of the Catholic idea of a divine plan, see John H. Wright, "The Eternal Plan of Divine Providence," *Theological Studies* 27 (1966), pp. 27-57; for a description of divine providence which corresponds to the idea of a divine plan suggested in the text, see the Protestant theologian Gordon D. Kaufmann, *Systematic Theology: A Historicist Perspective* (New York: Charles Scribner's Sons, 1968), pp. 299-302, 255-87.

[13]Louis F. Hartman and J. van Dodewaard, "Peace," *Encyclopedic Dictionary of the Bible,* col. 1782; cf. J. C. Hoekendijk, *The Church Inside Out,* trans. Isaac C. Rottenberg (Philadelphia: Westminster Press, 1964), p. 21.

[14]E. g., *Summa theologiae* I, ques. 105, Art. 5; II, ques. 23, Art. 2; *De Potentia,* ques. 3, Art. 7.

IV

CELEBRATION OF
THE PASCHAL MYSTERY

The word "celebration" evokes an image of a lively social gathering. To "celebrate" means to "throw a party" or "go to a party." Even this crude conception of celebration includes more than whimsical frivolity and purposeless merrymaking. It implies recognition of some unusual success or good fortune that inspires rejoicing and exaltation of the spirit. A family celebrates the wedding of one of its members, for instance, or a man celebrates his wife's giving birth to a child; students celebrate the completion of their examinations, and workers celebrate a raise in pay.

Part of celebration is recounting the good news which prompts the merrymaking. At a wedding banquet someone proposes a toast in honor of the newly wedded couple. A father tells about his newborn child as he offers cigars to his fellow workers. This announcement of the good news is not restricted to explicit verbal statement. People at a celebration may never mention, or hear mentioned, the event which occasions the gaiety; but they know about it, and the celebration itself declares that something extraordinarily good has come to someone.

Good fortune, achievement, and victory inspire joy. Therefore, rejoicing is an element in celebration. Because this blessing, accomplishment, or success is unusual, joy is particularly great and cannot be contained in the mind in a mild glow of satisfaction. It explodes into the whole of one's being, firing the emotions, quickening the senses and exciting the body to unusual action, for the stimulus is an extraordinary one. By "throwing a party," banqueting, listening to speeches, following a parade and shooting fireworks, joy is expressed in the whole person and even reaches out to include other things.

Celebration is human and personal; it belongs to beings endowed with intelligence and freedom. Only intelligent creatures are capable of the comparative understanding and evaluation that recognize an occasion for celebration. Only free beings can rejoice by creating the expressions of tribute and joy essential to celebration. Celebration is human and personal also because it engages all levels of one's being and, finally, because it provides an opportunity for rejoicing over the good which befalls men. This good may involve things which men have grown or tamed or made, but the celebration is for the good that comes to man because of these things. It is not for the horse who wins the race, but for the man who owns the horse or placed a bet on it.

Celebration is also social. In the strictest sense, a person does not celebrate alone. Happiness over an especial good impels him to tell someone about it, for telling the reason is part of celebration. A lonely man who gets a raise in pay "celebrates" by going to the corner tavern and buying himself a drink. He takes this opportunity to tell the bartender of his raise or feels, at least, that in facing the bartender and asking for the drink, he has in some measure shared his joy with another person. Celebration, the expression of unusual joy, is fully realized only socially.

As a psychosomatic and social phenomenon, celebration is capable of intensifying itself. A person may accept an invitation to a party with reluctance, and arrive in a melancholy mood. But the enthusiasm and gaiety of the group affects his senses, imagination, emotions, and mind. Soon reluctance and melancholy vanish. In this process, he may turn his thoughts to the celebration in a way different from before because now his emotional tone is keyed to the occasion. His fresh insight enkindles new and greater joy over the good which prompts the celebration. To express this joy, he throws himself into the merriment with greater enthusiasm. His enthusiastic participation provides a stimulus to others, who go through the same process, and thus the intensity of the celebration as a whole and in each of its participants grows.

Human energies are eventually exhausted, of course, but if the celebration comes to a close at the proper time, its participants leave as renewed human beings. They disperse with their joyfulness at a peak, so that it is carried into their ordinary, workaday life to give it new zest. Or they may disperse with their joy exhausted, but with their minds purged of cares and anxieties, refreshed for undertaking again life's difficult business.

So far this analysis of celebration has referred only to the announcement of and rejoicing over good fortune, achievement, and victory. But the word "celebration" is used in another seemingly opposite manner. We speak of "celebrating" a funeral, which is hardly a joyous affair. Death is grim and the source of sorrow rather than joy. The impressive funerals of President John F. Kennedy and Dr. Martin Luther King certainly deserve to be called celebrations, but they were sorrowful occasions.

Upon closer examination, however, even a funeral is seen as a celebration in the sense of its being an announcement of good news and the expression of joy over it. This should be obvious in the case of Christian death, for death in Christ is not a grim defeat; rather, it is victory over sin and eventually, at the resurrection of the dead, victory over death itself. If death is a source of only sorrow for Christians, then they are still in pagan ways. The feasts of the saints are celebrated (note "feasts" and "celebrated"), not on the anniversaries of their natural birth, but on the anniversaries of their death—their birth into eternal life, their victory in Christ. The new funeral rites in the liturgy of the Catholic Church demonstrate very well that a Christian funeral is a celebration announcing and rejoicing over the good news of a blessing and a victory.

Death, nevertheless, does involve loss and grief. For that reason the joy characteristic of a funeral celebration will be muted. It ought not to be completely drowned, however, by a flood of sorrow which flows from paying attention to only the loss of those who remain alive, while forgetting the triumph of the one who has died.

Even apart from the Christian context, a funeral is aptly defined in terms of a subdued but fundamentally joyful announcement of the good news of achievement. Death is an end of something. It is the completion of a life and of that life's achievements, however meager or great they may have been. A funeral, therefore, celebrates a life of achievement that has reached its completion, and the solemnity, elaborateness, and number of participants connected with it tend to be proportionate to the accomplishments of the deceased and to public knowledge of these accomplishments. The death of a well-known general, doctor, scientist, or writer will be celebrated more magnificently than the death of an unknown alcoholic on skid row. The elaborate funeral of President Kennedy, though occasioned by tragedy, was a celebration of the achievement that was his life.

Even in the celebration of events which appear to be purely joyful, a negative element linking them with death is discernible. It is not only to announce the good fortune of entering a new phase of life that a wedding celebration is held; it is also to announce the completion of a previous phase. Marriage entails the loss of bachelorhood with its freedom and the end of maidenhood surrounded with parental care and protection. To revel over successfully completed examinations or to buy a drink to celebrate a wage increase is to announce the end of the discipline of study or the end of frugal management. Bachelorhood, maidenhood, the discipline of study, frugal management—all these have their intrinsic value, and their cessation can be a source of sorrow, even as the cessation of life itself. But their cessation is both entrance into a new phase of life with its own value worthy of joyful acceptance, and completion of the achievement of that phase now coming to an end; both are occasions for rejoicing, for celebration.

Celebration, then, consists in joyfully announcing the good news of both that which is beginning and that which has been completed. Accomplishment, success, or blessing invariably entails the end of something good: a way of life, self-discipline, intense effort, even life itself. Various losses cause varying degrees of sorrow which more or less dampen the joy inspired by the gain. Different combinations of attainment and loss, and joy and sorrow give rise to various kinds of celebrations, from those wherein joy reigns supreme with only a trace of sorrow, to those wherein joy is a small jewel in a setting of sorrow.

One more rather subtle point remains to be noted.

Chronologically, celebration often follows the event that occasions it—for example, the victory dance is held in the evening after the football game has been won in the afternoon. But sometimes the occasion for celebration may be included in the celebration or, to put it another way, celebration may be the manner in which the occasion for celebration occurs. For example, a wedding celebration is not only the dinner after the ceremony, but the ceremony itself. The wedding ceremony includes: (1) the *occasion* for celebrating, namely, the great good which is the sealing of human love by marriage vows and the beginning of a new phase of life for a couple, and (2) *celebration* of this great good by the visible, audible exchange of vows, and by the words and actions surrounding it, all of which joyfully announce the marvelous good which has come to two people in their love and in their new life which arises from it. "To celebrate a marriage" sometimes means "to get married." Celebrating something can mean doing it or bringing it into existence in a way which simultaneously announces its goodness and expresses the joy it inspires.

In view of these ideas about celebration, it is apparent that celebration of the paschal mystery involves, first of all, recognition or acknowledgement of that mystery as a great good for men. It calls for the announcement of the paschal mystery as "good news" by means of speech, song, symbolic action, and other forms of expression. Celebration of the paschal mystery includes rejoicing over it, exuberantly or serenely, with the

whole of one's being, and employing things to help
express this joy. It involves gathering with others. It also
includes partial realization of the paschal mystery because, ideally, celebration of the paschal mystery is its
coming into existence in such a way that its goodness
at the same time is announced in joy. All these elements
are found in the most obvious celebration of the paschal
mystery, the liturgy of the Word and the Eucharist.[1]

In order to talk about actual celebrations of the paschal mystery, two types can be proposed—formal and
informal. These are abstract models that do not exist as
such in reality, but they are logical constructs to assist
understanding of the complexity of actual celebrations.
Any actual celebration of the paschal mystery will fall
between the two poles represented by these types, that
is, it will contain elements of both, tending more toward
one pole or the other.

Formal celebration is characterized by the participants' explicit awareness of the paschal mystery and of
what they are doing in its regard, namely, acknowledging it, announcing it to others, rejoicing over it, and
partially realizing it.[2] Formal celebration is also characterized by explicit reference in words and actions to
the paschal mystery or, in other words, to those persons,
events, institutions, history, and so on, of which it is
constituted. Finally, formal celebration is characterized
by stylized forms of speech and action, that is, ceremony or ritual.

This type of celebration is realized, insofar as it ever
is, in the liturgy of the Word and the Sacrament. This

liturgy explicitly refers to the paschal mystery, acknowledging it as a great good for men and for God's glory, and proclaiming it in word, song, and action as "good news." It is joyful, though often muted in varying degrees, and it is communal action. In it men are caught up in the realization of God's paschal plan by union with Christ in faith, hope, and love as well as by union with him sacramentally in Holy Communion. However, in actual performance this liturgy never perfectly realizes the pure, formal type of celebration. This is because of factors operative in the participants, who are often distracted and thus not always fully aware of the paschal mystery or of what they are doing in its regard. Their emotions are controlled by their personal thoughts or the weather, and consequently they do not respond with the feeling of joy which the paschal mystery should evoke. They have an imperfect sense of community, so that there is in their celebration little sharing of joy over a common blessing. The performance of this liturgy may make use of only the very general pattern proper to it and be otherwise quite unceremonial.

The other sacraments, the sacramentals, worship generally and even worship alone, tend toward this formal type of celebration of the paschal mystery. In all these there is some explicit recognition and announcement of the paschal mystery with some joy in it, however muted or however much it may be frustrated by the mood of the worshiper. Some customary formulas of words and actions are followed. But, again, in actual performance, all these forms of worship include informal elements and lie somewhere in the continuum between the two types of celebration.

The other type of celebration—the informal—is characterized by only implicit reference in words and actions to the paschal mystery and by the participants' implicit awareness of the mystery, of what they are doing in its regard, and of what is happening to them. It is characterized also by informal activity which is neither ceremonial nor ritualistic. This type of celebration is realized in everyday Christian life.

In seeking to do the will of God, the Christian is cooperating with God in realizing the paschal mystery. His activities, therefore, refer at least implicitly to the paschal mystery insofar as they realize it. The Christian thus goes about his daily activities in faith, with at least implicit awareness and acknowledgment of the paschal mystery as a great good for mankind and for himself. In addition, he is at least implicitly aware that he is realizing the paschal mystery in seeking to do God's will, and that he is bearing witness to it in the world. He has, as a result, an implicit joy, although he may not feel this joy very intensely. He lives his Christian life in communion with fellow Christians. Christian life itself, therefore, has the characteristics of celebration of the paschal mystery: joy, communal recognition, announcement, and realization of God's plan to bring life from death and being from nothingness. But this celebration is informal because of its implicit awareness, and its implicit and unstructured expression.

Informal celebration of the paschal mystery is not verified in anonymous (latent) Christian life. By definition, the anonymous Christian is unaware that he is cooperating in the realization of the paschal mystery in his good actions. His activities, considered in themselves apart from his subjective awareness of their value, may implicitly refer to the paschal mystery insofar as they realize it; but he is not subjectively aware, even implicitly, of the value of his actions in their Christian dimension. The anonymous Christian realizes the paschal mystery in his daily life, but he does not celebrate it; in other words, he does not realize it in a way which at the same time at least implicitly announces its goodness and expresses the joy which it inspires.

The informal celebration of the paschal mystery in daily Christian life becomes more nearly perfect as the Christian's awareness grows in relation to what he is doing and what is happening through his actions. He celebrates the paschal mystery more fittingly as he becomes more conscious that he is realizing it in cooperation with God, as he more consciously acknowledges the goodness of the mystery and its realization, as he becomes more desirous of having others share in it, as he rejoices more in it, and as he becomes more aware of his communion with others in its realization.

As this awareness, desire, and joy increase, they have a tendency to seek more explicit expression, in both the individual's mind and feelings and in his external behavior and actions. In other words, as the celebration of the paschal mystery found informally in everyday

Christian life reaches a greater awareness and emotional pitch, it tends toward the formal type of celebration, toward the explicitness found in the liturgy of the Word and the Sacrament and in other forms of ritual worship. The Christian who is going about his daily affairs and is suddenly struck by the insight that he is realizing God's paschal plan in healing this body or preparing this catechetical instruction, will feel an impulse to pause for a short prayer, even if it is no more than a familiar ejaculation uttered to himself. He will also feel an urge, however slight, to tell someone else about this wonderful thing of which he has become aware, although circumstances may deter him from actually doing so.

Conversely, a Christian will deliberately engage in the liturgy of the Word and the Sacrament with its explicitness about the paschal mystery in order to intensify his awareness, awaken his joy, and confirm his commitment to it, in view of those periods of daily life when he knows that his mind and heart will be explicitly occupied with other things. Thus, informal celebration of the paschal mystery tends toward formal celebration, and formal celebration nourishes informal celebration. The anonymous Christian, it is to be noted, does not informally celebrate the paschal mystery in his daily life because he never celebrates it formally.

It is pointless to ask whether formal or informal celebration of the paschal mystery is better. Both are necessary for the Christian life. The Christian life *is* the paschal mystery being realized by God and his adopted son, the Christian; it is not the whole of the paschal mystery, of course, but it is an integral part of it. When the Christian life is lived in the awareness proper to human beings, the paschal mystery is realized in a way in which it is simultaneously acknowledged, announced, and accepted in joy: it is celebrated. As awareness grows (and it should if there is to be growth in faith proper to a human being) there will be a tendency toward explicit acknowledgment, announcement, and joy, that is, toward formal celebration. On the other hand, in order to sustain and increase daily Christian awareness, formal celebration is necessary. It is as difficult to conceive of anyone persevering as a Christian for a very long time or developing a more intense Christian life without explicit expression of his faith, as it is to conceive of a Christian living by faith day in and day out and yet never feeling the impulse to express it explicitly.

The Christian Sunday as celebration of the paschal mystery can be located somewhere between the two types of celebration, tending more toward the formal. In its observance of worship, it certainly inclines toward formal celebration and realizes it to a great extent. In its observance of rest it also tends toward formal celebration, though this is not so obvious and requires some reflection.

There is something artificial, stylized, and ritualistic about Sunday rest. There is a rubric for Sunday's activities: they should not involve work or, more positively, they should involve play (as will be explained later).

The significance of Sunday rest in Christian tradition may be summarily stated as the anticipatory participation in the messianic rest of the new creation, the term of God's paschal plan begun at creation; the motive for Sunday observance is to honor the Creator who redeemed his creation by the death and resurrection of Jesus, which revealed the paschal mystery and inaugurated the messianic rest.[3]

Two characteristics of formal celebration begin to emerge here: explicit reference to the paschal mystery, and a stylized form of action. If a Christian, aware of the paschal mystery, observes Sunday rest for the purpose of acknowledging it as a benefit from God, witnessing to it before men, rejoicing over it, and advancing its realization, the third characteristic is added: explicit awareness. Thus Sunday rest is truly celebration of the paschal mystery, not so formal as the liturgy of the Word and the Sacrament but, because of the rubric for Sunday's activities, not so informal as everyday Christian life.

To see the liturgy of the Word and the Sacrament, the Christian Sunday in its twin observance of worship and rest, and daily Christian life as lying between two polar types and being simply different modes of celebrating the paschal mystery, serves to integrate Christian life. There is no opposition between liturgical worship and Christian life in the world, between the Christian Sunday and the Christian weekday; all are celebrations, in different ways, of the paschal mystery. There is no opposition between Christian activity in the sanctuary and in the marketplace; both celebrate the paschal mystery. All these modes of celebration reinforce one another and only together realize fully and celebrate adequately the paschal mystery.

Because of this intimate interrelationship, the problem of the celebration of the paschal mystery by Sunday observance cannot be resolved except in relation to its celebration by Christian life generally. The Christian Sunday must be so treated that it meets the need of daily Christian life in contemporary circumstances. Therefore, before a strategy for meeting the problem of the Christian Sunday can be proposed, it is necessary to reflect on Christian life.

Notes

[1]See Christopher Kiesling, "Celebration of the Paschal Mystery: The Eucharist," *Review for Religious* 27 (1968), pp. 284-86.

[2]In the following pages, the expressions "explicit awareness of the paschal mystery" and "explicit reference to the paschal mystery" do not mean that one must be aware in the sense of having in mind the precise concept, "paschal mystery," or that reference to the paschal mystery must use the very words "paschal mystery." What is meant is explicit awareness of or reference to the realities that go by the name "paschal mystery." Thus the words "paschal mystery" may not appear in the liturgy, though it explicitly refers to the mystery. Nineteenth century worshipers did not have the concept "paschal mystery" and yet they were explicitly aware of the reality which bears that name.

[3]See Franz X. Pettirsch, "A Theology of Sunday Rest," *Theology Digest* 6 (1958), pp. 114-16; Jean Daniélou, *The Bible and the Liturgy* (Notre Dame, Ind.: University of Notre Dame Press, 1956), pp. 242-86.

V

CHRISTIAN LIFE
AND THE CHURCH

The Christian life may be thought of as a lifelong striving to conform to certain standards of belief, conduct, and worship set forth by the Church in preaching the Gospel and handing on the traditional interpretation of it. This conformity is not necessarily an unthinking heteronomy unworthy of a human being. The right and indeed the duty of the Church to set forth the Gospel and its authentic traditional interpretation are freely accepted by the individual. Moreover, these standards are to be internalized, by prayer for divine help in understanding and fulfilling them, and by persevering reflection and discipline. Saintliness comes to Christian life to the degree that a person so internalizes these standards that he freely, from within his heart and with little effort and great joy, lives in conformity with them. Then he is indeed close to God. All this presupposes, of course, God's grace.

This view of the Christian life has been widely held. Evidence of this is the distress and even anger manifested by many Christians in recent years as a result of changes in the Church, whether official—as in the Catholic Church's liturgy or in the Lutheran Missouri Synod's ecumenical stance—or unofficial, as in the sermon content of Protestant ministers or in the statements of Catholic theologians regarding the presence of Christ in the Eucharist. Concrete standards of belief, conduct, and worship laid down by the Church, either by official acts or by the habitual repetition of phrases, practices, and forms, have come to be regarded as essential to Christian life, with little discrimination shown for their various values and little recognition made of their historical limitations. This development is to be expected if Christian life is seen as essentially a striving to live in accordance with standards. With these standards questioned and rendered dubious today, striving to conform to them makes little sense. Many Christians feel that they have been deprived of their religion and so cut off from God. Naturally, they are distressed and provoked even to anger.

But there is another way of conceiving Christian life; it can be thought of as a particular way of *being human.*

God's revelation, especially his definitive revelation in Jesus Christ, is not his invading the secular, profane world to reveal the existence of another far better one, which is to be won as a reward for internalized conformity to certain conditions—such as keeping the Commandments, adhering to approved formulas of faith, or worshiping according to schedules and rites prescribed by the Bible or by the instrument of God's will, the Church. Instead, God's revelation is his manifesting to men, and concretely showing them in the life, death, and resurrection of Jesus, his paschal plan for creation and mankind, and hence the true value of human life and the world. God himself became man: was conceived, born, and psychologically and personally molded by family life and a particular society with its unique culture; he worked, had friends and enemies, experienced the gaiety of a wedding feast and the sorrowful agony of death. God in Jesus Christ lived through his own paschal mystery, thus revealing it to us; God in Jesus Christ celebrated the paschal mystery.

Since God has done this, it means that, quite apart from what may come after temporal existence, human life in this world is a marvelously good and beautiful thing, in both its joys and sorrows.[1] God's revelation, especially in the Incarnation, tells men not to seek to escape the human and the secular, but to enter into them more fully than ever. Men are invited to collaborate with him in the adventure of the unfolding of his paschal plan. They are invited to share with him the task of bringing about a fullness of being and life—for themselves, by seeking rich human experience; for others, by unselfish love in interpersonal relationships; for society, by political participation; and for the world, by development of it through technology and art.

What is revealed by God in Jesus Christ confirms his previous revelation that he created a *good* world. The Book of Genesis says that after each of God's creative acts, he saw that what he had made was good, and that the whole of it was indeed very good. Hence a fundamental Judaeo-Christian vocation is to relish being-human-in-this-world, to savor it in all its dimensions, its joys and sorrows, its good and bad aspects,[2] while always doing the best one can in every situation to bring forth being and life from nothingness and death.

Again, Christian life is a *particular way* of being human. This includes openness to a personal transcendent yet immanent God who reveals himself especially in Jesus Christ as the ultimate reality and the norm of being and life. It involves openness to fellow men: respect, concern, care, even self-sacrifice for all men as persons, equal before God, his images, his children. It entails hope and optimism that the efforts expended in trying to be fully human and in developing society and nature to achieve *shalom* shall not be in vain but shall be fulfilled by God in what can be described only symbolically as a New Jerusalem in a new heaven and a new earth (Revelation, chaps. 21-22). Christian life may share one or another or several of these characteristics with other ways of being human—Jewish, Moslem, Marxist, humanist, and so on. But if all three characteristics and the peculiar content of each for the Christian are taken together, they sufficiently define the particularly Christian way of being human.

Another important factor of Christian life is implied in its being a particular way of being human. Christian life includes a ceaseless search for and pursuit of *shalom*, the fullness of being and life promised by God for mankind and creation. There is no resting, or no saying, "At last I am all that I can be; I have met the standards and I am close to God." There are always further possibilities to be realized—possibilities inherent in creation, possibilities inherent in the infinite power of God —which remain to be exploited or expected. This holds true not only for individual life, but for societies and nature; there are always possibilities to be exploited or expected to bring more life and being from death and nothingness.

Existing standards are guidelines from the past which indicate those that proved helpful then in promoting *shalom* and which suggest those that will promote it now and in the future. But with changing circumstances, with new possibilities for good and evil continually opening up as the universe is continually created by God and by man under God, these standards have to be continually reexamined, reinterpreted, and perhaps reformulated. Man can never say: "I have the final expression of truth; I know concretely exactly what must be done in every possible set of circumstances." He can only say: "I am pointed accurately in the direction of the truth and its final expression, but I must continue searching for them until they are finally given into my grasp in the vision of God. I am pointed in my habitual conscience in the direction of what should be done, but I must continually search for the particular right action in each particular complex set of circumstances in which I find myself at each moment."[3]

Thinking of Christian life as a particular way of being

human does not exclude that which is known as God's grace and man's vocation to eternal life with God. Grace and eternal life, it must be remembered, presuppose human life; they are qualifications of human life.[4] A pseudo-Christian humanism that recognizes nothing beyond man's native capacities and this temporal existence, but uses Christian words to describe them, is not being proposed here. On the other hand, to be avoided is a dualism of natural and supernatural worlds which regards the supernatural as a distinct existence parallel to human existence and alone of any value compared to the human. Persons exist humanly, and grace qualifies this human existence of persons; it does not replace it. A genuine Christian humanism gives full value to human life but sees human life permeated and enriched by God's grace and culminating in eternal life with him. Grace and eternal life were implied previously when it was said that being human in a Christian way includes openness to a personal God and hope for final fulfillment in a New Jerusalem.

The Christian life, then, does not consist primarily in the Christian's conforming to certain standards and thus thinking and doing certain things which other men do not think and do, such as going to church or resting from work on Sunday. The Christian life does indeed involve thinking and acting in ways in which other men do not, though more fundamentally it consists in being human like other men but with a particular awareness, or consciousness, of self and world. The Christian is human with the awareness that he is called by God, the creator of the universe, to cooperate with him in imitation of Jesus Christ in unfolding the paschal plan. The Christian lives human life in the awareness that he must give himself to perfecting human life and the world, even if it appears that his efforts are in vain, and even if men and the world take his life as they took the life of Jesus. The Christian lives humanly with a consciousness marked by the confident hope that, despite appearances, *shalom* is being realized by God, though often in a hidden way which only he perceives. The Christian engages in human life in all its dimensions in conscious dependence upon God and with gratitude for the privilege of being called to cooperate with him in working out his purpose.

If Christians think and do different things than non-Christians, if they gather to hear the Word of God and to break bread together, engage in ritual, adopt a discipline of life, go off on a "retreat," and observe Sunday with worship and rest from work, the purpose of all these special activities is to preserve and intensify the awareness in which they live human life, make history, create culture and, in all this, search for and pursue God's *shalom.*

The relevance of one's concept of the Christian life to the problem of the Christian Sunday is not difficult to discern. If the Christian life is conceived of as conforming to a given set of standards, then very likely one of the givens to be conformed to will be the Christian Sunday. It is certainly a most solid part of the whole of the Christian past, with roots in Jesus' own actions.

There is only one solution to the problem of the Christian Sunday: it must be retained and revitalized.

On the other hand, if Christian life is perpetual pursuit of being and life and the ceaseless search for *shalom* through human life, then a strategy for meeting the problem of the Christian Sunday will be flexible. It will seek to revitalize the Christian Sunday out of respect for tradition, and in view of the fact that there is no substitute obviously at hand; but it will also provide other means of serving the function which the Christian Sunday has served, and if the Christian way of being human is thereby fostered, will even admit the possibility of the Christian Sunday becoming less and less important for the sustenance of Christian life in the future.

Since the Church is the visible institution in which Christian life is led and supposedly nurtured, and since the observance of the Christian Sunday is promoted by that institution, something must be said here about the Church. The institutional aspects of the Church can help or hinder the Christian life of its members, and its attitude toward the Christian Sunday can be an adamant insistence upon preservation of the status quo, or an openness to adaptation and change in response to changing cultural conditions.

"Church" or "institutional Church" does not refer here solely to the Church's governing bodies, officials, hierarchy, clergy, and ordained ministry. It refers to the entire people of God—governed and governing, laymen and clergy. The shape of the visible Church and the style of its corporate activity are decided as much by the laity as by the ordained. A passive laity invites autocratic leadership and the structures that support it; an indifferent and lukewarm people invite a dull and mediocre clergy. Without doubt there is God-given authority in the Church to govern, and a charism to preach the Gospel and dispense the sacraments; but that does not exempt holders of authority or charism from listening to and cooperating with the faithful in whom the spirit also works, nor does it exempt the faithful from responsibility for the image of the Church in the world and for its mission.

The future of the Christian Sunday, therefore, is not the responsibility of only those who hold some office in the Church. It is the responsibility of every layman as well. If the Church should act to meet the problem of the Christian Sunday, the layman should not wait until the clergy or other officials decide what to do. The spirit of God may be calling him to initiate the response of the Church. Perhaps he can do no more than instruct his children about what appears to him to be the truly Christian approach to the problem, and guide the life of his family accordingly. Perhaps he can find like-minded people to support him in leading a style of Christian life that is adequate to the needs of the time as he and they see them. Through a priest or pastor who sees the problem, some changes in the style of ecclesial life in the local parish may be effected. There are many avenues that can be exploited by laity who see the need for change, although admittedly, as is the case in all

societies, it requires considerable patience, persever-
ance, and courage to bring about change in the Church.

Any pastoral effort today must recognize the division
in the Church between those who cannot adapt to new
styles of life, community, witness, and service, and
those who are eager to do so. Those who cannot adapt
to new ways—such as elderly people or middle-aged
people with not-so-flexible personalities—have to be
respected by the Church and helped to grow in their
faith and their manner of living it. The same holds true
for those who find a more meaningful expression of
their faith in new forms, such as youths and many
younger adults. If the Church consists of both these
groups and is going to provide for the growth in faith
of both, these groups have to respect and help one
another to live the Christian life as each sees that it
should be lived. Those for whom the Christian life is
mainly a matter of internalizing conformity to a set of
standards should not insist that others hold the same
view, or hinder others from living according to a different view. Similarly, those for whom the Christian life is
a particular way of being human, a ceaseless search for
shalom, should not expect everyone to share their view
or, as happens in many cases, to be able even to understand it because of psychological and social factors.

Any strategy, therefore, for meeting the problem of
the Christian Sunday must provide for both these
groups within the Church. Neither can be, with justifi-
cation, ridden over roughshod. Any pastoral program
must be broad enough to promote the welfare of all

members of the Church, not merely some at the expense of others. Some compromise may be called for, and the "haves" may be required to surrender some of their possessions so that the present "have nots" may be served. But somehow the Church, the whole people of God, should serve all its members as well as it can.

There are other divisions to be taken into account which do not correspond to the one noted in the foregoing paragraphs. The first is the division between those for whom religion is a very serious and prominent factor in life and those in whose lives religion plays only a small part. The possible reasons for this difference are several. It may be the result of having had or not having had a genuine, profound religious experience in the course of a lifetime. It may be a matter of temperament, character formation, or environmental influence, with or without significant religious experience. Another division is of recent origin and concerns the "third man" described by Gregory Baum in *The Credibility of the Church.*[5] The "third man" is the believer in the Christian faith who is disinclined to associate himself closely with the institutional Church, whether Catholic, Orthodox, or Protestant. There is, then, a division between members of the Church who participate fully in its institutional forms and those who do not. Any pastoral program should provide for the variety of religious needs of these different groups of people.

Again, the conception of the Church which one brings to the pastoral task of meeting the challenge to the Christian Sunday must include respectful trust and acceptance of other viewpoints on how Christian life should be led today. It must include a policy of freedom in the Church, so that different styles of Christian life can be led without constant harassment and charges of betrayal, and it must include positive provision for various viewpoints and styles of life.

This approach is not without precedent. All through its history the Church has positively provided for communities of religious men and women. These communities have been allowed to develop their own spirit, their own discipline, their own understanding of what it means to be a Christian. They have been given their own governments, although they have often surrendered a large part of their autonomy because they lacked the courage to bear responsibility for their own decisions. They have been given their own liturgies: the Dominican rite, the Carthusian rite, the Benedictine Office and calendar, and so on. Another precedent, even more striking in the variety for which it provides, is found in the Eastern Churches in communion with Rome. They have their own doctrinal expressions, theologies, canon law, mystique, liturgies, and conceptions of Christian life which members of the Latin Church often find difficult to comprehend. Why cannot similar provision for such autonomy within the Church also be made for groups of clergy, laity, and religious, in order that they may live the Christian life in the way which seems to them correct and enriching? Why cannot different parishes provide varieties of Christian spirit, discipline, understanding, government, and

liturgy for the Christian people, as religious congregations do for their people?

On the basis of the ideas of the Christian life and the
Church set forth in this chapter, it is possible to suggest
a pastoral strategy to meet the needs of the Christian
people in the face of the current threats to the Christian
Sunday.

Notes

[1] It may seem strange to talk about sorrow as good and beautiful,
yet seen in the larger context of life, it can have a good and beautiful
aspect. Viktor Frankl relates a thought-provoking incident: "Long
after I had resumed normal life again (that means a long time after
my release from camp), somebody showed me an illustrated weekly
with photographs of prisoners lying crowded on their bunks, staring
dully at a visitor. 'Isn't this terrible, the dreadful staring faces—
everything about it?' 'Why?' I asked, for I genuinely did not understand. For at that moment I saw it all again: at 5:00 A.M. it was still
pitch dark outside. I was lying on the hard boards in an earthen hut
where about seventy of us were 'taken care of.' We were sick and
did not have to leave camp for work. We could lie all day in our little
corner in the hut and doze and wait for the daily distribution of
bread. . . . and for the daily helping of soup. . . . But how content we
were; happy in spite of everything. All this came to my mind when
I saw the photographs in the magazine. When I explained, my
listeners understood why I did not find the photographs so terrible:
the people in it might not have been so unhappy after all." *Man's
Search for Meaning* (New York: Washington Square Press, 1963), pp.
75-77. See Frankl's ideas on the values which give meaning to life
in *The Doctor and the Soul*, trans. Richard and Clara Winston (New
York: Bantam Books, 1967), pp. 34-36.

[2] "Entering wholeheartedly into the bad aspects of human life"

does not mean that one should sin. It means that there are ugly, disagreeable, unpleasant experiences which must be accepted in the pursuit of being and life according to God's paschal plan. The child, for example, must curb his instinctual behavior if he is to develop behavior which is becoming to a mature adult. A married man must restrain any attraction he may feel toward other women if he is to intensify his marriage relationship with his wife. It means also that when one does sin, one does not persecute one's self by irrational feelings of guilt, but acknowledges that God in his paschal plan has taken this possibility into account and is so much the master of creation and its history that these failures can be factors bringing about being and life. In short, one can learn from one's mistakes, correct one's way, and bring *shalom* into one's own life and into the lives of others better than one could have done before the experience of failure.

[3]This is not relativism, the denial of truth and of absolute truth; nor in the ethical, moral sphere is it situational ethics such as that proposed by Joseph Fletcher (*Situation Ethics: The New Morality* (Philadelphia: Westminster Press, 1966). The truth possessed about things that by their nature change must necessarily be changing truth. The truth possessed about things that do not change will necessarily be limited by man's finite mind and by the historical cultural conditions in and from which he has a perspective on these things. This is particularly true in regard to what are essentially mysteries knowable by man only through revelation and never comprehensible to him. Such realities may be conceived in one way from one perspective, in another way from another perspective. There is absoluteness insofar as a particular statement may direct man accurately toward the ultimate, adequate statement of truth, whereas another statement may be an erroneous pointer. In the domain of morals or ethics, all final judgments are situational in a sense. Even in classical Scholastic moral theology as expounded by Thomas Aquinas, for example, ultimate moral judgments are situational. The function of the virtue of prudence is precisely to make a situational judgment, to determine what should be done in a par-

ticular set of circumstances (*Summa theologiae* II, ques. 47, Arts. 3, 7, 8; ques. 49, Arts. 6-8). Moral principles are just that, principles, not conclusions; they must be applied in particular circumstances by individual consciences. There is a natural moral law, but its dictates are very general; its particular expressions are conditioned by man's culture and must be worked out anew in each culture. The natural law's application is further conditioned by the situation in which the individual finds himself, so its application must be worked out by each individual. There is absolute truth in the theoretical and ethical realms, but it is not immediately, adequately, or easily discerned; it must be sought through a lifetime.

⁴Aquinas, *Summa theologiae* I-II, ques. 110, Art. 2.

⁵(New York: Herder and Herder, 1968), pp. 200-204.

VI

NUCLEAR COMMUNITIES

The appropriate response to the threats to the Christian Sunday suggested in Chapter Two is to preserve the Christian Sunday with a new understanding of and a new attitude towards the activities of the day, while at the same time developing a new style of Christian life, community, witness, and service which will support it and yet make Christian life less dependent upon it. Fundamental to this strategy is the development of a new style of Christian living.

In regard to Christian life, witness, and service, the new style will be in keeping with the Christian life regarded as a particular way of being human and as informal celebration of the paschal mystery. Thus the life, witness, and service of the Christian will adopt the styles and techniques of current culture. Sunday observance will not be an arbitrary intrusion into this new of community would entail, or because the only ideas they have are based on reports in the public press of sensation-making freak events in extremist groups which they find repulsive. The development of solid nuclear communities witnessing to genuine Christian brotherhood and fostering a new style of Christian life, and education through various media, should arouse the interest of many of these Christians in becoming members.

Christians who are content with the style of Christian living and ecclesial life which they now have in the average parish, and who even find that they have drawn close to God in this style of life, should not be pressured into joining a nuclear community. The same holds true for any other Christians: the lax, the fallen away, the "third men." It has already been noted that any pastoral plan for meeting the problem of the Christian Sunday must respect the various kinds of Christians and the various ideas of what Christian life should be. No coercion, therefore, is to be used in developing nuclear communities of Christian brotherhood.

There should be no arbitrary assignments of those interested in forming nuclear communities. For example, a parish should not be divided into territories with the people in each, who are interested in forming a nuclear community, required to belong to the community of that territory. The nuclear communities should be encouraged to develop more or less naturally through people who wish to form a community together. Thus a community may arise among a number of families in which the husbands are in the same profession, or among those in which the husbands and wives have similar educational backgrounds and already existing ties of friendship. It is important in the beginning to capitalize on spontaneous, natural groups.

This natural grouping presents a problem, of course, for Christian brotherhood should cut through natural divisions: "There are no more distinctions between Jew and Greek, slave and free, male and female, but all of you are one in Christ Jesus" (Gal. 3:28). This problem will be dealt with later.

Although people should not be assigned arbitrarily to nuclear communities on the basis of territorial divisions of parishes, it should be stressed that the development of nuclear communities need not wait for a change in the present parish system. Right now nuclear communities can be formed within parishes on more or less natural bases. Indeed, the immediate formation of such communities is highly desirable in order to begin the reformation of the present parish system, and especially desirable if some of the communities are allowed to cut across present parish boundaries. A host of vigorous nuclear communities scattered throughout the present parish system would be a firm base for the development of a new structural division of the Church to replace the present territorial parish system.

Another reason why existing parishes should not be regarded as obstacles to the development of nuclear communities now is that they provide services still required for those Christians who find the present structure sufficiently satisfying and even beneficial to them in leading their Christian lives. Existing parishes are a help, not a hindrance, in the pastoral strategy proposed here; they have a service to perform.

Small nuclear communities of Christian brotherhood are extremely important for the future. The Church is supposed to be the sign and realization of the brotherhood of men in Christ under God. No other human community, fraternity, or society fulfills this role. Whatever defects are apparent in the Church as it is made up of men, God's grace creating visible brotherhood manifestive of that grace is its deepest reality. The Church's institutional structure, creedal statements, canon law, and forms of worship are meant to express and serve this reality; though they may often be deficient, God's grace is not.

If the Church is to be the sign and realization of God's grace creating brotherhood among men and thus realizing the *shalom* which is the term of God's paschal plan, several requirements are necessary. The Church's teaching must be properly presented and the life of the Church, collectively and in its individual members, must be what it is supposed to be, so that God the Father and his incarnate Son and their Spirit are present and, in some sense, visible among men. But "what does the most to reveal God's presence. . . . is the brotherly charity of the faithful who are united in spirit as they work together for the faith of the Gospel and who prove themselves a sign of unity."[1]

A primary objective of renewal in the Church today,

therefore, must be the development of communities of genuine Christian brotherhood. Only in such communities can the Church be what it is supposed to be; there alone can the faithful "prove themselves" a sign and realization of the brotherhood of men in Christ and thereby reveal God's presence in the world among men.

No one will object to this statement, but it is necessary to stop playing with words and face reality. Authentic communities of brotherhood in Christ cannot be formed of thousands or hundreds of people. In such large groups people cannot even know one another's name. At present, most of the energies of the Christian people are being invested in renewal and reform of secondary aspects of the Church: international, regional, and diocesan governments; universal, national, and religional liturgies; new catechetical formulations of faith; universal and regional canon law. Renewal of the deepest reality of the Church, that which in the last analysis touches the hearts of men—brotherhood in Christ—has scarcely begun.

The masses of the Christian people have never experienced profound unity among themselves in Jesus Christ. They have no idea of what genuine brotherhood in Christ is. Fortunately more and more people are having a taste of what Christian community is in its deepest reality through retreats of the Cursillo and sensitivity types, intimate Eucharists, experimental communities, and so on. But the vast majority of people in churches on Sunday simply have not experienced Christian brotherhood in any deep sense. They may have experienced great consolation from their religion and their fellow Christians. But this is not the same as experiencing the unity of mankind in Jesus Christ. The time has come for the Church to bring its own members and mankind, not only salvation through the consolations of religion, but also salvation through the brotherhood of men in Christ. This calls for the development of small nuclear communities in which it will be possible to generate a keen sense of community in Christ and to experience deeply the Eucharist for what it is, "a sacrament of love, a sign of unity, and a bond of charity."[2] This development is not only a responsibility of all Christians, in order to fulfill Christ's will for his Church, but also a right to which individual members of Christ's Church have a claim and which those governing the Church have a duty to provide.

The vigor of an individual's Christian life in the future will depend to a great extent upon the support of a small nuclear community. As Peter Berger points out, faith needs a plausibility structure to support it.[3] Of the various elements which constitute a plausibility structure, association and conversation with like-minded people are extremely important. A man continues to accept as true what he knows about reality as long as he finds that knowledge confirmed by others; when others question it, he becomes less certain. If the Christian style of life in the future is going to be a life of full involvement in a pluralistic society, where many world views will compete with Christian faith in the marketplace, then a vigorous Christian life will be in special need of the kind of support that only a small nuclear community can supply.

Every available means should be used to develop nuclear groups whose members are united by strong bonds of Christian love. This love is supernatural, and therefore the primary means for developing Christian community will be, to name but a few, common prayer, study of the Bible, days of recollection, charitable and apostolic projects, and the religious education of the children who belong to a primary community. Care should be taken, however, to see that external projects do not become the end of nuclear communities. Their primary purpose is not to be Christian social service centers, but to provide Christian community, and the support and inspiration which Christian community can give to Christian life in the world. Nuclear communities should not become Christian social service centers but provide dedicated Christians for secular social service centers.

Many psychic and social barriers prevent communication and consequently community among people, thus hindering God's gift of Christian love for neighbor from being exercised to the full extent of its power. Therefore natural means should also be employed to promote community, such as purely social gatherings and group dynamics or sensitivity sessions presided over by trained and prudent moderators. Such purely natural means are more often than not indispensable in disposing people toward the free flow of Christian love and the achievement of genuine Christian community.

As a general rule, nuclear communities should meet biweekly or twice a month. Certainly primary communities should meet at least this often. Some secondary nuclear communities—for example, those made up of college students away from home—should perhaps meet every week. Other secondary communities, such as those composed of business men who would also be members with their wives and families of primary communities, should meet only once a month; these men would find it practically impossible to participate in both biweekly meetings of their respective primary communities and in biweekly meetings of their specialized group, unless they felt some extraordinary need which compelled them to assume the sacrifices that this would entail. Each group should decide on the frequency of its meetings, but primary communities should provide for at least biweekly or twice-a-month meetings at which the liturgy of the Word and the Eucharist will be celebrated.

Attendance at these meetings must be taken as seriously as good Christians now take attendance at church on Sunday. The nuclear communities are not to be regarded, as might be a parish women's organization, as dispensable additions to the fundamentals of Christian life. They are the fundamentals of a new style of Christian life. If a regular day for meetings is established by common agreement, or a schedule of meetings planned for the year, members can then arrange their social calendars so that they will be free to attend at those times when their community meets.

Meetings of nuclear communities will have to take

place during the week, and at the meetings at which the liturgy of the Word and the Eucharist will be celebrated, a priest or fully ordained minister will be required. On Sunday—and increasingly on Saturday evening for Catholics—priests and ministers will have to provide worship for the parish, particularly for those who prefer the traditional style of Christian life, but also for clusters of nuclear communities. To expect priests and ministers to preside several times over the worship of several separate nuclear communities also meeting on Sunday would be expecting too much, although there may be situations, in rural areas, for example, in which there would be no problem. The meetings of nuclear communities, therefore, particularly the biweekly meetings which include the Eucharist, will have to be held on weekdays.

Many primary nuclear communities, because of their peculiar composition, will have to meet in the early evening after men are through work and before younger children go to bed. Other primary communities with few young children could meet later in the evening. Supplementary communities could meet during the day or in the evening depending on their membership; business men, for instance, could meet after working hours. As each group must decide upon the frequency of its meetings, so it must decide upon the day of the week and the time most convenient to meet. A particular person's or family's choice of a nuclear community will sometimes be determined by the meeting time of a particular community rather than by its locality or its members.

Primary nuclear communities should, if possible, meet in the homes of their members. If the communities are too large to do this, they should then meet in some parish or cluster center so built or remodeled that it has two, three, or four rooms (perhaps divided by folding walls) which have a homelike atmosphere, that is, carpeted floors rather than vinyl flooring, table and floor lamps rather than overhead lighting, some upholstered furniture supplemented by folding chairs rather than all folding chairs, wood bureaus rather than steel cabinets for storing things, pictures on the wall, and so on. The center of a cluster of nuclear communities should have a building similar in design and furnishings—though not in spirit—to a funeral home, with its flexible interior which can be made into one or several rooms.

Secondary nuclear communities should meet somewhere in their own milieu. A room in an office building might be the meeting place for a specialized community of secretaries or professional men. A cell of nurses and doctors might meet in a conference room in a hospital.

Nuclear communities should not meet in a church or chapel, even when their meetings include the liturgy of the Word and the Eucharist. An aim of nuclear communities is to emphasize that the Church is people; it is not a special set of buildings down the street or in Vatican City. Moreover, it is people who live, work, and play in the world, and the Church must more obviously appear to be the Church-in-the-world. In addition, people today are not coming to the church to hear the word of God and to participate in the Eucharist. It is therefore the responsibility of the Christian people to bring the Word and the Sacrament to men where they live, work, and play. The Word and the Sacrament must be released from the prison of the sanctuary so that they can exercise their influence on men in the world, which is the purpose for which God has given them to his people. The dichotomy between worship and worldly activity must be overcome, not by destroying either worship or worldly activity, but by worshiping in a way that shows that worship, together with secular activity, is an integral part of Christian life which both informally and formally celebrates the paschal mystery.

The agenda of the regular meetings of nuclear communities has already been partially noted in passing: common prayer, Bible study, planning and reporting on charitable or apostolic projects, activities to promote fraternity and communication, and so on. Since the aim of nuclear communities is to develop and support a new style of Christian life, community, witness, and service, each community should work out its own agenda for its own meetings. However, some items in the agenda are so essential that they are normally to be preferred if time is limited.

The first essential item is the biweekly or twice monthly liturgy of the Word and the Eucharist—the Mass, in Catholic terminology. The Word and the Eucharist together, not only one or the other, are the heart of Christian life and community, witness and service. Both Catholics and Protestants must reform their thinking in this matter and restore integral Christian worship.[4] The primary immediate objective of nuclear communities is the best possible liturgy of the Word and the Eucharist. Every other item in the agenda of the meetings is either to prepare for this worship or to exploit and extend its inspiration.

To make worship the primary objective of nuclear communities is not to promote withdrawal from involvement in the world. Granted that there are strains of Christianity and notions of worship that would lead to this conclusion, authentic Christian faith and worship are not of that sort. Authentic Christian worship does not attempt to escape from the world, time, place, history, the things of everyday life, physical and moral evil. On the contrary, it faces all these things, takes them up into itself, seeks their origin and purpose, weighs their value for life, and searches for the hand of the Creator and Savior in them. Authentic Christian worship does not take men out of the world but sends them into the world with new light in which to see it, penetrate its being and discern all that is in it—good and evil, truth and falsehood, the beautiful and the ugly. It teaches men that it is in and through this world, and their working with it and for it, that they will encounter its Creator and Savior who reveals himself and man's destiny by realizing in the world his paschal plan.

Good liturgies of the Word and the Sacrament in nuclear communities' weekday meetings will be powerhouses of Christian life in the world. They will give birth to new styles of Christian life, community, witness, and ministry, and indirectly improve Sunday worship, for they will teach people by experience what the liturgy of the Word and the Eucharist means and can be. People can then carry this experience over into Sunday worship and use it to guide and vitalize the worship of the larger community.

Another item on the agenda of nuclear communities' meetings should be the occasional celebration of the liturgy of the sacrament of forgiveness—Penance—or something comparable for Protestants. A team of priests could come for the meeting of a Catholic community to hear individual confessions and pronounce God's forgiveness individually, or the local bishop could give permission for the use of common absolution on these occasions, in accordance with the new rite of the sacrament of forgiveness.

Baptism also should be carried out in the meetings of the nuclear communities. Though this will most often affect primary nuclear communities which include families, it may also affect secondary ones. Baptism celebrates incorporation into the Christian community,[5] and Christian community will be most fully realized experientially in nuclear communities. The meaning of Baptism will be more clearly recognized when celebrated in these groups.

All members of a nuclear should be concerned about sick and dying members—visiting them, and when they can, helping them and their families. The sacrament of the anointing of the sick should also be the concern of the whole nuclear community, and although it will usually be celebrated in the home of the sick person or in a hospital, at least some members should be present for it if at all possible. This is one more means of drawing together in Christian charity the members of these communities.

The manner of celebrating the liturgy in nuclear communities should be appropriate to the setting, which will not be a church or a chapel. The presiding celebrant should normally wear some simple sign of his office—a stole, for example. The utensils employed should be ordinary; decoration should be simple and in good taste. The ritual action, though following an approved general pattern, should be natural in its execution and detailed procedure. The texts provided by the universal Church should be followed, with provision made for spontaneity and the contributions of the particular group.

Two extremes in the liturgy are to be avoided: first, the elaborateness and formality which is appropriate and even necessary in churches and chapels, especially those with large congregations and, secondly, a verbalized liturgy which excludes the non-verbal communication inherent in ritual gestures, vestments, candles, special chalices, and so forth. Official commissions of the Church responsible for providing liturgical rites, texts, and books will have to do additional work beyond what has already been done, in order to provide legitimate ways of appropriately celebrating the liturgy in nuclear communities in the world outside churches and chapels. Many clergymen and laymen on the other hand, will have to resist the temptation of thinking, as so many do today, that good liturgy can exist without symbolism that escapes immediate intellectual comprehension.

Following the principle of subsidiarity, the government of nuclear communities should be, as much as possible, in the hands of each community. It should be democratic. Elected officers, chairmen, or leaders for the whole group or for task committees within the group should be laymen or religious, not clerics. A clergyman should be attached to each community, but his role should not be to govern but to serve it. He should do this by presiding over its liturgy, encouraging its growth in community, suggesting ways of witness and ministry that it might undertake and assisting it to undertake them, aiding in the religious instruction of the members, counseling both the group and individuals, and performing whatever other services the community deems necessary for their spiritual well-being. He should be the man of God to whom the community can turn for an understanding of God's Word as they seek to know and live it, and at times he should be the man of God who pronounces God's prophetic judgment.

The development of nuclear communities would help to solve the identity crisis currently troubling many priests and ministers. Since their function would be to move from one to another of the several communities for which each would be responsible, they would not be confined to the church and rectory or parsonage, waiting for people to come to them. Catholic priests would not daily celebrate early morning Masses in parish churches with only a handful of people present, but would celebrate perhaps two or three Masses a day in morning, afternoon, and evening meetings of nuclear communities, in schools, office buildings, homes, and other places.

In addition to this activity—since those Christians who still prefer the old style of Christian and ecclesial life must be served—the clergy would have to continue with the present services which the parishes now offer: Sunday worship, daily Mass, Saturday confessions, and so on, although these would have to be cut down so that priests and ministers could serve the nuclear communities. For private counseling they may, like doctors, have to set up office hours during the day or on certain evenings only, and people will have to make appointments to see them. The priesthood and ordained ministry would be full-time jobs, especially if there is a shortage of clergy to care for a large number of nuclear communities.

In areas where the number of communities is large, where they meet quite frequently, or where relatively few priests or ministers are available, members of a permanent diaconate could assist in serving the nuclear communities. They would be able to preside over and explain the liturgy of the Word; they could distribute the Eucharist in Catholic communities, administer Baptism, and should be sufficiently trained to help the communities in developing their Christian lives. But the government of nuclear communities should not be in the hands of deacons any more than in the hands of priests and ministers. Permanent deacons might also serve in the center of a cluster of nuclear communities, as will be discussed in the next chapter.

The ecumenical possibilities of nuclear communities should not be overlooked. On a regular basis, perhaps a few times a year, a community of Catholics could meet with an Orthodox, Lutheran, or Anglican community for a liturgy of the Word, Bible study, and fellowship. Or a nuclear community could extend an invitation to a family or a single person of another faith to join in one or another of their regular meetings, with respect always being paid to individual consciences and the rules of Churches regarding participation in the Eucharist. Nuclear communities should also bear responsibility for lax or fallen away Christians and the "third men." These people are more likely to return to a vigorous practice of their faith or participate in the institutional life of the Church as a result of the more personal contact and atmosphere of a nuclear community than as a result of radio and subway advertisements exhorting them to worship in the church of their choice on Sunday.

The establishment of nuclear communities would, in effect, shift the center of ordinary ecclesial life from the sanctuary or church building to a genuine *ecclesia,* a community of God's people called together to worship him and witness to his marvelous deeds wherever this *ecclesia* might meet—in a home, conference room, office building, or recreation center. Nuclear communities would realize in a dramatic way the Church-in-the-world. Such nuclear communities initiated now—and they can be initiated now in any parish whose clergy and people are interested enough—would absorb the restlessness of many Christians dissatisfied with present ecclesial life. They would prevent the Church from becoming split into a huge impersonal religious service organization on one side, and on the other, a mass of people—some only nominally Christian and others conscientiously seeking deeper Christian life and community in "underground churches." Well-established nuclear communities with biweekly liturgies of the Word and the Eucharist would provide a ready alternative to Sunday worship if cultural conditions ever made it impossible to be maintained. Henceforth, this liturgy of the Word and Sacrament in nuclear communities, rather than Sunday worship, should be regarded as *the* fundamentally essential liturgy of the Church. This liturgy is not meant to abolish Sunday worship, however, but to give it new meaning.

Notes

[1] *Pastoral Constitution on the Church in the Modern World* 21, in *The Documents of Vatican II,* ed. Walter M. Abbott (New York: America Press, paperback ed., 1966), p. 219.

[2] *The Constitution on the Sacred Liturgy* 47, in *The Documents of Vatican II,* p. 154.

[3] *A Rumor of Angels* (Garden City, New York: Doubleday & Company, Inc., 1969), pp. 42-46; *idem,* with Thomas Luckmann, *The Social Construction of Reality* (Garden City, New York: Doubleday, Anchor Book, 1966), pp. 92-97, 104-116, 147-56.

[4] Of all the suggestions made in this book, Protestants generally

will find the frequency of the Lord's Supper and its celebration on weekdays the most difficult to accept in view of their traditions. With regard to the frequency of the Eucharist, Protestant scholars of early Church history acknowledge that the Eucharist was an integral part of Christian worship every Sunday in the earliest days of Christianity (e.g., J. J. von Allmen, *Worship: Its Theology and Practice* (New York: Oxford University Press, 1965), pp. 148-50; Willy Rordorf, *Sunday: The History of the Day of Rest and Worship in the Earliest Centuries of the Christian Church*, trans. A. A. K. Graham (Philadelphia: Westminster Press, 1968), pp. 239, 243-47, 271-72, 305-306), © SCM Press, Ltd., 1968. Used by permission. They also acknowledge that neither Luther nor Calvin intended that the Eucharist not be celebrated every Sunday. It was their followers who eventually squeezed the Lord's Supper out of the normal worship of the Christian people on Sunday (e.g., Gustav Aulen, *Eucharist and Sacrifice*, trans. Eric H. Wahlstrom (Philadelphia: Muhlenberg Press, 1958), p. 32; J. J. von Allmen, *op. cit.*, pp. 150-52; Kenneth G. Phifer, *A Protestant Case for Liturgical Renewal* (Philadelphia: Westminster Press, 1963), pp. 71, 86, 129; Cyril C. Richardson, "Word and Sacrament in Protestant Worship" in *Liturgical Renewal in the Christian Churches*, ed. Michael J. Taylor (Baltimore: Helicon Press, Inc., 1967), pp. 35-37, 40). Protestant advocates for liturgical renewal insist that this means restoration of the Eucharist to its rightful place as complementary to the Word of God in worship (e.g., Phifer, *op. cit.*, pp. 127-33; Richardson, *op. cit.*, pp. 48-52).

Some Protestant scholars insist that the Eucharist should be held every Sunday and only on Sunday (e.g., Rordorf, *op. cit.*, p. 303; von Allmen, *op. cit.*, p. 226). However, Luther's idea (Rordorf, *op. cit.*, p. 302) that worship of God is not bound to particular times seems more in accord with the New Testament message, especially Paul's idea of Christian freedom from the law and from the elements of this world (Gal. 4:3-11; Col. 2:8-23). With regard to Rordorf's contention that because the Lord instituted the Eucharist a second time, as it were, on the evening of his resurrection on Sunday, he therefore determined Sunday as the Christian day of worship (*op. cit.*, pp. 233,

303-304), it should be pointed out that what is most important on this "first day of the week" is not merely the objective fact of Jesus' resurrection, but the newly risen Lord's appearance to his disciples and his sharing with them the glory of his exaltation as Lord and head of the Church, the *shalom* of God (cf. John 20:20). If this encounter had occurred on a day of the week other than Sunday, that day would most likely have been chosen as the day for Christian worship in the early Church, even though it did not coincide with the basic fact of the Lord's resurrection. The time for the celebration of the Lord's Supper is not nearly so important as the achievement of its purpose, the union of the Risen Lord with his people, the building up of the body of Christ, the Church. If in the twentieth or twenty-first century this purpose can be achieved better on a weekday than on Sunday, the Christian people should not hesitate to celebrate the Lord's Supper on a weekday.

While Protestants regain an esteem for the Lord's Supper as an integral part of normal Christian worship, Catholics must regain a similar esteem for the Word of God. Since the biblical movement in the Catholic Church, and especially since Vatican Council II, particularly the *Constitution on the Sacred Liturgy* (24; 35:2, 4; 51; 52; 92:a), Catholics have made notable progress in this restoration, though much remains to be done.

[5]See Christopher Kiesling, "Infant Baptism," *Worship* 42 (1968), pp. 617-26.

VII

NEW MEANING
FOR SUNDAY WORSHIP
AND REST

The development of nuclear communities will make Christian life less dependent upon the Christian Sunday for regular spiritual nourishment. The center of ordinary ecclesial life will be transferred from the church on Sunday to meetings of nuclear communities in the world on weekdays. Instead of weakening the Christian Sunday, however, this shift should give it new meaning because it will become the day for nuclear communities to worship together in clusters, for the Church-in-the-world to witness that it is also the Church-for-the-world.

Important as they are for the future of Christian life, small nuclear communities cannot afford to be introverted and isolated from each other. The Church is the sign and realization of *universal* brotherhood in Christ. The mutual love of its members must extend in affection and action to men and women of every race, color, social status, natural talent, and acquired ability. Nuclear communities that were exclusive clubs of naturally compatible people providing one another with a religious massage every other week could not be the basic cells of Christ's body, the Church.

The Church, moreover, is a brotherhood sent by God through Jesus Christ to herald and promote the paschal mystery, to cooperate with God in accomplishing his *shalom:* the resurrection of the body, a kingdom of truth, justice, love, freedom, and a new heaven and earth. The Church's mission is not simply to console or prick individual consciences, to provide individuals with the comfort of human community, or to offer, like the arts, an outlet for men's need to transcend the objective order of an industrial, technological society that impersonally and relentlessly follows its intrinsic laws of supply and demand and of maximum efficiency. The Church's mission is to change both the subjective realm of human conscience and the objective realm of society.[1] It must bring its influence to bear on the structures of society in order to change them toward an ever more perfect embodiment of truth and justice, love and freedom, toward an ever closer approximation to God's *shalom.*

This mission to promote the establishment of God's reign in society means that Christians must think and work together, and that small nuclear communities must be in communication with one another, for the time will inevitably come when the whole Christian people will have to offer strong prophetic protest or assume courageous intitiative in regard to grave social issues affecting neighborhoods, cities, nations, and the world itself. Nuclear communities should therefore be grouped into clusters.

A cluster of nuclear communities constitutes a new form of parish, much more loose and decentralized than the old. The new parish as a cluster of nuclear communities is not the basic unit of the Church, which is now the nuclear community of brotherhood in Christ. It is, rather, a center for ensuring communication between the communities themselves, and between the communities and the bishop of the diocese.

The nuclear communities which form a cluster need not be located in the same area, just as the Christians who form a community need not be from the same immediate neighborhood. The new parish, in other words, need not be territorial. An argument for nonterritorial clusters is that they could be established so that each contains a good cross section of the Christian population: a nuclear community of white suburbanites, another of inner-city blacks, another of college students, another of workers, another of professional people. When the cluster of nuclear communities then meets for the liturgy of the Word and the Eucharist, it will be more truly representative of what God's people should be, and the challenge to Christian brotherhood in such an assembly will have been prepared for by the activity within each of the cells. On the other hand, in many situations such an arrangement may be unmanageable. In such case, a cluster of nuclear communities in the same territory may be more workable, but they should not be established by simply dividing the territory like a piece of pie; free, more or less natural groupings must be retained even within a territory.

More important at the moment than making a final decision as to whether new parishes should be territorial or non-territorial is the development of nuclear communities and community clusters. Right now territorial parishes can and should be organized into clusters of nuclear communities. If in the process of this organization communities or individual Christians cross present parish boundaries, all parties concerned should make whatever concessions necessary. The present territorial parish system and structure, which many believe is no longer appropriate or adequate, will change in the future only if it is changed now. Organization of a parish into a cluster of nuclear communities is feasible now, and enlightened clergy and laity in some parishes should begin the process.

Organizing present territorial parishes into clusters of nuclear communities is also necessary in order to continue providing for those who still prefer the old style of Christian life. Present territorial parishes can serve two functions: they can continue to serve Christians who are satisfied and even benefited by the way things presently are, and they can initiate a new style of Christian life by forming within their boundaries some nuclear communities for those interested. When these nuclear communities become numerous in territorial parishes, they can be regrouped into new clusters that may or may not respect the old parish boundaries, depending on what will prove the most practical in each locality. Most of the present territorial parishes may then be abolished, with their buildings left to serve as centers for the new clusters.

A cluster of nuclear communities should be presided over by the several priests or ministers and permanent deacons who serve the individual communities of the cluster, and by delegates from each of the communities. This team should meet periodically to review the life of the individual communities and of the cluster as a whole. It should exchange information that ought to be shared by each of the communities, see if the communities can help one another in any particular way, and determine whether the communities of the cluster should undertake any projects together; in addition, it should assess the needs of the area, nation, world, or Church about which the communities ought to share a common concern.

This team of clergy and delegates—lay and religious —should be considered the center of the new parish. In other words, just as the Church is to be thought of as people gathered in nuclear communities, so centers of nuclear communities should be thought of as people, rather than as groups of buildings. However, the team will need some place to conduct their meetings and carry out other functions. This could be rented space; it could be a multipurpose building erected precisely for the functions of the cluster's center, or an existing parish building appropriately remodeled. Here again thought must be given to making use of existing facilities which cannot or will not be disposed of by Church authorities, since present parishes with their buildings afford a framework in which a new style of Christian and ecclesial life can be inaugurated now.

The center of the cluster of nuclear communities should also be responsible for the keeping of necessary records, such as baptismal, marriage, and financial records. It should handle other business which may be necessary for the life of the individual communities, such as the purchase of hymnals, missalettes, and liturgical books. But its chief responsibility must always be the pastoral care of the Christian people, both those who prefer the old style of Christian life and those who desire the new.

This pastoral care entails providing for Sunday and weekday worship as usual, confessions on Saturday, religious counseling, visitation and anointing of the sick, baptisms, funerals, and other services for those Christians who are satisfied with the present manner of ecclesial life. It must also, of course, serve the nuclear communities of which it is the center. But before detailing this service, it should be pointed out again that existing parishes are helpful in fulfilling this total pastoral task. While the development of nuclear communities and the shift into them of ordinary ecclesial life is taking place, these existing parishes can continue with their present services, although they will have to curtail them to some degree in order to free the clergy and the permanent deacons for the care of the nuclear communities. Even a new parish in a suburb, for example, which can begin as a cluster of nuclear communities, should provide pastoral care for those in the area who wish the old style of Christian life. To provide this service, of course, buildings of some sort, rented or built, will be required.

For those Christians incorporated into nuclear communities the center should provide for Confirmation, marriages, and funerals. Confirmation should be celebrated in the physical center of the cluster or new parish because it is that phase of Christian initiation which incorporates the Christian into the Church with a direct responsibility for the mission of the universal Church. A child or minor serves the good of his country by developing his own body and mind in order to be a good citizen; his direct responsibility is to his own good, whereby he indirectly but truly serves the whole society. When he reaches adulthood he receives a direct responsibility for the welfare of society by being given the right to vote and the duty of paying taxes and doing military service, things not expected of a minor; as an adult he pursues his own good indirectly by fulfilling his direct responsibility to his country. Thus, the baptized person's direct responsibility is the development of his own Christian maturity, whereby he indirectly serves the good of the Church and its mission. With Confirmation he receives a direct responsibility for the good of the Church and its mission, and thereafter, by serving these, indirectly serves his own maturity. It is appropri-

ate then that Confirmation, unlike Baptism, be celebrated with the larger unit of the Church, the cluster of
nuclear communities, which more obviously witnesses
to the Church-for-the-world, and which also testifies to
the role of the bishop as the symbol of Christ the Head,
to whom the members of all the nuclear communities
are united.

Marriages and funerals should also be celebrated in
the physical center of the cluster of nuclear communities. One reason for this is purely a matter of expedi-
ency: at marriages and funerals there will usually be
more people in attendance than merely the members of
any one nuclear community or even a cluster of communities; consequently, more space will be needed. But
there are also theological reasons. Marriage in particular is of concern to the total society and to the whole
Church; in it, moreover, Christ's union with his whole
Church is symbolized. Funerals mark the end of life
toward which all Christians are tending—death in
Christ.

Most importantly, however, the center of the cluster
must provide for the liturgy of the Word and the Eucharist celebrated by all the nuclear communities. The
Christian people, assembled to hear the Word of God
and participate in the Eucharist, is *the* ritual expression
of the Church-for-the-world even as it is of the Church-
in-the-world. As the Christian people confirm themselves as a primary community of love through the
Word and the Sacrament, so they confirm themselves as
a secondary community of universal mission through
the liturgy of the Word and the Sacrament. True, these

two aspects of the Christian community cannot be separated; one cannot be confirmed without the other also being strengthened. But a large congregation provides a particularly suitable situation in which to promote the sense of belonging to a worldwide community with a universal mission. Since both aspects of the Christian community should be fostered, a sensible pastoral program will consciously seek to nourish both, utilizing the liturgy of the Word and the Eucharist in nuclear communities to promote the one, and the liturgy of the Word and the Eucharist in clusters of nuclear communities to promote the other.

Another reason for the liturgy of the Word and the Sacrament in a cluster of nuclear communities is to remind the members that the Church to which they belong includes all men, that their Christian love must extend in deed as well as in affection to *all* men. It will be recalled that nuclear communities are to be developed freely and naturally, encouraging interested people to come together on more or less natural bases, whatever they may be: profession, work, education, geographical proximity. But true Christian community transcends natural bonds. A cluster of nuclear communities embraces groups which differ from one another sociologically, especially if the cluster is non-territorial and sweeps through a whole town or part of a major city. Transcendent Christian community will be expressed and realized most aptly through the liturgy of the Word and the Sacrament celebrated in a cluster of nuclear communities.

Appropriate times for the assembly of all the nuclear

communities of a cluster for the liturgy of the Word and the Eucharist would be the major Christian feasts and Sunday, the Lord's Day, the day on which Christians from the beginning have assembled to nourish their unity in Christ and to give public testimony of their faith by worshiping together. The members of nuclear communities should be encouraged (not obliged) to participate every Sunday in the worship of the cluster's center. In any case, there will have to be worship in the cluster's center every Sunday to provide for those Christians who consider Sunday worship as the heart of their Christian life, in contrast to those who will have opted to regard the biweekly worship of their nuclear community as the heart of their Christian life.

To think that encouraging the members of nuclear communities to participate in the Sunday worship of the cluster or new parish is asking them, in view of their fundamental biweekly worship on a weekday, to do more than is necessary, is to have missed the difference between the two worships. It is not a matter of asking them to do more than is necessary, but of asking them to do what is basically necessary for a full appreciation of Christian community. Rarely will appreciation of Christian community as a primary community of love be generated in large congregations. It is experience of this dimension of Christian community, sadly lacking in the past, which is craved today, and which the weekday worship of Word and Sacrament is meant to provide. Those seeking a new style of Christian life presumably desire a full Christian experience. For this it is necessary to have both the worship of small nuclear communities and the worship of a cluster of nuclear communities. Only if one is thinking in terms of fulfilling an obligation to worship, without any consideration of the quality of the worship involved, does this recommendation appear to ask more worship from members of nuclear communities than from those who prefer the old style of Christian life.

Members of nuclear communities are not to be obliged by law or by the threat of offending God to participate every Sunday in the worship of the cluster's center. Hopefully, the members will frequently reflect upon their need and responsibility to cultivate the broader Christian community beyond the limits of their little groups. As a result they will develop a conscience that inclines them to participate in the Sunday worship of the cluster as part of their celebration of the paschal mystery on Sunday by both worship and play.

Certain Sundays of the year, however, should be singled out as days on which a very special effort must be made by all members to participate in the cluster's worship of Word and Sacrament. Toward this Sunday worship a genuine serious obligation of conscience should be developed. Two of these Sundays would be Easter and Pentecost which, with Christmas, constitute the major feasts of the year. But other Sundays also should be singled out for celebration by the entire cluster. One would be in September at the beginning of the social year, when schools start, clubs resume meetings, and city life takes up after the summer months of vacation.

A second would be the first Sunday of Advent, a third the first Sunday of Lent, and a fourth late in May, when the social life of the city is closing down for summer vacation. Other Sundays could also be stressed, for example, the one before Thanksgiving (the Sunday after the holiday may not be practical because of weekend traveling) or the Sunday before the Fourth of July.

The liturgy of the Word and the Sacrament on these selected Sundays should be very special, not only in the sense that an attitude of serious obligation toward it is developed in the members of the nuclear communities, but also in the sense that it becomes a genuine celebration of the cluster or new parish, a true expression of the people's faith. The liturgy for these Sundays, as well as for the major feasts, should be planned by the communities' members. The talented musicians, singers, dancers, and artists of every kind who belong to the cluster should be called upon to contribute their skills and arts to a really grand liturgy that truly expresses the faith, love, and hope of these people who constitute this unit of the universal Church. It probably will not be possible to do this for every one of the major feasts and special Sundays decided upon by the cluster, but for only three or perhaps four in the course of a year. A less magnificent liturgy, but one still arising from the people, might be celebrated on the remaining feasts and special Sundays by having one nuclear community in a cluster plan the liturgy for the first Sunday of Advent, another plan the liturgy of the first Sunday of Lent, and a third the liturgy for the final Sunday of the social year in spring. People will participate with greater interest and enthusiasm in the Sunday liturgy when they have participated in its planning and have contributed their own talents to the praise of God. The liturgy then will be more efficacious in building up a sense of community, not only in the secondary sense, but in the primary sense as well, even though the congregation will be large.

The theme of every Sunday's worship should emphasize the universality of the Church, its social mission, and the service of the Christian people to the world. It should not be directed to consoling the congregation; this is more proper to the weekday worship of nuclear communities and to special occasions in the worship of the cluster. Sunday worship should be directed to stimulating Christian conscience regarding social issues that are genuine threats to the welfare of men generally and that can be solved only by communal action: pollution of natural resources, underdeveloped countries struggling with poverty, pornography and drugs peddled among youngsters, racial discrimination, and other such issues. Perhaps the sermon on Mother's Day should not be in praise of good Christian mothers, but about the plight of unwed mothers and the social implications of this phenomenon. If its theme is carefully selected so that it is steadily directed to the universal Church and its mission to society and culture, Sunday worship will assume a meaning distinctive from that of weekday worship in nuclear communities. This weekday worship will usually be directed to the development of personal love of God and interpersonal charity to strenghen the sense of primary community; when it does concern the universal Church and its social mission, it will view these much more in terms of their significance for personal spiritual growth in Christ and for authentic brotherly love within the nuclear community. If the theme of the universal Church and its mission is emphasized in the cluster's Sunday worship, this worship will not seem to the members to be simply a duplication of their biweekly liturgy of Word and Sacrament. It will be seen instead as a valuable complement and enrichment which extends their Christian experience, even as the biweekly worship intensifies it.

Needless to say, much more imaginative implementation of existing liturgical regulations and much more creative reform of the liturgy for Sunday will have to be undertaken if Sunday worship is going to provide the unique sort of worship which has been suggested. The choice of Scripture readings, the content of prayers, and the message of sermons or homilies will have to reflect more social awareness than they do at present. Sunday worship will have to be much more explicit in its celebration of the paschal mystery as God's plan leading to the bodily fulfillment of mankind in the resurrection of the dead in a new heaven and a new earth.

New meaning can be given to the Christian Sunday's observance of worship, therefore, by making it the worship of a cluster of nuclear communities that expresses the unity of the people in the universal Church sent by

Christ to herald and promote God's reign among men in society. The experience of worship in the large congregation in the center of a cluster on Sunday complements, confirms, and broadens the experience of worship in the small congregations of the nuclear communities on weekdays. By removing the pressure to participate in the worship of the new parish every Sunday and yet encouraging participation on several special Sundays with special liturgy, the uniqueness of Sunday as the Lord's Day is retained generally and, at notable times of both the liturgical and civil year, assumes exceptional significance. The uniqueness of Sunday as the Lord's Day can also be preserved by a new understanding of Sunday rest.

What is proposed here concerning the Christian observance of rest on Sunday is similar to that which has been proposed concerning the observance of Sunday worship. Sunday rest and Sunday worship of the large Christian community both have value, and for that reason should be maintained as long as possible. If they are to be preserved, however, cultural conditions require that they be regarded in a new light. These same cultural conditions also require recognition of the fact that the Christian people may have to abandon Sunday worship and rest as impractical in the future, and with this possibility in mind, preparations must be made for the retention of the values which they embody. By retaining Sunday worship for the cluster of nuclear communities while shifting ecclesial life to small nuclear communities which meet on weekdays, Sunday worship is preserved for the present with new significance; at the same time the Christian people are becoming accustomed to another way of regularly nourishing their life by worship. By promoting a positive use of Sunday rest as play in the new creation to celebrate the paschal mystery, the Sunday observance of rest is retained with new meaning and, simultaneously, Christians are being prepared to bear witness to the paschal mystery through the good use of leisure at other times.

The Sunday observance of rest can be conceived as a celebration of the paschal mystery which lies between the informal celebration which is Christian daily life, and the formal celebration which is the liturgy of the Word and the Eucharist. Sunday rest does not announce the paschal mystery with the explicitness of the liturgy; but insofar as it is observed for the purpose of bearing witness to the paschal mystery manifested by the Risen Lord to his disciples on "the first day of the week," and because it limits Christians' activities to those which are not "work," it does announce the paschal mystery in a quasi-stylized or ritual form. Thus Sunday rest is a celebration of the paschal mystery which tends toward the formal type of celebration.

Through the paschal mystery, men enter into the freedom of the sons of God, into the joy of life which is God's, and into the new creation. Men have this freedom, joy, and new creation in an imperfect manner— by faith, in hope, fragmentarily and anticipatorily, *in mysterio,* however one wishes to phrase it.

On all sides men are seen oppressed and in bondage

either to their own uncontrolled instincts and emotions, to forces destructive of physical integrity and life, or to unjust social structures and cultural conditions. Sorrow, depression, boredom, despair, and pain seemingly smother joy in the world of experience. When one rides by train through the slums of large cities and sees shabby apartments, grubby little factories, and yards full of junk, one finds it difficult to speak of freedom and joy in a new creation now.

Yet the Christian in his faith believes that freedom, joy, and the new creation are realities, however imperfectly they may be realized at present or however much they are objects of hope rather than of possession. It is the Christian's mission to announce this to all mankind, not merely by speaking about it, but by striving to live it in cooperation with God's grace. Sunday rest is the announcement and realization, the celebration by living of the freedom and joy of the new creation of the paschal mystery.

In the light of these thoughts, rest from work on Sunday must be interpreted as abstention from whatever curtails freedom, suppresses joy, and prevents enjoyment of the goods of this world. It is abstention, or better, an escape from the slavery of an existence made difficult and miserable by sin in a world made ugly by sin. It means escape from those ordinary activities to which men are bound by the sheer necessities of human existence infected by sin.

The Scriptures present the picture of man as enslaved by the things of this world because of sin. Adam is cast out of paradise and condemned to earn his bread by the sweat of his brow because of sin (Gen. 3:19). Eve's human condition as subject to her husband is due to sin (Gen. 3:16). St. Paul writes about slavery to the elements, or elementary religious notions, of this world (Col. 4:3). St. John speaks of men as belonging to this world unless they are freed from it by Christ (John 8:23; 16:33).

To be a slave or to belong to this world is to be caught in the web of sinful human existence, with all its anxieties and cares, some merely for bodily needs, some for needs of the human mind and spirit. Not only servile work but judicial proceedings as well have been banned on Sunday because both, as actually experienced, are the result of sinful man's needs. The United Nations General Assembly and the United States Congress spend their time thinking, talking, discussing, debating—activities which moral theologians have never classified as the kind of work forbidden on Sunday. But neither organization ordinarily meets on Sunday because everybody knows that in the concrete historical situation these activities are in fact work, a slavery to which men are condemned by their sinful human condition: their animosity toward one another, their failure to communicate and understand one another, their envy of one another in the struggle for survival.

Abstention from work on Sunday means men's wresting themselves free from the dominion of sin and refusing to become involved in those activities (in kind or quality) which must ordinarily be engaged in to keep sin-infected human existence going in all spheres: bodily, mental, spiritual. Men wrest themselves free from slavery to sinful human existence by celebrating their freedom and joy as sons of God in the new creation in the Risen Christ. They celebrate their freedom by doing what they wish to do rather than what they must do. They celebrate their joy by enjoying themselves. They celebrate the new creation by appreciative, creative use of the world. In a word, they celebrate the paschal mystery by play in the new creation.

Many activities which have been classified as work or cooperation in work can be seen now in a new light and hence as suitable for the Christian Sunday. Shopping on Sunday, for example, can be seen in an affluent society as play. The Christian can perceive in the abundance of goods which fill the stores of the nation something akin to the wealth which Israel's prophets foretold as characteristic of messianic fulfillment: caravans from Midian, ships from Tarshish with silver and gold, flocks of Kedar, and rams of Nebaioth, the cypresses of Lebanon and the pines (Isaiah 60). The abundance of goods and the money with which to purchase them can be viewed as the realization of man's dominion over creation which, according to the story of Genesis, was entrusted to him by God. For the woman busy with household chores from one end of the week to the next, a leisurely shopping tour on Sunday may be a truly free act with special enjoyment, a way of celebrating her share in Christ's victory over the difficulties of human existence. It can be play to examine and admire the marvelous goods which man makes and to exchange dollars for these goods, thus bringing convenience and beauty into the clothes, home, and life of one's family.

Those who own and operate stores on Sunday, such as people who work in restaurants or movie theatres, can be seen as sacrificing their own freedom and enjoyment out of charity, so that others may enjoy themselves in freedom from work. Or better, if the celebration of the paschal mystery by play on Sunday is seen as a cooperative action by the whole Christian people, then those who operate stores on Sunday are cooperating with their fellow Christians in the celebration of the paschal mystery by play; they, too, are observing the Christian Sunday.

This positive interpretation of Sunday rest as play in the new creation is not novel. The early Christians did not cease from work on Sunday, except when it was necessary for participating in corporate worship.[2] The Sabbath commandment of the Old Testament was not applied to Sunday, but was seen as having been fulfilled in Christ. The Christian in his everyday life, by abstention from sin and, positively, by the performance of good deeds, is united to Christ and fulfills the Sabbath commandment spiritually, that is, according to its ultimate significance in God's intentions. Even when civil legislation under Constantine and subsequent emperors made Sunday a holiday, the Fathers of the Church stressed, not abstention from work, but worship and upright conduct becoming to Christians. It was only because of growing moral laxity on the civil holiday that the Sabbath commandment was applied to Sunday rest and with it the restrictions about work which, in the centuries following, became the focal point of concern.

To say that Sunday rest means joyful play in the new creation is to use the language of today's theology in the light of its evaluation of the secular in order to say what the Fathers of the Church said in their day—namely, that Christians should not sin but do good deeds every day, especially on Sunday, the day on which Christ rose from the dead and appeared to his disciples as Lord.

If Sunday rest is understood in this new way as joyful play in the new creation, then a positive attitude toward Sunday's activities must be adopted. Sunday must not be regarded simply as a day free from work, but as a day for the exercise of freedom, the expression of joy, and enjoyment of the world. Sunday rest must not suddenly come upon Christians, leaving them with nothing other than time on their hands, time to be killed. Sunday must be approached with the will to act, perhaps even with forethought and planning of the day's activities. The time available on Sunday must be seized and filled with suitable activities for which the idea of play in the new creation provides criteria.

Notes

[1]See Jürgen Moltmann, *The Theology of Hope*, trans. James W. Leitch (New York: Harper & Row, 1968), pp. 323-38.

[2]For this and the following statements, see Franz X. Pettirsch, "A Theology of Sunday Rest," *Theology Digest* 6 (1958), 114-20; for a

detailed historical study see Willy Rordorf, *Sunday: The History of the Day of Rest and Worship in the Earliest Centuries of the Christian Church,* trans. A. A. K. Graham (Philadelphia: Westminster Press, 1968), pp. 54-173. © SCM Press, Ltd., 1968. Used by permission. For the views of the Fathers of the Church on Sunday's meaning and its appropriate activities, see Jean Daniélou, *The Bible and the Liturgy* (Notre Dame, Ind.: University of Notre Dame Press, 1956), pp. 222-86 *passim.*

VIII

CRITERIA FOR
SUNDAY ACTIVITIES

If Sunday activities are celebration of the paschal mystery by play in the new creation, then they should have the characteristics of play: freedom, joy, recreation, creativity. These four characteristics taken together provide a handy norm for determining which activities are suitable for Christians. They are more positive than the negative norm of "no work" or the outmoded rule of "liberal work" but not "servile work."

Sunday activities should be free. "Free" is to be understood here existentially, that is, as a quality of a particular person's activity in its total complexity and in the context of his whole life. It is not to be understood essentially, that is, as a characteristic of an action viewed abstractly, apart from the circumstances of its actual performance by the person, solely in terms of its immediate object. "Free" refers to a quality of lived action, not of conceptualized action as in a manual of moral theology.

The word is to be understood as people generally understand it. Basically people associate free action with what they wish to do, rather than with what they must do because of some pressure, whether social, moral, physical, or any other kind. A professional writer who sweats over his book on Sunday to meet a publisher's deadline is engaged in free activity, a "liberal work" as opposed to a "servile work," only in theory and not in fact.

The freedom spoken of here is Christian freedom from the slavery of sin and the human condition which follows upon it. From the instant of conception, man is caught in the web of sinful humanity. He struggles to escape from it but cannot. Because of his sinful condition, man's freedom is curbed, sometimes by physical violence; sometimes by unjust laws and corrupt judges; sometimes by undisciplined emotions and bad habits. Even the guidelines for the development of freedom— just laws and the demands of love—become curbs upon freedom, for the freedom of man in the web of sin tends to turn in upon self and to find justice and love confining rather than liberating. In Christ, the Christian believes, man can begin to escape from this web and experience true human freedom. A Christian's activity on Sunday should somehow embody as lived experience this freedom of Christ from the sinful human condition. His Sunday activity should give him a sense of being a free son of God.

Christians should be so formed that they learn to sense whether their activity is imposed upon them by the sinful human condition or whether it is free—or at least relatively free—from the slavery resulting from sin, for in this life men never extricate themselves completely from the entangling web of sin and its consequences. The curse put upon Adam for sin was that he should gain his livelihood by the sweat of his brow. Sunday activity should not be that kind of activity, unless, of course, it is absolutely necessary. A Christian should have some "feel" for the kind of activity that is not a burden placed on man because of sinfulness.

Doubt will surely arise about whether or not some activity is really a part of the curse on man. Instead of becoming entrapped in moral casuistry by his efforts to resolve the doubt, the Christian should examine his intention and mood and, if both seem innocent, should then, in faith and trust, pursue the activity with the conscious intention of trying to celebrate joyfully his freedom as a son of God in the new creation.

Some may object to this approach on the grounds that it opens the door to subjectivity in moral judgment. Certainly there will be subjective judgment concerning some activity or other, but the norm for judging is not subjective: Sunday activity should be the exercise of Christian freedom from the bondage of sin and its consequences. This norm is quite objective. Moreover, if a person conscientiously judges that this objective norm is embodied in a particular action and he proceeds to that action in the spirit of Christian freedom,

the action, unless obviously evil from some other point
of view, is objectively good in the concrete; it is therefore a genuine celebration of the paschal mystery appropriate for Sunday.

A Christian acting in a spirit of Christian freedom,
although engaged in an activity that preachers or moralists would classify as "servile work" because of its
nature, is actually, existentially, more truly Christian
than one who is performing an action which fulfills the
moralists' idea of a "liberal work" but who is engaged
in this liberal activity under the pressures of the sinful
human condition. The file clerk who digs up his backyard for a vegetable garden in a spirit of freedom from
lifeless file cabinets is acting more truly as a Christian
than an author who spends Sunday doing the same
thing he does the rest of the week to earn a living.

Subtle casuistry must not be used to justify certain
activities on Sunday on the pretext of freedom. Some
activities are necessary for human existence or must be
performed in response to the demands of justice or
charity. A doctor, for example, may have to perform an
emergency operation. A mother must prepare meals for
her family. An intricate discussion could begin about
how these actions flowing from virtue are truly free, but
such understanding of "free" is more refined than the
understanding proposed for this first criterion. The doctor who spends three or four hours in an operating
room, or the mother who spends three or four hours in
a kitchen, usually does not regard such activity as
"free." They may *conceive* of it as free after a theolo-

gian explains it to them, but their *lived experience* is not one of freedom. This lived experience, not conceptualized experience, is what must be free in order to justify an activity as suitable for Sunday.

Whether or not lived experience is free depends greatly upon the individual person and his circumstances. A career woman may find four hours in the kitchen on Sunday a free activity. The individual is the ultimate judge in the light of the objective norm. The preachers' and moralists' task is not to name the activities which are free, but to describe the freedom which the Christian should seek in the activities which he chooses for Sunday.

A second criterion for Sunday activities is the joy which they afford. The conviction of Christian faith has always been that God created man for happiness, that he raised Christ from the dead in fulfillment of that promise and as a pledge that all men shall some day experience its fulfillment if they submit to God's creative action and do not reject it. Lack of joy is un-Christian. This does not mean that Christians admit no sorrow or sadness into their lives, or that they should continually wear false smiles and go about like giggling schoolgirls. It means that joy is an integral part of Christian life. It ought to dominate life in the long run even during earthly existence, although only beyond this existence will it be untroubled by any sorrow. Entangled six days a week in the cares and anxieties of human existence tainted by sin, the Christian on Sunday should attempt to extricate himself from these worries and the sorrow they engender by doing what he finds enjoyable, in order to proclaim and exercise his joy as a participant in Christ's victory over sin and death.

Freedom and joy tend to go together. If what a person does is freely done, if it is not done under the pressure of everyday existence, the chances are that he will enjoy it. (If he does not enjoy it, then perhaps he is neurotic, infected with a compulsion to work.) The joy found in an activity, on the other hand, enables a person to engage in it with greater spontaneity and enthusiasm or, in other words, greater freedom.

In a Sunday family gathering, a Sunday picnic, baseball game or tennis match, beach or ski party, in attendance at a movie or a concert, a Christian should find a pleasure and joy which are a confirmation of the goodness of creation and an assurance of the new creation in Christ's paschal victory. No apology need be made for the exhilaration of the senses, the pleasure of the eyes or ears, the limberness of the body, the play of the imagination, and the response of the emotions to nature's wonders and man's skill which are found in these Sunday pastimes. Indeed, these activities ought not to be called "pastimes," with the implication that they have little or no intrinsic value and serve only to take up time and prevent boredom. These activities are joyful and thus necessary ingredients of any celebration, including celebration of the paschal mystery. By engaging in these enjoyable activities on Sunday, Christians announce the paschal mystery to the world, not by explicit words, but by acting out the reality, by tasting the joy intrinsic to God's victory over sin and death in Christ.

If joyfulness, together with freedom, is a criterion for Sunday activities, a place is found for the carpentry which the office worker enjoys doing on Sunday when away from his desk and official forms, or the knitting a busy waitress enjoys on Sunday when she can sit down for more than an exhausted moment and do something more permanent and constructive than taking orders, carrying trays, and cleaning tables. The premed student, busy with biology and books all week long, may find ecstatic joy on Sunday in overhauling his car.

As it is in the case of the freedom of an activity, so it is with the joy of it: doubts may arise as to whether its joy is appropriate to Sunday. But again, of primary importance are the intention and the attitude, the spirit of celebration. Sundays will be more truly Christian if preachers encourage a spirit of paschal celebration in the activities of Sunday, rather than warn against work. They will be more truly Christian if moral theologians do not engage in casuistry about the use of that machine of manual labor known as the typewriter, but instead instruct Christians on how they can make human activity celebration of the paschal mystery.

The third criterion for Sunday activities is their re-creative quality.

Men do not have to be Christians in order to see the need for at least one day a week free from ordinary pursuits, so that human energies—physical, emotional, and mental—may be replenished. For this necessary recreation, Sunday is as good a day as any. Men of the post-Christian era will be (or are) quite willing to devote Sunday to recreation.

The Christian observance of Sunday, however, calls for recreation not simply as a necessity for the recuperation of human energies, but as celebration of the new creation of the paschal mystery. The renewal of bodily energy and muscular tone, the purgation of emotions and the restocking of the imagination, the unburdening of the mind and the calming of the spirit which accompany the enjoyment of Sunday's free activities make men new again and thereby foreshadow the restoration of humanity which will be definitively accomplished in the resurrection of the dead.

The Sunday recreation of the Christian and the refreshed humanity which follows from it symbolize the renovation and new condition of humanity at the resurrection of the dead. If it is true that a symbol, in contrast to a sign, contains the reality to which it points, then Sunday recreation and the resulting human condition contain something of the renewal and condition of man in the resurrection. This assertion may sound fantastic, but there are grounds for it.

A Christian person is radically a new man by God's grace in Christ, even though not yet entirely new, not yet new through and through to the very last fiber of the person. Growth in Christian life consists precisely in cooperating with God's grace to extend this radical renewal of humanity into every area of personal being. This renewal should proceed primarily in man's spirit, in virtue of which he transcends the limits of bodily being and is related personally to God. But the process of renewal pertains also to the mind and the body. Every conquest of mental illness, bodily disease, mental or bodily fatigue, injury, and deformity anticipate the ultimate renewal of humanity that God intends in his paschal plan revealed in Christ's resurrection from the dead. Jesus' miracles in healing minds and bodies inaugurated the messianic kingdom of God, the new creation. They were not merely tricks employed by Jesus to attract attention or to "prove a point." They were an integral part of his mission to save men, not merely souls.

The renewal of humanity in its mental and bodily being lags behind renewal of the spirit, of course, for it will be definitively accomplished only in the resurrection of the dead. The reason for this difference in the restoration of the various components of humanity is a mystery which escapes our comprehension. God restored the humanity of Jesus after three days; men know not the day nor the hour of their final renewal. All they know is that they are heirs of God and fellow heirs with Christ, provided they suffer with him in order that they may also be glorified with him (Rom. 8:17).

In the Christian person, therefore, recreational activity is the actualization of human nature radically transformed, made new, in Christ. To the eyes of faith, Christian recreation is qualitatively different from merely human recreation, for it exists in a new humanity, a humanity rightly ordered to God in Christ;

thus recreation is also rightly ordered to God. The Christian does not have to be explicitly conscious of this ordination to God in order for it to exist; the habitual orientation of his life will tend to shape his recreation so that it is ordered to God in Christ. To the extent that this recreation is not rightly ordered to God, and to the extent that this disordered recreation is deliberately engaged in, it is sinful.

The bodily and mental refreshment which follows upon a Christian's recreation will likewise be ordered to God in Christ, will be a condition fulfilling God's design for man's well-being in Christ. If the resultant state of humanity after recreation does not conform to God's intention for man, the recreation leading to this state has been sinful to some extent, provided the situation was within man's control. A hangover that incapacitates a man for a day leads to the suspicion that the recreation which preceded this state of humanity was not entirely according to God's will.

The Christian's recreation and the condition of humanity which follows upon it are in line with what God will accomplish in men at the resurrection of the body. They are foreshadowings of the renewal and pristine vigor of humanity fully accepted into the new creation. What that experience of renewal will be like, and what the condition of humanity after its accomplishment will be like, are impossible of description. But whatever they will be like, they will be a sublimation of that exhilaration and euphoria which men can experience now, and however utterly different they necessarily will be, however distant in their likeness from what men know now, they are foreshadowed in the recreation and refreshed humanity which men now enjoy.

This third criterion for Sunday's activities—their recreative quality—helps to determine what Christians should do on Sunday. The professor may busy himself on Sunday with the work that comes across his desk: lectures to be prepared, books to be reviewed, reports to be compiled, papers to be researched, agendas for seminars to be planned. He may excuse himself as he wrestles with this "work" (that is the word which best describes it for him) on the grounds that it is not "servile work" but "liberal work" allowed on Sunday. If he is busy with this sort of activity five or six days a week, however, more of the same on Sunday will not be recreation. On the contrary, it will continue to exhaust his energies, confine his emotions to the same objects, deplete further the stock of his imagination, occupy his intellect with the same problems, and leave his spirit in the same degree of anxiety. Activity with this destructive effect abounds and brings much pressure to bear on men in their sinful condition. Such activity may very well be a symbol of enslavement to the sin of the old creation, rather than an anticipation of the freedom and joy of the new.

The professor's activity just mentioned "may very well be" and not "necessarily is" a symbol of enslavement to sin, for if this activity is engaged in freely, and if it is done joyfully, it may be truly recreative. It will have these qualities of freedom, joy, and recreativeness if it is carried out in a way which differs from the way it is performed the other days of the week, so that it turns the mind and body in a new direction. The writer of prose may find recreation in writing poetry on Sunday. The professional philosopher may find recreation in the arts on Sunday. The construction worker may find recreation building fine cabinets or a rock garden. Such a shift of activity, slight though it may be, can provide genuine recreation, and it is a declaration of freedom and joy in spite of the human condition under sin.

As with the other criteria for Sunday activities, doubts may arise as to whether this or that activity is recreational. Much depends upon the individual's needs, of which he is normally the best judge. When doubt arises, the criterion of freedom can help to resolve the doubt, for what is freely done and what is not part and parcel of ordinary activities to keep existence going, is more likely to be restorative because it will release emotions, mind, and spirit from their usual concerns and divert them to other objects. Doubt can be settled also by the heightened enjoyment found in an activity. Enjoyment admits of degrees of intensity, and tends to wane with prolongation of the activity which gives rise to it. A modicum of enjoyment may be a sign that what is being done is part of normal human existence. Even work in the strict sense of earning a living offers some joy, otherwise it could not be carried on sanely day after day; but its joy is low-keyed because it has become customary. Heightened joy is a sign that what is being done is different, hence giving rest to body and mind, restoring them, recreating them.

Although heightened joy alone may not be a sufficient criterion for determining suitable activity for Sunday, the criteria of freedom, joy, and recreation, if combined, create a helpful norm. If it is necessary to engage in enervating "liberal work" on Sunday so that the activity is not free, enjoyable, and recreative, it would be better to justify the activity on the grounds of service to fellow men out of charity, rather than to justify it on the grounds of being a liberal kind of work. Thus the journalist may work hard at his writing on Sunday to serve men's need for and right to information, but let this activity be called what it is for him— work.

The fourth criterion for Sunday activities is creativity. As the book of Genesis says, God created man in his image and gave man a share in his dominion over creation (Gen. 1:26). Genesis portrays man as placed by God in a garden to cultivate and care for it (Gen. 2:15). Man is to continue God's creation-out-of-nothing by fashioning new things out of the goods God has given him. If Sunday activities should be celebration of the new creation, Christians most appropriately exercise their creativity on that day. If Adam in the garden was destined to create in freedom, joy, and personal fulfillment, so are those men who are incorporated by faith and baptism into the New Adam.

By means of this fourth criterion of creativeness, place is found on Sunday for gardening, carpentry, needlework, gourmet cooking, as well as for more obviously "liberal works," such as reading poetry or listening to music. Making steel and building houses are creative also, but normally such activities are part of everyday human existence with its burden of sin, so they are not symbolic of man's freedom from sin in the new creation. Moreover, the creativity which is appropriate to Sunday is very personal, for the person who works should be master over what is done, as God intended Adam to be. In addition, making steel and building houses usually are not done with the freedom, the unusual enjoyment, and the recreation of human energies which should characterize Sunday activity. Hence, this criterion of creativity, taken in conjunction with the other criteria, does not encourage the operation of Pittsburgh's steel mills, the construction of homes, or many other activities which Christian custom has long regarded as unsuitable for Sunday.

On the other hand, a sculptor may weld steel on Sunday, perhaps even make the steel by some special process he has developed. A man and his companions may leisurely put together a little cottage on a lakeshore where they regularly go for camping and fishing. Each of these instances presupposes that the creative activity involved is under personal mastery, is free, enjoyable, and recreative. If the sculptor is welding steel six days a week, or the man and his companions are building houses all week long, their activity on Sunday will not be recreative and especially enjoyable if it is substantially the same as during the week. Their celebration of the paschal mystery on Sunday must be through truly creative activity which somehow is different from what they do every day so that it will be particularly enjoyable, reinvigorating, and significative of their freedom in Christ from the net of sinful human existence in which they are bound by their daily work.

If Sunday activities have these four qualities, they will be play. Play stands over against work in the freedom with which it is done, in the more intense joy it provides, in the recreation of mind and body which it affords, and in its creativeness which produces something personal, whether this be as transient as a well-made serve in a tennis match or as permanent as an oil painting. And if Sunday activities are play, then they are appropriate for the celebration of the paschal mystery and the new creation. The question which the Christian should ask about his Sunday activity comes down to this: Is this activity play for me? If it is, then it is suitable for the day without further question. If it is doubtful, then he should go ahead with it in the spirit of play with the intention of celebrating the new creation; he should make it play.

The pastoral strategy suggested here for preserving the Sunday observance of rest does not consist in decrying those who work on Sunday, in repeating the ancient injunctions against work, in pointing out the evils which will befall men if they work on Sunday, in boycotting shopping centers open on Sunday, or in pressuring legislatures to pass laws against work on Sunday. Some of these tactics, at times, may be appropriate in particu-

lar situations. But in the long run it is more important
to disseminate a very positive understanding of Sunday
rest as celebration of the paschal mystery by play in the
new creation. It is important to develop an attitude in
Christians which impels them to seize the opportunity
of leisure on Sunday for activities which are free, joyful,
recreative, and creative. If Christians will learn to see
Sunday rest as play in which they deliberately engage
for the purpose of celebrating the paschal mystery, or
see their work as enabling others to engage in play,
then, however secular Sunday may be for society in
general, for Christians it will be Christian. At the same
time, Christians will learn that the value embodied in
the Sunday observance of rest can be preserved in
other periods of leisure on other days, if social and
cultural conditions ever change so much that it
becomes impossible to maintain the traditional Christian observance of rest on Sunday.

CONCLUSION

The purpose of this book has been to examine the plight of the Christian Sunday today and to propose a strategy to meet the threats to its future. The strategy finally suggested and the theological bases for it have involved many other aspects and elements of Christian life besides the observances of worship and rest on Sunday. Much will have been accomplished if the result of this book is only a more widespread awareness of the important place occupied by the Christian Sunday in the fabric of the life of individual Christians and the Church, so that the future of the Christian Sunday cannot be left out of explicit consideration when renewal of Christian life and the Church is under discussion. Above all, however, a proposal of strategy calls out for at least a serious attempt to implement it. Unless a strategy is patently unrealistic from the beginning, its validity is determined only by trial in action. It is hoped, therefore, that some Christian pastors and people will put the strategy proposed in these pages to the test by trying to implement it in their parishes. They certainly will discover ways to improve it and they may discover a different but far better strategy for meeting the problem of the future of the Christian Sunday.

CLASSIC SERMONS
ON THE
ATTRIBUTES OF GOD

KREGEL CLASSIC SERMONS Series

Classic Sermons on the Attributes of God

Classic Sermons on the Birth of Christ

Classic Sermons on Christian Service

Classic Sermons on the Cross of Christ

Classic Sermons on Faith and Doubt

Classic Sermons on Family and Home

Classic Sermons on Heaven and Hell

Classic Sermons on Hope

Classic Sermons on the Names of God

Classic Sermons on Overcoming Fear

Classic Sermons on Praise

Classic Sermons on Prayer

Classic Sermons on the Prodigal Son

Classic Sermons on the Resurrection of Christ

Classic Sermons on the Second Coming and
Other Prophetic Themes

Classic Sermons on the Sovereignty of God

Classic Sermons on Spiritual Warfare

Classic Sermons on Suffering

Classic Sermons on Worship

CLASSIC SERMONS ON THE ON THE ATTRIBUTES OF GOD

Compiled by
Warren W. Wiersbe

Grand Rapids, MI 49501

Classic Sermons on the Attributes of God, compiled by Warren W. Wiersbe. © 1989 by Kregel Publications, a division of Kregel, Inc., P. O. Box 2607, Grand Rapids, MI 49501. All rights reserved.

Library of Congress Cataloging-in-Publication Data

Classic Sermons on the Attributes of God, compiled
 by Warren W. Wiersbe. (Classic sermons series)
 Includes index.

 1. God—Attributes—Sermons. 2. Sermons, American.
3. Sermons, English. I. Wiersbe, Warren W. II. Series:
Kregel classic sermons series.
BT130.C56   1988   231'.4—dc19   88-12842

ISBN   0-8254-4038-6 (pbk.)

3 4 5 Printing/Year 94

Printed in the United States of America

Dedicated to the memory of

AIDEN WILSON TOZER (1897-1963),

whose prophetic ministry of the Word made our hearts burn within us and moved us to seek the beauty of holiness.

CONTENTS

PREFACE

THE *KREGEL CLASSIC SERMONS SERIES* is an attempt to assemble and publish meaningful sermons from master preachers about significant themes.

These are *sermons*, not essays or chapters taken from books about themes. Not all of these sermons could be called "great," but all of them are *meaningful*. They apply the truths of the Bible to the needs of the human heart, which is something that all effective preaching must do.

While some are better known than others, all of the preachers, whose sermons I have selected, had important ministries and were highly respected in their day. The fact that a sermon is included in this volume does not mean that either the compiler or the publisher agrees with or endorses everything that the man did, preached, or wrote. The sermon is here because it has a valued contribution to make.

These are sermons about *significant* themes. The pulpit is no place to play with trivia. The preacher has thirty minutes in which to help mend broken hearts, change defeated lives, and save lost souls; and he can never accomplish this demanding ministry by distributing homiletical tid-bits. In these difficult days, we do not need "clever" pulpiteers who discuss the times; we need dedicated ambassadors who will preach the eternities.

The reading of these sermons can enrich you own spiritual life. The studying of them can enrich your own skills as an interpreter and expounder of God's truth. However God uses these sermons in your own life and ministry, my prayer is that His Church around the world will be encouraged and strengthened.

Back to the Bible Broadcast   WARREN W. WIERSBE
Lincoln, Nebraska

The Love of God

Dwight Lyman Moody (1837-1899) is known around the world as one of America's most effective evangelists. Converted as a teenager through the witness of his Sunday school teacher, Moody became active in YMCA and Sunday school work in Chicago while pursuing a successful business career. He then devoted his life to evangelism and was used mightily of God in campaigns in both the United States and Great Britain. He founded the Northfield School for Girls, the Mount Hermon School for Boys, the Northfield Bible Conference, and the Moody Bible Institute in Chicago. Before the days of planes and radio, Moody traveled more than a million miles and addressed more than 100 million people. This message on God's love is from *Glad Tidings*, published by E. B. Trent, New York, 1876.

Dwight L. Moody

1

THE LOVE OF GOD

And the God of love and peace shall be with you
(2 Corinthians 13:11).

WE HAVE FOR our subject this evening, "Love." I have
often thought I would need only one text. If I thought I
could only make the world believe that God is love, I
would take that text alone and go up and down the
earth trying to counteract what Satan has been telling
people—that God is not love. He has made the world
believe that lie.

It would not take 24 hours to make the world come
to God if you could just make people believe that God
is love. If you can really make a man believe you love
him, you have won him; and if I could only make people
really believe that God loves them, what a rush we
would see for the kingdom of God! Oh, how they would
rush in! But man has a false idea about God, and he
will not believe that He is a God of love. It is because
he doesn't know Him.

God Is Love

Now, in Paul's farewell letter to the Corinthians he
says, "Finally, brethren, farewell. Be perfect. Be of good
comfort. Be of one mind. Live in peace, and the God of
love [he calls Him the God of love] and peace shall be
with you" (2 Cor. 13:11).

Then John, who was better acquainted with Christ
and told us about the love God has for this perishing
world, writes in his epistle, in the evening of his life,
these words: "Beloved, let us love one another, for love
is of God, and every one that loveth is born of God and
knoweth God, and he that loveth not, knoweth not
God, for God is love" (1 Jn. 4:7, 8).

We built a church in Chicago a few years ago, and we were so anxious to make people believe that God is love that we thought, if we could not preach it into their hearts, we would burn it in. So right over the pulpit we had the words put in gas jets, "God is love," and every night we had it lighted.

A man walking past there one night glanced in through the door and saw the text. He was a poor prodigal, and he kept going. And as he walked away, he said to himself, "God is love? No. God is not love. God does not love me. He does not love me, for I am a poor, miserable sinner. If God was love, He would love me. God is not love." Yet there the text was, burning down into his soul. He went on a little further, turned around and came back, and went into the meeting. He didn't hear what the sermon was, but the text got into his heart, and that is what we want.

It is of very little account what men say if only God's Word gets into the heart. And he stayed after the meeting was over, and I found him there weeping like a child. But as I unfolded the Scripture and told him how God had loved him from his earliest childhood all along, the light of the gospel broke into his mind, and he went away rejoicing. This would be the best meeting we have had today if we could only make this audience believe that God is love.

Now, our brother who opened the meeting with prayer referred to the difference between human and divine love. That is the very trouble with us. We are all the time measuring God's love by ours. We know that we love a man as long as he is worthy, and then we cast him off. But that is not divine love. There would be no hope for any of us if the Lord did that.

I have the idea that our mothers are to blame for a good deal of that, because of their teaching during their children's youth. They tell them that the Lord loves them when they are good children; when they are bad children the Lord does not love them. That is false teaching. God loves them all the time, just the same as you love your children.

Suppose a mother should come in here with a little child, and after she has been here a while, the child begins to cry. She says, "Keep still," but the child keeps on crying, so she turns him over to the police. She tells them "Take this child; I don't want him." What would you say of such a mother as that?

Teach a child that God loves him only as long as he is good and that when he is bad the Lord does not love him, and you will have problems. When he grows up, if he has a bad temper, he will have the idea that God hates him. He will think God doesn't love him when he has a bad temper, and as he has a bad temper all the time, he will conclude that God does not love him at all, but hates him all the time.

Now God hates sin, but He loves the sinner. There is a great difference between the love of God and our love—all the difference in the world between the human and the divine love.

God's Love Is Unchangeable

Now, turn a moment to John 13:11: "Now, before the feast of the Passover, when Jesus knew that his hour was come that he should depart out of this world unto the Father, having loved his own which were in the world, he loved them unto the end." His love is unchangeable. That night He knew very well what was going to happen. Judas had gone out to betray Him. He knew it. He had already left that little band to go out and sell Christ.

Do you tell me Christ did not love Judas? That very night He said to him, "Judas, what thou doest, do quickly" (13:27), and when Judas, meeting Him in the garden, kissed Him, He said, "Betrayest thou thy Master with a kiss?" (Luke 22:48). Was this not the voice of love and compassion that ought to have broken Judas' heart? He loved him in the very hour that he betrayed Him.

That is what is going to make hell so terrible —you go there with the love of God beneath your feet. It is not that *He* doesn't love you but that you despise His love. It is a terrible thing to despise love.

"He loved them unto the end." Jesus knew very well that Peter was going to deny Him that night and curse and swear because he was mistaken for Jesus' companion. He knew that all His disciples would forsake Him and leave Him to suffer alone. Yet He "loved them unto the end."

And the sweetest words that fell from the lips of the Son of God were the night when they were going to leave Him. Those words will live forever. How they will live in the hearts of God's people! We could not get on very well without the 14th of John, and the 15th and 16th chapters.

It was on that memorable night that He uttered those blessed words, and it was on that very night that He told them how much God loved them. It seems as if that particular night, when He was about to be deserted by all, His heart was bursting with love for His flock.

Just let us look at John 16:27 to see what He says. "For the Father himself loveth you, because ye have loved me, and have believed that I came from God." I don't know but what Christ felt that there might be some of His disciples who would not love the Father as they loved Him.

I remember that for the first few years after I was converted, I had a good deal more love for Christ than for God the Father. I looked upon God as the stern Judge, while I regarded Christ as the Mediator who had come between me and that stern Judge to appease His wrath. But when I got a little better acquainted with my Bible, those views all fled.

After I became a father and woke up to the realization of what it cost God to have His Son die, I began to see that God was to be loved just as much as His Son was. Why, it took more love for God to give His Son to die than it would to die Himself. You would a thousand times sooner die yourself in your son's place than have him taken away. If the executioner was about to take your son to the gallows, you would say, "Let me die in his stead; let my son be spared."

Oh, think of the love God must have had for this world that He gave His only begotten Son to die for it. And that is what I want you to understand. "The Father himself loveth you because ye have loved me." If a man has loved Christ, God will set His love upon him.

Then, in John 17:23 is that wonderful prayer Jesus made that night: "I in them, and thou in me, that they may be made perfect in one, and that the world may know thou hast sent me, and hast loved them as thou hast loved me." God could look down from heaven and see His Son fulfilling His will; and He said, "This is my beloved Son, in whom I am well pleased."

But when it is said, "God loved us as he loved his own Son," it used to seem to me to be downright blasphemy, until I found it was in the Word of God. That was the wonderful prayer He made on the night of His betrayal.

Is there any love in the world like that? Is there anything to be compared to the love of God? Well may Paul say, "It passeth knowledge" (Eph. 3:19).

And then I can imagine some of you saying, "Well, He loved His disciples, and He loves those who serve Him faithfully; but I have been untrue." I may be speaking now to some backsliders, and if I am, I want to say to everyone here, "The Lord loves you."

A backslider came into the inquiry room night before last, and I was trying to tell him God loved him. He would hardly believe me. He thought because he had not kept up his love and faithfulness to God, and to his own vows, that God had stopped loving him.

Now, it says in John 13:1, "He loved them unto the end," that is, His love was unchangeable. You may have forgotten Him and betrayed Him and denied Him, but nevertheless, He loves you; He loves the backslider. There is not a man here who has wandered from God and betrayed Him but what the Lord Jesus loves him and wants him to come back.

Now, in Hosea 14:4, God says that He will heal every backslider. "I will love them freely." So the Lord tells the backsliders, "If you will only come back to me, I will forgive you." It was thus with Peter who denied his Lord. The Savior forgave him and sent him to preach His glorious gospel on the Day of Pentecost when 3,000 were won to Christ under one sermon of a backslider.

Don't let a backslider go out of this hall this evening with such hard talk about the Lord. No backslider can say God has left him. He may think so, but it is one of the devil's lies. The Lord has never left a man yet.

God's Love Is Everlasting

Just turn to Jeremiah 31:3. "He hath loved us," He says, "with an everlasting love." Now, there is the difference between human and divine love: the one is fleeting, but the other is everlasting. There is no end of God's love.

I can imagine some of you saying, "If God has loved us with an everlasting love, why does it say that God is angry with the sinner every day?" Why, dear friends, that very word "anger" in the Scriptures is one of the very strongest evidences and expressions of God's love.

Suppose I have had two boys, and one of them goes out and lies and swears and steals and gets drunk. If I have no love for him I don't care what he does. But just because I do love him, it makes me angry to see him take that course. And it is because God loves the sinner that He gets angry with him. That very passage shows how strong God's love is.

Let me tell you, dear friends, God loves you in all your backslidings and wanderings. You may despise His love and trample it under your feet and go down to ruin, but it won't be because God doesn't love you.

I once heard of a father who had a prodigal son, and the boy had sent his mother down to the grave with a broken heart. One evening the boy started out as usual to spend the night in drinking and gambling. His old father, as he was leaving, said, "My son, I want to ask a favor of you tonight. You have not spent an evening with me since your mother died, and now I want you to spend this night at home. I have been very lonely since your mother died. Now, won't you gratify your old father by staying at home with him?"

"No," said the young man. "It is lonely here, and there is nothing to interest me, and I am going out."

The old man prayed and wept, and at last he said, "My boy, you are just killing me, as you have killed your mother. These hairs are growing whiter, and you are sending me, too, to the grave."

Still the boy would not stay, and the old man said, "If you are determined to go to ruin, you must go over this old body tonight. I cannot resist you. You are stronger than I, but if you go out you must go over this body."

And he laid himself down before the door, and that son walked over the form of his father, trampled the love of his father under foot, and went out.

God's Love Is for Sinners

That is the way with sinners. You have to trample the blood of God's Son under your feet if you go down to death —to make light of the blood of the innocent, to make light of the wonderful love of God, to despise it. But whether you do or not, He loves you still.

I can imagine some of you saying, "Why does He not show His love to us?" Why, how can it be any further shown than it is? You say so because you won't read His Word and find out how much He loves you.

If you will take a concordance and run through the Scriptures with the one word "love," you will find out how much He loves you. You will find out that it is all one great assurance of His love. He is continually trying to teach you this one lesson and to win you to Himself by a cross of love.

All the burdens He has placed upon the sons of men have been out of pure love, to bring them to Himself. Those who do not believe that God is love are under the power of the evil one. He has blinded you, and you have been deceived with his lies.

God's dealing has been all with love, love, love—
from the fall of Adam to the present hour. Adam's
calamity brought down God's love. No sooner did the
news reach heaven than God came down after Adam
with His love. That voice that rang through Eden was
the voice of love, hunting after the fallen one—"Adam,
where art thou?"

For all these thousand years that voice of love has
been sounding down through the ages. Out of His love
He make a way of escape for Adam. God saved him out
of His pity and love.

In Isaiah 63:9 we read, "In all their affliction he was
afflicted, and the angel of his presence saved them: in
his love and in his pity he redeemed them; and he bare
them, and carried them all the days of old." In all their
afflictions He was afflicted. You cannot afflict any of
God's creatures without afflicting Him. He takes the
place of a living father.

When a man has a sick child burning with fever,
how gladly the father or the mother would take that
fever and put it into their own bosoms. The mother
would take from a child its loathsome disease, right
out of its body, and put it into her own—such is a
mother's love. How she pities the child, and how gladly
she would suffer in the place of the child! That
illustration has been often used here—"As a mother
pitieth her children."

You cannot afflict one of God's creatures but God
feels it. The Son of His bosom came to redeem us from
the curse of the world. I do not see how any man with
an open Bible before him can get up and say to me
that he does not see how God is love.

"Greater love hath no man than this, that a man lay
down his life for his friend." Christ laid down His life
on the cross, and cried in His agony, "Father, forgive
them, they know not what they do." That was wonderful
love.

You and I would have called fire down from heaven
to consume them. We would have sent them all down
into the hot pavement of hell. But the Son of God lifted

up His cry, "Father, forgive them, they know not what they do."

I hear someone say, "I do not see, I do not understand, how it is that He loves us." What more proof do you want that God loves you? You say, "I am not worthy to be loved." That is true. I will admit that. And He does not love you because you deserve it.

It will help us to get at the divine love to look a little into our own families, and at our human love. Take a mother with nine children—all good children except one. One is a prodigal. He has wandered off and he is everything that is bad. That mother will probably love that prodigal boy as much or more than all the rest put together. It will be with a love mingled with pity.

A friend of mine was visiting at a house some time ago where quite a company was assembled. The guests were talking pleasantly together. My friend noticed that the mother seemed agitated, and was all the while going out and coming in. He took her aside and asked her what troubled her. She took him out into another room and introduced him to her boy. There he was, a poor wretched boy, all mangled and bruised with the fall of sin. She said, "I have much more trouble with him than with all the rest. He has wandered far, but he is my boy yet." She loved him still. So God loves you still.

God's Love Is Undeserved

It ought to break your hearts to hear of God's love and it ought to bring you right to Him. You may say you do not deserve it, and that it true. But because you do not deserve it, God offers it to you.

You may say, "If I could get rid of my sins God would love me." In Revelation 1:5, John said, "Unto him that loved us, and washed us from our sins in his own blood." It does not say He washed us from our sins, and then loved us. He loved us first, and then washed us clean.

Some people say, "You must turn away from sin, and then Christ will love you." But how can you get rid of it until you come to Him? He takes us into His own bosom, and then He cleanses us from sin.

He has shed His blood for you. He wants you, and He will redeem you today, if you will it.

An Englishman told me a story once that may serve to illustrate the truth that God loves men in their sin. He does not love sin, but He loves men even in their sin. He seeks to save them from sin.

There was a boy, a great many years ago, who was kidnapped in London. Long months and years passed and the mother had prayed and prayed. All her efforts had failed, and they had given up all hope. But the mother did not quite give up her hope.

One day a boy was sent into the neighboring house to sweep the chimney, and by some mistake he got down through the wrong chimney. When he came down he came in by the sitting-room chimney.

His memory began at once to travel back through the years that had passed. He thought that things looked strangely familiar. The scenes of the early days of youth were dawning upon him; and as he stood there surveying the place, his mother came into the room.

He stood there, covered with rags and soot. Did she wait until she had sent him to be washed before she rushed and took him in her arms? No, indeed; it was her own boy. She took him to her arms, all black and sooty, hugged him to her bosom, and shed tears of joy on his head.

You have wandered very far from Him, and there may not be a sound spot on you; but if you will just come to God He will forgive and receive you.

I think a good deal of Isaiah 38:17. It reads: "Thou hast in love to my soul delivered it from the pit of corruption; for thou hast cast all my sins behind thy back." Notice, the love comes first. He did not say that He had taken away sins and cast them behind Him. He loved us first, and then He took our sins away.

I like that little word, "m-y," "my." The reason we do not get any benefit from the Scriptures is that we are always speaking in generalizations. We say God loves nations, God loves churches, and God loves certain classes of people. But here it says that out of love to my soul, He has taken all my sins and cast them behind his back.

If they are behind His back, they are gone from me forever. If they are cast behind His back, how can Satan ever get at them again? I will defy any fiend from hell to find them. Satan can torment me with them no more.

God's Love Is Unfailing

There are three thoughts I have tried to bring out tonight:

> God is love,
> God's love is unchangeable;
> God's love is everlasting.

The fourth thought is this:

> God's love is unfailing.

Your love is not. His is. When people come to me and talk about their love of God, it chills me through and through; the thermometer goes down 50 degrees. But when they talk about God's love for them, I know what they would say.

So, do not think for a moment that God does not love you a good deal more than you love Him. There is not a sinner here; there is not an unsaved man here tonight but He wants to save—just as a father loves his child, only a thousand times more.

Is there a poor wanderer here who has wandered far from Christ? He sends me to invite you to come to Him again. I don't care how sinful you are; let this text sink deep into your soul today, "God is love."

The Majesty of God's Mercy

J. Stuart Holden (1874-1934), Vicar of St. Paul's
Church, Portman Square, London, was an Anglican
preacher of great ability. Possessing an engaging
personality and persuasive manner, Holden was
known on both sides of the Atlantic for his convention
ministries. Holden was leader of the Keswick
movement for almost 30 years and guided it ably.
Skilled as a diagnostician of the deeper spiritual life,
he helped guide many in discerning the difference
between spurious and genuine faith. This message on
God's mercy is from *Life's Flood-tide* by J. Stuart
Holden, published by Roxburghe House, London, 1913.

J. Stuart Holden

2

THE MAJESTY OF GOD'S MERCY

He healeth the broken in heart . . . He telleth the number of the stars (Psalm 148:3, 4).

WHAT A SURPRISING conjunction is found in this twin attribute of God—active pity in the small circles of human experience and unmeasured power in the great realms of creation! Here is God manifesting Himself in both the remotest and the nearest things of which we have any knowledge—the universal and the personal.

At first sight, it seems incongruous to suggest that these two things have anything in common. Surely there can be little, if any, connection between the starry heavens above and the suffering hearts below; between that which is so infinitely great and that which is so infinitely little; between that of which no man knows much and that of which all men know a great deal; between that which transcends in its greatness all our thoughts, and that which in its bitterness touches all our lives.

But in this declaration of the majesty and mercy of God, the psalmist is not indulging in mere flights of fancy. Nor is he doing violence to the separate revelations of God's power and love, as though these could ever be in contrast.

Instead, he is pointing to an underlying relationship between stars and sorrows—one that unerringly points to the overruling care of God. If we can understand this truth as we should, it will direct our hearts into the safe anchor of His love as nothing else could do.

Heaven's Glories and Earth's Griefs

This is the very glory of the gospel—anticipated here by the psalmist, but only fully revealed in Jesus

Christ—that heaven with its glories is close kin to earth with its griefs. Heaven with its holiness is always touching earth with its heartbreaks.

The God of the stars is the God of the saints—and of the sinners too! More and more clearly do we see this as we read the record of Christ's life and work—His unveiling of the glory of the Father.

Jesus seems always to be striving to convince men of the greatness of God so they may be subdued. And He tells them of the gentleness of God so they may be wooed into surrender and submission to His claims upon them.

The Father He reveals is all majesty, but all mercy too. He is certainly the God of lofty transcendence, but just as certainly He is also the God of loving tenderness.

His comprehension is universal; so too is his compassion. "He telleth the number of the stars," and by the same power "He healeth the broken in heart."

So what is the purpose of this word of testimony from the early days of men's dealings with God? It may well come to us—interpreted as it is now by the light that Christ's Evangel sheds upon it—as just another of the many calls we are always receiving to fear of God, to have faith in Him, and to acknowledge our indebtedness by gratefully yielding our strength to His service.

Two Conceptions of God

Let us examine two popular conceptions of God, neither of which, taken by itself, is either right or adequate. The first idea is that God is so remote from men in the perfection of His power and greatness that He has little if any concern with the trifling sorrows and cares of their lives.

In the other concept, God is regarded as being so friendly and—shall I say it?—human that He is almost one of us. In the first instance, He fails to get our love. In the second, He fails to inspire us with fear.

If we are in danger of having a God too far off we are

also in danger of having a God too near—One with whom familiarity has bred in our hearts a kind of affectionate contempt. We are apt to forget the God who "telleth the number of the stars" in our happiness at finding the God who heals the broken hearts.

The person who falls into the error of thinking of God as nothing more than the Great Architect of the Universe—One who is far removed from the poor human concerns of life—inevitably fails to realize His personal grace and care.

Life for him may develop a sense of duty, but he never comes to regard himself as a son of God, the child of His love. What an eternal loss is his!

On the other hand, the person who rejoices in knowing God's nearness and goodness but forgets that He is "the high and lofty One who inhabiteth eternity," is inclined to lose sight of God's superintending care and guidance in the larger things of life.

As a result, he is apt to be seized with panic and to yield to a faithless pessimism when things seem to be going wrong. He loses sight of the conjunction of mercy and majesty. Worse yet, he is no longer effective in service for God.

An old writer has said that God has two thrones—one in the highest Heaven, the other in the humblest heart! We need always to remember this balance of truth, which is just another way of saying that "He telleth the number of the stars" and that "He healeth the broken in heart."

Stars and Broken Hearts

The connection between stars and broken hearts is not as obscure as we may at first think, for there is a general likeness between them that is far more than mere poetic imagination. For instance, both are the common possession of all men.

No one has a monopoly on the starlit heavens. Rich men whose human instincts have not kept pace with their material prosperities may fence in their land and deny to others access to mountain or glen. But they cannot stop anyone from gazing upon the heavens above their properties.

The brightest and remotest stars are the possession of the poorest and richest alike. So too are the sorest heartbreaks. From the prince in his palace to the peasant in his cottage, not a man among us is exempt from the ordinary workings of human experience. All of us, sooner or later, come to know what it means to be crushed, wounded, and broken. It is part of the price we pay for living.

Also, both stars and heartbreaks bring men to a realization of their own littleness and feebleness. Who has gazed out on the starry skies in mid-ocean or on some countryside where the light of the cities does not obscure the panorama without realizing his infinite smallness?

Who has seen the grand constellations without saying in the awe of great loneliness, "What is man, that Thou are mindful of him?" (Ps. 8:4).

There is nothing that makes a man feel so tiny and so powerless as the sight of God's myriad worlds— nothing, perhaps, but the heartbreaks of life, his own and those of others.

For we stand silenced before them, utterly powerless to avert or alleviate them. They are as great in their power to teach us our limitations as are the stars. Together they unite in this ministry to us.

Millions of the stars are hidden from our gaze even when we are assisted by the strongest telescopes. And as for counting them! Well, that is entirely beyond all human power.

How like our heartbreaks! Their causes are often hidden, and their number is incalculable. Both are the secret of God, and both will drive us back—if we rightly consider them—to His saving majesty and mercy.

These simple and obvious analogies lead us to a clear and necessary understanding of this great fact: It takes the God of the stars to heal our sorrows and to bind up our broken hearts.

There is no greater folly than that of the man who either cynically or in mere bravado makes light of his heart's needs. The fact is, our needs are the greatest things we have—far greater than our possessions or accomplishments or desires.

Our needs testify to our immortality. And none of our needs do so more clearly than the need of our broken hearts for solid comfort and lasting assurance. Indeed, it is our heartbreaks that prove there is something within us which refuses to answer to material comforts or to be satisfied with anything temporal.

This fact establishes our relationship to God, who has made us for Himself. Perhaps we cannot comprehend His "telling of the stars," but we can understand the healing of our own heartthrobs.

Things that are intellectually incomprehensible are always spiritually necessary, for it takes the same power to do the one as the other. In our hours of pain and loneliness and misery, we instinctively turn to the greatness and majesty of God for unfailing comfort. We rely on the stupendous might of His grace. Is He not the One to whom great things are little and little things are great?

Why Do Our Hearts Break?

To illustrate this and to bring it home to us, think of some of those most common causes of heartbreak. When a man's inner being is undergoing a great revolution, it is in no exaggeration that he cries out, "My heart is broken!"

For instance, when the conviction of sin is upon him, scourging him with its stinging lash, wrapping him round with its Nessus robe of condemnation, and haunting him with the sense of his sin-created exile from God and love and Heaven. Who does not know that kind of broken heartedness?

More common is the heart that is broken and crushed by sorrow and loss. I came across a person in that situation not long ago.

He poured out his heart in his sorrow over a prodigal son—one who had left home and gone into sin's far country. Despite his father's love and prayers, this son had shown no signs of return.

If ever I saw into a broken heart, I did that day. I had no difficulty in recognizing its kinship with Him whose heart has long been broken over His prodigal children.

Still more common is the heartbreak of the young man (for middle life and old age have no monopoly in this matter) who feels that in his endeavors to live an upright and clean life he is contending against unequal forces. He senses that temptation is stronger than his strength of resistance, and that failure, with all its bitter humiliation, is inevitable.

Many a young man, who bravely tries to turn a bright face toward others, weeps scalding tears in the secrecy of his own room at the discovery that he is in the grip of destructive forces, and he cannot liberate himself. His heart is broken, for he is an undone man.

Then there is the heartbreak of betrayal, when human love proves unstable and the light seems to be blotted out of the sky. All of life becomes drab and desolate.

And to us all, sooner or later, comes the heartbreak of separation. Death, with its ruthless blows and strange mocking silence, crushes the very life out of those who stand round the open grave, hopeless and paralyzed.

Yes, the heartbreaks of life are very many and very real! This mere mention of some of them verifies the truth already stated: It takes the God of the stars to deal with and heal them.

He alone is able to bind up and repair the bruised life. He alone can set it free in the field of renewed opportunity. He alone can cause us to live and witness to the still greater reality of His compassion—which is His power shot through with the light of His love.

Indeed, both stars and heartbreaks are definitely related to His central government. The stars, as we know, run their courses and keep their places in the heavens entirely in virtue of their relation to the great solar center. Thus it is that He telleth their number.

So too is it with our many heartbreaks. They have a distinct and definite relationship to Him who is the Sun of Righteousness. And it is only as that relationship is recognized by faith and love that we may know His healing power, just as the stars know His guiding might.

The Proof of Experience

Does not our personal experience prove all this? What is it that has helped us in our most trying hours, when all has seemed lost or not worthy of the struggle?

What has made it possible to rise above unkindly circumstance and organize victory out of defeat? What has brought joy and peace into sorrow and storm?

Surely just the great fact of God's majesty and mercy—His greatness and His grace, His sovereignty and His sympathy, His powerfulness and His pity.

The certainty of the power of God's might, which "telleth the number of the stars" is at the disposal of the "broken in heart" to help and heal them.

And doesn't it help to know the assurance that it is offered in Jesus, God's full and final Word of power! He alone meets the need and answers the instinct of the life which, because it has been created for Him, can never find its comforts anywhere else.

> What can it mean? Is it aught to Him
> That the nights are long, and the days are dim?
> Can He be touched by the griefs I bear,
> Which sadden the heart and whiten the hair?
> About His throne are eternal calms,
> And strong, glad music of happy psalms
> And bliss unruffled by any strife;—
> How can He care for my little life?
>
> And yet I want Him to care for me,
> While I live in this world where the sorrows be.
> When the lights die down from the path I take;
> When strength is feeble and friends forsake;
> When love and music that once did bless

Have left me to silence and loneliness;
And my life-song changes to sobbing prayers;—
Then my heart cries out for the God Who cares.

Yes, this ever-present positive instinct of the soul, as well as its past experiences of His power, proclaims the great truth that the God of the stars, who stoops and speaks to us in Christ, alone satisfies the aching need of any brokenhearted man.

Remote Enough to Awe
Close Enough to Satisfy

And what is the ultimate significance of this message of the kinship of the stars of heaven with the sorrows of earth? Surely an inspiration to hope and cheer and peace, in the knowledge that He who nightly works a miracle in the skies is the very One who cares and pities and stands by to strengthen us when we are broken in heart from any cause.

What joy to know that He "healeth," with no thought of harshness or suspicion or criticism or of magnifying the fault which has caused the trouble, or of condemnation. And that we may, by reason of our need, draw near and yet nearer to Him who draws near to us in the person of His dear Son.

We shall always find Him remote enough to awe, but close enough to satisfy.

NOTES

The Jealousy of God

George H. Morrison (1866-1928) assisted the great
Alexander Whyte in Edinburgh, pastored two
churches, and then became pastor in 1902 of the
distinguished Wellington Church on University
Avenue in Glasgow. His preaching drew great crowds;
in fact, people had to line up an hour before the
services to be sure to get seats in the large auditorium.
Morrison was a master of the use of imagination in
preaching; yet his messages are solidly biblical. From
his many published volumes of sermons, I have chosen
this message, found in *The Wind on the Heath*,
published in 1915 by Hodder and Stoughton, London.

3

THE JEALOUSY OF GOD

I, the Lord thy God, am a jealous God (Exodus 20:5).

JEALOUSY IS SO associated with evil that we hesitate to attribute it to God. We would never have ventured to think of God as jealous without the authority of the Holy Scriptures.

A jealous nature in a man or woman is not one that commands our admiration. We do not despise it as we do a mean nature, but we certainly do not admire it.

And all our associations with the Word, gathered from the experience of life, create in us an instinct to avoid attributing jealousy to God.

The Darker Side of Jealousy

Among the passions portrayed for us by William Shakespeare, there is one unrivalled picture of jealousy. Jealousy is the absorbing passion, as it is the ruin, of Othello. And so ingrained into the minds of students is that unrivalled creation of the dramatist, that it has tended to color the jealousy of God.

Here is a nature, essentially great, goaded into the madness of a beast. There is in Othello a certain grand simplicity such as is always found in noble natures. And yet Othello becomes blind and mad, and he ends by murdering the woman he worshipped—all under the overmastering power of jealousy.

It is such things that make Francis Bacon in his *Essays* speak of envy as the vilest of all passions. It distorts everything, blinds the vision, and is the mother of profound unhappiness. That is why we naturally shrink, as our experience of life increases, from attributing the passion of jealousy to God.

Nor is the Bible, to which we owe the thought,

ignorant of that darker side of jealousy. It too, in its picture gallery, like Shakespeare, has wonderful portraitures of jealous men.

There is Cain, for instance, on the verge of history, madly jealous of his brother Abel. There is Saul, who was not unlike Othello in a certain heroic simplicity of nature. And yet when the women cried in the day of victory, "Saul hath slain his thousands and David his ten thousands" (1 Sam. 18:7), the heart of the kingly Saul was turned to bitterness.

He who could fight like a lion in the battle, could not tolerate his rival's eminence. It was as gall and wormwood to his spirit that David should have the precedence in praise. He missed that crowning touch of our own Lord Nelson, who, when the fleets were closing at Trafalgar, said, "See that gallant fellow, Collingwood, how he carries his ship into action."

We find also in the New Testament an ample recognition of the darker side of jealousy. We see it in the disciples when they forbade the man who was casting out devils in the name of Christ. We see it also in the Scribes and Pharisees, who were so madly jealous of the Master that nothing but his death would satisfy them.

The jealousy of neighboring towns or villages is too notorious to be disputed. In Galilee, for instance, there were two neighboring villages: Cana and Nazareth. It illuminates the page of Scripture to remember that it was Nathanael of *Cana* who asked the bitter and derisive question, "Can any good come out of *Nazareth?*" (John 1:46).

We do not need to turn to Shakespeare, then, to understand the darker side of jealousy. In all its tragedy and all its pettiness, it is known and registered in the Holy Scriptures. And yet the Bible, which knows our human hearts and searches out the latent evil in them, assures us of the jealousy of God.

Jealousy: Love's Shadow

We begin to see the solution of this difficulty when

we recall the connection of jealousy with love. Jealousy is the shadow cast by love. That is the difference between jealousy and envy.

For envy, the meaner word, is also by far the broader word. It applies to the intellect as well as to the heart and to ambitions as well as to affections. Envy touches relationships where love is never thought of.

One scholar may be envious of another, and one actor may be envious of another. But in our common speech, we do not say that a husband is envious of his wife. We say that a husband is jealous of his wife, because marriage is a relationship of love.

That is why we speak of Cain as jealous—because he and Abel had once loved each other. That is why we speak of Saul as jealous—because his heart had been knit to that of David. And even the disciples, when they forbade the man, were not envious of rival power; they were jealous because they loved their Lord.

We may be envious of other people although it has never been our lot to love them. But an indifferent wife cannot be jealous; she only becomes jealous when she loves. And so in human life, as witnessed in our speech, jealousy is one side of love, though often a very dark and tragic side.

God's Jealousy: His Right

It is along such lines that we begin to fathom the possibility of jealousy in God. For the God of the Bible, His essential nature is revealed to us as love. And if that love flows out upon humanity in an infinite and everlasting mercy, it also, if it be deep and mighty, can scarcely lack the attribute of jealousy.

There is no spiritual peril in attributing jealousy to God. God alone has the right to the undivided devotion of the creature. That is where human jealousy is evil. That is the source of all its bitter tragedy.

It is the passionate claim of one poor human creature to the undivided devotion of another. However noble such a claim may be, it is always selfish and forever wrong. No human heart is large or deep enough entirely to absorb another heart.

We are all finite creatures at our highest, and one such creature cannot fill another. So our jealousy tends to become sinful, because it is our assertion of a claim that is proper to the infinity of God.

Only God can satisfy the heart—even the poorest and the meanest heart. Only He can absorb it without wronging it, for in Him we live and move and have our being. Only He has the full right to say, in the highest spiritual interest of His children, "My son, give me thine heart" (Prov. 23:26).

Therefore, the jealousy of God does not differ from the jealousy of man. They are alike in this, that both are born of love—a love that cannot tolerate a rival. But the jealousy of man grows dark and terrible because it makes a claim that is impossible. But for God, the jealousy is His right.

How closely associated divine love and jealousy are, is witnessed in a very simple way. It is in the Bible, and in the Bible only, that we meet with the thought of the jealousy of God.

That the unseen powers are envious of man is one of the oldest conceptions of the race. You light on it far back in ancient Greece; you detect it in a hundred superstitions. That the gods are envious and always on the watch and filled with a bitter grudge against too great prosperity, is one of the oldest conceptions of the human mind.

I need hardly point out to you that such divine envy is wholly different from divine jealousy. It does not spring from a great pity; it springs from the malevolence of spite. And not till there had dawned upon the world that truth so wonderful—that God is love, do you ever have the truth that God is jealous.

That is why you find it in the Bible—and nowhere else. It is the Bible, and the Bible only, that has convinced the world that God is love. And it is the very depth and splendor of that love, sealed in the gift of the Lord Jesus Christ, which has given us the jealousy of God.

God's Jealousy: Revealed in Jesus

I want you to note again that the same attitude is very evident in our Lord Himself. It is something we are apt to overlook.

As we recall how Jesus walked in mercy, we lift up our hearts assured that God is merciful. As we remember His compassion of the fallen, we are filled with the certainty that God is love.

But no one can read the story of the gospels, believing that God was incarnate in humanity, without awaking to the awful truth that the Lord our God is a jealous God.

As surely as God will tolerate no rival, Jesus Christ would tolerate no rival. He makes a claim upon the human heart of absolute and unconditional surrender. Even had we never heard from the Old Testament that there was such a thing as divine jealousy, we should conclude it from the life of Jesus.

There were many things Jesus tolerated that we should never have thought to find Him tolerating. He bore with social abuses—with personal discourtesies—in a way that is sometimes hard to understand.

But there was one thing Jesus *never* tolerated, from the first hour of His calling to the last, and that was the division of His empire. "The Father . . . hath committed all judgment unto the Son" (John 5:22). "I am the way, the truth, and the life. No man cometh unto the Father, but by Me" (John 14:6). "No man knoweth the Father but the Son" (Matt. 11:27). That is either the most stupendous arrogance that was ever listened to from human lips—or else it is the jealousy of God.

That the Lord our God is a jealous God is abundantly evident in Jesus Christ. It is more plainly written in the Incarnate Word than in any reason annexed to the commandment. And it is good that we should remember this whenever we are tempted to presume upon that Fatherhood, which is infinitely merciful and kind.

God's Jealousy: Its Influence

This deep thought of the jealousy of God has been powerfully influential in two ways. It has, in the first place, given tremendous impulse to the vital doctrine of monotheism.

It has been of supreme importance to the race to learn the lesson that God is one. All spiritual progress has depended on it; all true knowledge has depended on it. And that great doctrine, so vital to humanity, has been tremendously deepened in appeal by the truth that ran out on the ear of Israel, "The Lord thy God is a jealous God."

The first thing that had to be impressed on men was that the worship of many gods was quite intolerable. They had to be taught that for reasons yet unknown to them, it was infinitely offensive to Jehovah. And it was taught, sublimely and yet simply, to men who as yet were spiritually children, by the ascription of jealousy to God.

It is not easy for you and me today to appreciate the attraction of polytheism. Yet every reader of the Old Testament knows how tremendous were its attractions to the Jew.

And if the office and calling of the Jews was to give to humanity the truth that God is one, do you not see that some mighty thought was needed to keep them true to their spiritual leading? That mighty thought was the jealousy of God: "The Lord thy God is a jealous God." It burned itself into the heart of Israel that God would tolerate no rival claim.

And thus, not without many a lapse, was the world led to that profound conviction, without which there is no unity nor peace.

That thought, lastly, has been very powerful in making ready for the incarnation. It is really the herald—the strange and shadowy herald—of the love that has been revealed in Jesus Christ.

A jealous God may be a dark conception, but a jealous God can never be indifferent. When love is jealous it may do cruel deeds, but at least it is a love intense and passionate.

So in the Old Testament you seem to find divine sanction for very cruel deeds, but you never find a God who does not care. He loves with a love so burning and intense that He is passionately jealous for His people. "He that toucheth you," He cries to them, "toucheth the apple of His eye" (Zech. 2:8).

And it was that great love, purged of its grosser elements, and shown in a beauty that man had never dreamed of, that was at last revealed in the Lord Jesus Christ. The jealousy of God is the true key to some of the darkest deeds in the Old Testament. But do not forget that it also is the key to the coming of the Lord and Savior. For it tells of a love so deep and strong and wonderful that it will go at last to any length of sacrifice—even to the giving of the Son of God.

The Sovereignty of God

John Daniel Jones (1865-1942), "Jones of
Bournemouth," was one of England's best-known
preachers and denominational leaders. Ordained in
1889, Jones pastored in Lincoln and then became a
New Testament lecturer in the Nottingham
Theological Institute. In 1898 he went to Richmond
Hill Congregational Church, Bournemouth, where he
ministered with distinction for 40 years. He published
many books of sermons, but perhaps his best work is
his *Commentary on Mark*. "The Sovereignty of God" is
from *The Gospel of the Sovereignty and Other
Sermons,* published by Hodder and Stoughton.

John Daniel Jones

4

THE SOVEREIGNTY OF GOD

The Lord reigneth; let the earth rejoice (Psalm 97:1).
The Lord reigneth; let the people tremble (Psalm 99:1).

THE GREAT NEED of our day is not the discovery of new truths but the vitalization of old ones. The man of the hour would be he who could breathe new life into certain simple, elementary truths that have been in the church's possession throughout her history.

We have quite enough articles in our creed. What we want is sincerely to believe in them, for every truth that we honestly believe in becomes an energy in our life. Every genuine belief is a force.

But many of the beliefs we profess to hold are as void of life and power as the dry bones in the valley of the prophet's vision. Some of the primary truths of our Christian faith would come upon us with all the surprise of new revelations if we once really felt their power.

Among the truths that need to be vitalized and restored to potency and influence among us is the great and blessed truth of the sovereignty of God. It is a primary article in our creeds, but to a large extent it has passed out of the category of effective beliefs. It has ceased to be an energizing faith. It is not today a force in our lives.

Yet there is nothing which, in the interests of a deep, virile, serious religion, we need more than to know the power of the truth that "the Lord reigneth;" that our God is not a dead God, not an inert God, not an absentee God; but a living God, a Sovereign God, a present God, a working God who is actively engaged in directing, overruling, and shaping the affairs of nations and of men.

Sovereignty and Calvinism

Now, there was a time when the sovereignty of God was a great, influential truth—a time when men had a subduing, almost overwhelming sense of the ruling and shaping will of God. Those were the days when Calvinism was at the height of its influence.

Happily, we have arrived now at the time when the fires of the old controversy between Calvinists and Arminians have died down, and there is not a spark left in the ashes. Therefore, without the risk of misunderstanding, we can recognize and appreciate the truths for which each party stood.

The sovereignty of God was the central doctrine of the Calvinistic system—the vital truth for which Calvinism stood. I agree that there was much that was stern and forbidding and even repulsive in the Calvinistic creed. Some of its repulsiveness was due to the pitiless and remorseless logic with which the doctrine of the sovereignty of God was pushed to its most extreme consequences. As a result, man seemed to be a helpless puppet and God an irresponsible tyrant, saving some and damning others out of His mere good pleasure.

However, when we speak with contempt and scorn of Calvinism and the Calvinists, we show ourselves both ignorant and foolish. We are ignorant because whatever else Calvinism may be, it is a mighty and reasoned system; it is a sublime creation of the human intellect.

The world has perhaps never produced two subtler thinkers, two men who have exercised a greater mastery over the human mind, than those two great exponents of the Calvinistic creed—John Calvin of Geneva, and Jonathan Edwards of America.

We show ourselves foolish, because this Calvinism, of which we speak so contemptuously, produced some of the greatest and most heroic men the world has ever known. Merely to mention the fact that Calvinism gave to the world William the Silent of Holland, Admiral Coligny of France, John Knox of Scotland, and Oliver Cromwell of England, ought to make gibes at Calvinism impossible and ought to make us realize that the world owes to it a debt it can never repay.

We may repudiate, and we do, the extreme Calvinistic dogmas, but let us frankly acknowledge what was great and noble in it. It was an iron creed, but it made iron men, so that the world never knew braver or stronger men than those Calvinism produced.

This humbling creed, which laid a man prostrate before his Maker, made holy men, so that the world numbers among its choicest saints John Bunyan, Richard Baxter, Samuel Rutherford, and Jonathan Edwards. This ennobling creed, which made a man feel he was the instrument and messenger of Almighty God, made mighty men, men who would neither bend nor bow, who feared none but God, and who with splendid courage crashed against all sorts of tyrannies and wrongs.

Listen to what J. A. Froude (not a prejudiced witness) says in one of the volumes of his short essays about the Calvinists:

> They attracted to themselves every man in Europe that "hated a lie." They were crushed down, but they rose again. They were splintered and torn, but no power could melt or bend them. They abhorred, as no body of men ever more abhorred, all conscious mendacity, all impurity, all moral wrong of every kind so far as they could recognize it. Whatever exists at this moment in England and Scotland of conscientious fear of wrongdoing is the remnant of the convictions which were branded by the Calvinists into the people's hearts.

And though there may be a little of Froude's rhetoric in that glowing passage, this witness is substantially true.

Our Puritan Heritage

We are fond, on such occasions as these,* of boasting of our descent from the Puritans. Surely this is a lineage upon which we may well pride ourselves. On the whole, the Puritan is the noblest and most heroic figure upon the pages of our English history. It was the Puritan who broke the back of tyranny in the state; it was the Puritan who preserved personal and vital religion.

And it was Calvinism that made the Puritan. The Puritan's fundamental belief was his belief in the sovereignty of God. He had a overmastering sense of the presence of God; he regarded himself as but the instrument of the divine will.

It was that sense of God as sovereign that produced the humbling consciousness of sin which you find, for instance, in John Bunyan's *Grace Abounding.* It was that same sense of God as sovereign that gave the Puritan his resistless strength.

"Deus vult, Deus vult," cried the crowd of princes, barons, and knights who listened to Urban's fiery advocacy of a crusade to rescue the tomb of Christ from the hands of the infidel: "God wills it, God wills it."

"Deus vult" might have been taken by the Puritans for their motto, "God wills it, God wills it." For that is exactly how they regarded themselves—as agents of the divine purposes, instruments of the divine will.

And there you have the secret of their pertinacity, their strength, their indomitable courage. The man who believes he is *sent,* that he has a mission, that back of his own will is the divine and almighty will, is always a terrible person.

What wonder that Rupert's cavaliers were scattered, like chaff before the wind, before that terrific onset of Cromwell's Ironsides? What chance had men whose inspiration was loyalty to a prince when brought into collision with men who believed themselves to be the

---

* Referring to the setting of this sermon, preached as the official sermon of the National Free Church Congress at Norwich.

instruments of the divine will? What wonde.
gallant soldiers who sang their joyous songs as ...
rode into battle were as stubble to the swords of men
who shouted as they swept to the charge, "The sword
of the Lord and of Gideon"!

It was in virtue of this central faith in the sovereignty
of God that the Puritan lived his strenuous life and
accomplished his mighty work. He lived as ever "in the
great Taskmaster's eye." His one and absorbing aim
was to bring himself into line with that holy and perfect
and acceptable will of God, which he saw working out
its purposes in the world.

The Soft Church

Calvinism is almost a reproach and a byword and a
hissing amongst us in these days. Yet we are faced by
the fact that never did this land of ours possess men so
great and strong and God-fearing as she did when this
iron creed was at the height of its influence. The day of
the supremacy of this doctrine of the sovereignty of
God was also the day when English piety come to its
consummate flower.

I am profoundly convinced that if we want to recover
that deep, serious, masculine religion which characterized the Puritan, we must recover this doctrine of the
sovereignty of God. We must restore it to its proper
place of influence and power.

I do not suggest that we should commit ourselves to
all that the Calvinists believed about election and
reprobation and the divine decrees. In all these things
they were the victims of their own logic, and they spoke
of God the things that were not right.

But life will never be great and dignified, and religion
will never be deep and serious until we realize God as
they did—as the living, present, sovereign God. Until
we are subdued and possessed and mastered by the
sense of His presence; until we regard ourselves as the
agents of His purposes and the instruments of His will,
we will not experience these realities.

We are living in a rather limp and flaccid time. The intellectual temper of our day is that of a genial humanitarianism. Our manners are soft, and our beliefs invertebrate.

And the church's condition corresponds somewhat to the condition of the age. For years now we have been bemoaning our ineffectiveness and lack of power. The fact is, a genial humanitarianism will never carry a church to victory.

What we need is a new vision of God—the Mighty God. Men have called the Puritan religion, "the Hard Church." But is it not time, as Professor Peabody says, to face the perils of "the Soft Church"?

That is our peril today—the peril of the Soft Church. We want a breath of the Puritan's bracing faith. For churches and for men it remains eternally true—"the fear of the Lord is the beginning of wisdom" (Ps. 111:10).

Sovereignty and Godly Awe

The texts I read out at the beginning of my sermon are from the royal Psalms. The main subject of these Psalms, from Psalm 93 on, is the sovereignty of God. And I have chosen my two texts just because they set forth a double result that will follow upon a realization of the truth of the sovereignty of God.

First, we will gain a *new sense of awe.* "The Lord reigneth; let the people tremble." There was a note of seriousness and solemnity about the religion of the Puritan that is all too often lacking in the religion of today. It was born of his sense of the sovereignty of God. It has passed away because, to a large extent, that doctrine has lost its hold upon us.

The characteristic of the teaching about God of the past 25 or perhaps 50 years has been the stress and emphasis on the Fatherhood. We have emphasized what is tender and gracious and benign in the divine character.

This has been partly, no doubt, a reaction against the harsher views that previously prevailed. Now, lest there be any misunderstanding, let me at once say that I too rejoice in the Fatherhood of God. I delight to proclaim God's tenderness and compassion and infinite love. But, as so often happens in our reaction from one extreme, we have swung right across to the other.

If our fathers emphasized God's "awful purity" at the expense of His love, we have emphasized His love at the expense of His "awful purity." We delight in these days to say, "Gentle, gentle, gentle, is the God and Father." We have almost forgotten that cherubim and seraphim, with veiled faces, continually cry, "Holy, holy, holy is the Lord of Hosts."

In our absorption in the thought of God as Father, we have almost lost sight of the fact that He is the Holy Sovereign, ruling the world in righteousness. The result has been that to a large extent we have lost the sense of *religious awe,* of *reverence,* and of *godly fear.* There is a verse in a hymn in which the writer says:

> Oh, how I fear Thee, living God,
> With deepest, tenderest fears;
> And worship Thee with trembling hope,
> And penitential tears.

That verse, I have often thought, is almost foreign to our modern religious experience. We do not "fear" God. We do not "tremble" in His presence. We do not worship Him with "penitential tears." We have lost our sense of God's holy sovereignty, and the awe has passed out of our religion.

God has become to many of us an easy-going, good-natured, indulgent parent who can be coaxed and wheedled and cajoled by His children, and who can deny them nothing—*le bon Dieu* of the Frenchman.

We have become "familiar" with God; we are on "easy terms" with Him; we speak to Him and about Him as we would to and about our next-door neighbor. We scarcely know what it means to worship God acceptably "with reverence and godly awe." And with our shallow and emasculated ideas of God we get a shallowness and superficiality and flippancy in our religious life.

The seriousness and the solemnity have gone out of it. There is no depth of earth.

To make our religious life deep and strong we need to recover that lost sense of awe. We need to be taught afresh the fear of the Lord. And to recover that lost sense of awe, to create within us the feeling of reverence, we need a new vision of God as the Holy Sovereign. "The Lord reigneth; let the people tremble."

If you will look at the Psalm from which this text is taken, you will notice that it is divided into three stanzas, and the last line in each stanza supplies the reason why the thought of the sovereignty of God should fill us with holy fear.

"The Lord reigneth; let the people tremble." Why? "Holy is He," answers the first stanza. "Holy is He," answers the second stanza. "For the Lord our God is holy," answers the third stanza. Put the two statements together, "The Lord reigneth . . . the Lord our God is holy," and what do you get? You get *holiness upon the throne*.

We have only to realize that God is the Holy Sovereign, and the awe is bound to come back. "The Lord reigneth. Holy is He. Let the people tremble." The Lord reigneth, a Holy God is on the throne, *therefore let us fear*.

To believe that an Almighty God is on the throne, working out His own holy and perfect and acceptable will, maintaining and asserting the eternal law of righteousness—is there not enough in that to fill the hearts of sinful men with "godly fear"? Is there not enough in that to make us "tremble"?

The Puritan's religion was a serious religion. He was *afraid* of God—afraid of Him in a worthy sense. He conceived of God as with him and about him always, and he was afraid of sinning against His holiness.

And is there not enough in the mere realization of the fact that a Holy God sits upon the throne, a God who is actively and unceasingly asserting His holiness— is there not enough in that one fact to make us, who are so prone to sin, serious and fearful?

We are constantly deploring our lack of the sense of sin. Is that because we have obscured God's holiness? Sometimes I wonder whether the very emphasis we have laid on the tenderness and gentleness and patience of God's fatherly love has made it easy for men to sin. We have made God's forgiveness so cheap that sin has come to appear a light and trivial matter.

If that is so, let us this day remind ourselves of the holiness of God; let us lift up our eyes to the shining peaks of the "awful purity." Let us remind ourselves that this Holy God is on the throne—that He is on the throne to maintain purity and righteousness. The will that rules is a holy will. The power that governs is a holy power.

All who sin bring themselves into collision with the sovereign will and power of the universe. Wherefore our Lord said, "Whosoever shall fall on this stone shall be broken, but on whomsoever it shall fall, it will scatter him as dust" (Matt. 21:44). "The Lord reigneth. Holy is He. Let the people tremble."

Sovereignty and Happy Confidence

If the realization that a Holy God is sovereign fills us sinful men and women with awe and godly fear, that same realization of God as sovereign ought to fill those of us who love goodness and long for the triumph of Christ with a *happy confidence*.

"The Lord reigneth; let the earth rejoice." "God's in His heaven," sang Pippa as she passed along the streets of Asolo, "all's right with the world." "In *His* heaven," that is, not as being absent from the earth, but as being in the place of supreme power and dominion. Anybody who believes that—who believes in the sovereignty of God, in God's actual rule and government—can add in happy trust, "All's right with the world."

"The Lord reigneth; let the earth rejoice." Here is the real ground of our confidence in the coming of a better day—"The Lord reigneth." There are many things in the condition of modern society to depress and sadden us. The touching faith men had in the natural and inevitable "progress" of the race has received many a shattering blow.

Society seems to be turning toward barbarism rather than away from it. The one thing that will keep our faith in the coming of the new earth, where righteousness dwells undimmed, is to believe in the sovereignty of God.

The destinies of the world are not, for instance, at the mercy of fleets and armies—*the Lord reigneth*. We want a new grip on this mighty fact, for the whole world seems to be subscribing to the atheism of force and fear. Nations seek their safety in a multiplication of guns and battleships. Here in England we are spending more on munitions of war than we have ever done in our history.

But it is not armies and alliances that settle the destinies of people. "The Lord reigneth." It is God who decides the fate of nations. He makes low and raises up, and none can usurp His power. And in that thought, let us be glad. "The Lord reigneth; let the earth rejoice."

To believe in the active sovereignty of God is to believe in the strength and supremacy of righteousness. The man who looks out on the world and can see only kings and emperors, scheming politicians, and armies and fleets all ready at the first signal to deal out death and destruction may well fall into distraction and something like despair. But the man who believes in and recognizes the sovereignty of God can be happy and confident.

When the Northern States of America braced themselves up for that gigantic struggle on behalf of the freedom of the slave, there were plenty of people— and among them many Englishmen—to prophesy defeat. But there were some men, like Ward Beecher, Whittier, Lowell, and the great Lincoln himself, who contemplated the issue with confidence. They believed they were on God's side and that God would not belie His own character by permitting the triumph of iniquity and wrong.

At first, it seemed as if the prophecies of those who foretold defeat were all going to come true. Things went badly for the North, and after one fierce engagement in which victory rested with the South, the hearts of the bravest failed them.

It happened that a meeting was being held in Washington at the time the news of the defeat arrived. Frederick Douglas, the slave orator, was speaking. The news was brought to the platform, and when he heard it, Frederick Douglas gave way to despair and burst into tears. The news passed from seat to seat through the hall, and as they heard it, the hearts of the people stood still with fear.

But there was one old black woman sitting way in the back gallery whom temporary defeat could not dishearten. When she saw the meeting falling into something like a panic—with even Douglas in despair—she cried out with a shade of reproach in her tone, "Frederick Douglas, God is not dead."

It was a simple word, but it brought the courage back to the hearts of all, because it reminded them of Him in whose hand the destinies of nations are, and by whom kings rule and princes decree justice. The Northern cause was a righteous cause; the event in time showed that "God was not dead."

"God is not dead." This is the truth we need for our good hope to realize today. He is not dead and He has not abdicated His throne. "The Lord reigneth; let the earth rejoice." To know that God rules—to realize His sovereignty—is to be delivered from fear and despair. His ways often transcend our feeble range of sight; clouds and thick darkness are often round about Him.

But to know that God rules, is to know in spite of all anarchism and militarism, that the kingdoms shall become the kingdoms of our God and of His Christ. "Fret not thyself because of evil-doers." "The Lord reigneth," and "He shall make righteousness to go forth as the light, and justice as the noonday" (Ps. 37:1, 6).

Sovereignty and the
Triumph of the Church

"The Lord reigneth." This is the ground of our confidence in the *triumph of the church.* The church has not, in recent years, been in a triumphant frame of mind. She has been depressed, nervous, harassed, and anxious. She has talked continually about "reaction" and "arrest." She has been conscious of strained resources and inadequate powers.

My brethren, what we want for a recovery of our courage and confidence is the recovery of our faith in the sovereignty of God. In Dr. Paterson's book *The Rule of Faith,* there is a sentence that I commend to the serious consideration of my brethren.

Here it is: "The value of a religion depends on the truth and sufficiency of its idea of God." Not only on *the truth* of it, you notice, but on the *sufficiency* of it as well. If we start with a little God, we shall have a little peddling religion, utterly insufficient to meet the greater needs and wants of man.

For the idea of God is the ground plan in religion. If the ground plan is cramped and meager, the building erected upon it is bound to be cramped and meager too. You cannot build a bigger building than your base will safely carry. On a narrow base, a big building would simply topple over. And in exactly the same way, you can never build a big religion upon a little God.

A great religion demands a great God for its starting point. Whatever else our Christian gospel claims to be, it claims to be a *great* religion. It claims the world for its province, and it preaches a salvation that reaches down to the last and the least.

But to make this Christian religion of ours, with its worldwide redemption—its universal salvation—even credible, we need a mighty conception of God. If we are to believe that it will win its way to the ends of the earth, we must start with a great idea of God.

And perhaps that is what we need for a revival of our faith and courage—an enlarged conception of God.

Our doubts and timidities and despairs arise from the fact that we have made Him altogether like ourselves.

If that's all He were, we might well despair. For no magnified and glorified man is equal to the great salvation of which our gospel speaks. But our God is a great God and a great King above all gods. The Lord reigneth—that is our confidence.

We need a vision of the sovereign Lord. The triumph of the church does not depend on us, but on Him. It is He—the mighty God— who has said, "Ask of Me, and I will give thee the heathen for thine inheritance, and the uttermost parts of the earth for thy possession" (Ps. 2:8). It is He who has said, "I will yet set my King upon my holy hill of Zion" (Ps. 2:6). Whatever God, the Almighty God, said, shall He not do it? Whatever He has spoken, will He not make it good?

We have lingered perhaps too long among the gentleness of God; we need today the bracing vision of His majesty and power. Perhaps we have dwelt overmuch on the meek and lowly Jesus; the vision we need to see today is that of the glorified Christ, with His sword upon His thigh, marching on prosperously because of truth and righteousness, the mighty to save. The vision of the Throned Lord is the antidote to fear.

Do you remember that antithesis at the close of Mark's gospel? "Then the Lord was received up into heaven, and sat down at the right hand of God. And they went . . . everywhere" (16:19, 20). The Lord on the throne—the servants out in the field. The Lord in the place of power—the disciples flinging themselves with resistless dash and courage on all the strongholds of heathenism. A true vision of the King produces exactly the same effect today.

"Do you expect to convert China?" asked the captain of the ship in which Robert Morrison sailed. "No," replied that indomitable missionary, going out alone to claim China for Christ, "but I expect God will." That is the secret of courage! The Lord reigneth; let His church rejoice!

To realize that God is King will change our sobs into shouts of triumph. A new faith in the sovereignty of God will send us back to our tasks with the assurance born of a mighty faith. What if obstacles are great and enemies are many? Greater is He that is with us than all that are against us. The Lord reigneth, and He will not fail or be discouraged until He has brought forth justice unto victory.

Sovereignty and Personal Peace

I finish with this personal word. "The Lord reigneth,"—it is just the realization that God is sovereign that will bring us *calm and peace amid the varied experiences of our individual lives.* Horace Bushnell has a sermon on the text, "I girded thee, though thou hast not known Me" (Isa. 45:5), and to the sermon he gives the title, "Every Man's Life, a Plan of God."

I know the difficulty there is in reconciling this with our faith in human freedom. I am not going to try to solve the antinomy. I believe that man is free, and I also humbly believe that every man's life is a plan of God.

God compasses our path; He is acquainted with all our ways; He orders our steps. The temptations, the trails, the joys, the sorrows of our lives—they are all of His ordaining. The niche we occupy, the sphere we try to fill, the work we seek to do—they are of His appointment.

"The Lord reigneth." In this fact let us rejoice. For this Lord who reigns—who girds us though we do not know it—is the God and Father of our Lord Jesus Christ. I have said that He is the holy God. But He is also the loving God. "Holy Father." That is His full and perfect name.

This is one of the commonplaces of our religion, but it is one of those commonplaces that sorely needs to be revitalized. When we come to account for our trials and difficulties and hardships—if we believe in the living God at all—we come ultimately to this: they happen to us because they are God's will for us. But that will is a loving will, a perfect will. Once we realize that, we shall arrive at Paul's sunny faith that all things work together for good to them that love God (Rom. 8:28).

Our lives get broken and harassed just because we forget that it is the Lord who reigns. "Be still," says one of the psalmists, "and know that I am God" (46:10). Once we realize that He who gave His Son for us all is on the throne, we shall find it easier, amid life's manifold perplexities, to be still.

Life is not easy for any one of us. It brings its burdens, its cares, its sorrows. Perhaps I am speaking to some burdened and sorrowful hearts. You have been laboring in a hard place; you have had grievous disappointment to bear; you have had sickness in the home; you have perhaps seen a dear one go down to the gates of death.

What have I—what has anyone—to say in the face of these things? Just this: "The Lord reigneth." And that Lord gave His Son. Holy love is sovereign. Love girds us though we may not know it.

To believe this is to possess that deep and central calm which neither sorrow nor pain nor trouble nor even death can disturb, for we shall know that underneath us are the everlasting arms. We shall be able to make those familiar lines of Whittier our own and say:

> I know not what the future hath
> Of marvel or surprise,
> Assured alone that life and death
> His mercy underlies.
>
> I know not where His islands lift
> Their fronded palms in air;
> I only know I cannot drift
> Beyond His love and care.

"The Lord reigneth; let the earth rejoice."

The Unknowable God

Joseph Parker (1830-1902) was one of England's
most popular preachers. Largely self-educated, Parker
had pulpit gifts that soon moved him into leadership
among the Congregationalists. He was a fearless and
imaginative preacher who attracted both common
people and the aristocracy, and he was particularly a
"man's preacher." His *People's Bible* is a collection of
the shorthand reports of the sermons and prayers
Parker delivered as he preached through the entire
Bible in seven years (1884-91). He pastored the
Poultry Church, London, later called The City Temple,
from 1869 until his death. This sermon is taken from
Volume 1 of *The People's Bible* (London: Hazell,
Watson and Viney, 1900).

Joseph Parker

5

THE UNKNOWABLE GOD

God is great, and we know him not (Job 36:26).

GOD IS THE unknown and the unknowable. Yet He is also the one Reality and the one Energy of the universe. What it is possible to *know,* it must be possible to explain—to put into words, which, being all set together, sum themselves into the exact measure of the thing that is known.

What can be known may, of course, be contained by the faculty that knows it. The vessel is of necessity larger than its contents. If, then, any faculty of mine knows God, that faculty contains God, and is in that sense larger than God, which is impossible and absurd.

Whatever I can know is, by the very fact that I can know it, less than I am. It may by bigger as to mere size in length and breadth, such as a huge disc that glares with light or a globe flying fast. Yet its speed can be set down in so many ciphers or lines of ciphers on a child's slate, so clearly that we can say: It is so much an hour the great wings fly, and not one mile more.

What is that but mere bigness, an appeal to our easily excited wonder, a size that shakes our pride and bids us mind our ways, or a weight that may fall upon us from the sky? It is nothing, nothing but an ascertainable quantity and intensity of fire—a wide and high stair leading to nothing!

Tiring of the Known

Unknown—Unknowable. Thanks. I am tired of the Known and the Knowable, tired of saying this star is fifty millions of miles in circumference, that star is ninety millions of miles farther off than the moon, and yonder planet is five million times larger than the earth. It is mere gossip in polysyllables, getting importance by hugeness, something that would never be named in inches and that owes its fame to the word *millions*.

It is in this manner that men want to make a mouthful of God! A great mouthful, no doubt, say even to the extent of super-millions squared and cubed into a whole slateful of ciphers, but pronounceable in words! Failing this, they suppose they have destroyed Him by saying He is Unknowable and Unknown.

It makes me glad to think He is! That any One or any Thing should be unknowable and should yet invite and stimulate inquiry is educationally most hopeful. O soul of mine, there are grand times in store for thee!

I cannot rattle my staff against the world's boundary wall and say, "The End!" Poor staff! It thrusts itself into a cloud; it goes over the edge; it is nearly pulled out of my hand by gravitation that pulls even the earth itself and keeps it from reeling and falling.

Yes, prying staff. You can touch nothing but a most ghostly emptiness. Soul of man, if you would truly see— see the Boundless, see the Possible, see God—go into the dark when and where the darkness is thickest. That is the mighty and solemn sanctuary of vision.

The light is vulgar in some uses. It shows the mean and vexing detail of space and life with too gross a palpableness, and it frets the sensitiveness of the eyes. I must find the healing darkness that has never been measured off into millions and paraded as a nameable quantity of surprise and mystery.

Deus absconditus. God hides Himself, most often in the light; He *touches* the soul in the gloom and vastness of night, and the soul, being true in its intent and wish, answers the touch without a shudder or a blush. It is even so that God comes to me.

God does not come through man's high argument, a flash of human wit, a sudden and audacious answer to an infinite enigma, or a toilsome reply to some high mental challenge. His path is through the pathless darkness—without a footprint to show where he stepped; through the forest of the night he comes, and when he comes the brightness is all within!

My God—unknown and unknowable—cannot be chained as a Prisoner of logic or delivered into the custody of a theological proposition or figured into literal art. Shame be the portion of those who have given Him a setting within the points of the compass, who have robed Him in cloth of their own weaving, and surnamed Him at the bidding of their cold and narrow fancy!

For myself, I know that I cannot know Him; that I have a joy wider than knowledge, a conception that domes itself above my best thinking, as the sky domes itself in infinite pomp and luster above the earth whose beauty it creates.

God! God! God! Best defined when undefined; a Fire that may not be touched; a Life too great for shape of image; a Love for which there is no equal name. Who is He? God. What is He? God. Of whom begotten? God. He is at once the question and the answer, the self-balance, the All.

Defining God

We have tried to build our way up to Him by using many words with some cunning and skill. We have thought to tempt Him into our cognition by the free use of flattering adjectives. Surely, we said, He will pour his heart's wine into the golden goblets we hold out to catch the sacred stream.

We have called Him Creator, Sovereign, Father; then Infinite Creator, Eternal Sovereign, Gracious Father, as if we could build up our word-bricks to heaven and surprise the Unknown and the Unknowable in His solitude, and look upon Him face to face. We have come near to blasphemy herein.

What wonder had we been thrust through with a dart! We have thought our yesterday roomy enough to hold God's Eternity and have offered Him with every show of abounding sufficiency the hospitality of our everchanging words as a medium of revelation.

Our words! Words that come and go like unstable fashions. Words that die of very age; words that cannot be accepted unanimously in all their suggestions and relations even by two men. Into these words we have invited God, and because He cannot come into them but as a devouring fire, we have stood back in offense and unbelief.

God! God! God! Ever hidden, ever present, ever distant, ever near; a Ghost, a Breath, making the knees knock in terror, ripping open a grave at the very feet of our pleasure; a mocking laugh at the feast, filling all space like the light, yet leaving room for all His creatures; a Terror, a Hope—Undefinable, Unknowable, Irresistible, Immeasurable. God is a Spirit!

Undefinable, Unknown, Unknowable, Invisible, Incomprehensible. These are grim negatives, emptinesses that deceive us by their vast hollowness. The wrong word is to blame for the wrong conclusion.

We have chosen the very worst word in our haste, and we have needlessly humbled ourselves in doing so. We have made a wall of the word when we might have made it into six wings—two to cover the face, two to cover the feet, and two with which to fly.

Instead of Unknowable, Invisible and Incomprehensible, say Superknowable, Supervisible and Supercomprehensible. Then the right point of view is reached and the mystery is made luminous.

From the *Un*knowable I turn away humiliated and discouraged; from the *Super*knowable I return humbled, yet inspired. The *Un*knowable says, Fool, why bruise your knuckles in knocking at the final granite as if it were a door that could be opened? The *Super*knowable says, There is something larger than thy intelligence; a Secret, a Force, a Beginning, a God! The difficulty is always in the lame *word* and not in the solemn *truth*. We make no progress in religion while we keep to our crippled feet; in its higher aspects and questionings it is not a road to walk upon, it is an open firmament to fly in.

Alas, he who mistakes crutches for wings! Yet this absurdity has so recommended itself to our coldness as to win the name of prudence, sobriety, and self-suppression. We have lost the broad and mighty pinions that found their way to heaven's gate and the eye of burning love that looked steadfastly into the sacred cloud.

We have now taken to walking, and our lame feet pick their uncertain way over such stones as Unknown, Unknowable, Invisible, and Incomprehensible, and we finish our toilsome journey exactly where we began it.

Enthusiasm sees God. Love sees God. Fire sees God. But we have escaped the revealing, sympathetic fire and have built our prudent religion upon the sand. On the sand! Think of it! So we go to it, and walk around it, and measure it, and break it up into propositions, and placard it on church walls, and fight about it with infinite clamor and some spitefulness.

My soul, amid all Unknowableness, Incomprehensibleness, and other vain and pompous nothings, hold fast to the faith that you can *know* God and yet know nothing merely *about* Him. You can know Him by love and pureness, and not know *about* Him by intellectual art or theological craft.

Looking for the Invisible

Invisible! This is what the Bible itself says. The invisibleness of God is not a scientific discovery; it is a biblical revelation; it is a part of the Bible. "No man hath seen God at any time" (John 1:18)—"No man can see God and live" (Ex. 33:20). This is the difficulty of all life, and the higher the life the higher the difficulty. No man can see *himself* and live! He can see his incarnation, but his very *self*—the pulse that makes him a man—he has never seen, he can never see!

Anatomy says it has never found the soul, and adds, "Therefore there is no soul." The reasoning overleaps itself and takes away its own life by rude violence. Has anatomy found *genius?* Has the surgical knife opened the chamber in which *music* sings and sees the Singer? Or has anatomy laid its finger upon *imagination* and held it up, saying, "Behold, the mighty wizard"?

But if there is no soul simply because anatomy has never found one, then there is no genius, no music, no imagination, no chivalry, no honor, and no sympathy, because the surgeon's knife has failed to come upon them in wounding and hacking the human frame!

Anatomise the dead poet and the dead ass, and you will find as much genius in one as in the other; *therefore* there is no genius! Who that valued his life would set his foot on such a bridge as the rickety "therefore"? But some men will venture upon any bridge that seems to lead away from God.

A very simple anatomy will find the reason; it is because "they DO NOT LIKE to retain God in their hearts" (Rom. 1:28). It is not because of intellectual superiority, but because of moral distaste. An internal cancer accounts for this invincible aversion.

Yes, God is Unknown and Unknowable. But that does not make Him unusable and unprofitable. That is a vital distinction. If the master of science humbly avows that he has not developed a theory of magnetism, does he therefore ignore it or decline to inquire into its uses? Does he reverently write its name with a big M, and run away from it shaken and whitened by a great fear? Verily he is no such fool. He actually *uses* what he does not *understand.*

I will accept his example and bring it to bear upon the religious life. I do not scientifically know God. The solemn term does not come within the analysis that is available to me.

God is great, and I know Him not: yet the term has its practical *uses* in life, and into those broad and obvious uses all men may inquire. What part does the God of the Bible play in the life of the man who accepts Him and obeys Him with all the inspiration and diligence of love? Any creed that does not come down easily into the daily life to purify and direct it is imperfect and useless.

Courage and Sacrifice Comes From God

I cannot read the Bible without seeing that God (as there revealed) has moved His believers in the direction of *courage* and *sacrifice*. These two terms are multitudinous, involving others of kindred quality and spreading themselves over the whole space of the upper life.

In the direction of courage, this is not mere animal courage, for then the argument might be matched by many gods whose names are spelled without capitals. No, this is *moral* courage, noble heroism, fierce rebuke of personal and national corruption, sublime and pathetic judgment of all good and all evil.

The God-idea made mean men valiant soldier-prophets; it broadened the piping voice of the timid inquirer into the thunder of the national teacher and leader. For brass it brought gold; for iron, silver; and wood, brass; and for stones, iron. Instead of the thorn it brought up the fir tree, and instead of the brier the myrtle tree, and it made the bush burn with fire.

Wherever the God-idea took complete possession of the mind, every faculty was lifted up to a new capacity and borne on to heroic attempts and conquests. The saints who received it subdued kingdoms, wrought righteousness, obtained promises, stopped the mouths of lions, quenched the violence of fire. Out of weakness they were made strong, waxed valiant in fight, turned to and fight the armies of the aliens.

Any idea that inspired life and hope in man is to be examined with reverent care. The quality of the courage determines its value, and the value of the idea that excited and sustained it.

What is true of the courage is true also of the *sacrifice*, which has ever followed the acceptance of the God-idea. This is not the showy and fanatical sacrifice of mere blood-letting. Many a Juggernaut, great and small, drinks the blood of his devotees.

But spiritual discipline, self-renunciation, the esteeming of others better than one's self, the suppression of selfishness—these are the practical *uses* of the God-idea. It is not a barren sentiment. It is not a color vapor or a scented incense, lulling the brain into partial stupor or agitating it with mocking dreams.

It arouses courage. It necessitates self-sacrifice. It touches the imagination as with fire. It gives a wide and solemn outlook to the whole nature. It gives a deeper tone to every thought. It sanctifies the universe. It makes heaven possible. Unknown—Unknowable. Yes, but not therefore unusable or unprofitable.

Creating the Creator?

Say this God was dreamed by human genius. So be it. Make Him a creature of fancy. What then? The man who made or dreamed or otherwise projected such a God must be the author of some *other* work of equal or approximate importance. Produce it! That is the sensible reply to so bold a blasphemy.

Why would man make a Jehovah and then take to the drudgery of making oil paintings of Him and ink poems about Him and huts to live in indeference to Him? Where is the congruity?

A man says he kindled the *sun,* and when asked for his proof, he strikes a match that the wind blows out! Is the evidence sufficient? Or a man says that he has covered the earth with all the green and gold of summer, and when challenged to prove it, he produces a wax flower that melts in his hand! Is the proof convincing? The God of the Bible calls for the *production* of other gods—gods wooden, gods stony, gods ill-bred, gods well-shaped, and done up skillfully for market uses. From His heaven he laughs at them, and from His high throne he holds them in derision.

He is not afraid of competitive gods. They try to climb to His sublimity but only get high enough to break their necks in a sharp fall. Again and again I demand that the second effort of human genius bears some obvious relation to the first. The sculptor accepts the challenge, so does the painter, so does the musician; why should the Jehovah-dreamer be an exception to the common rule of confirmation and proof?

We wait for the evidence! We insist upon having it. Then, so we don't waste our time in idle expectancy, we can meanwhile call upon God, saying, "Our Father which art in heaven, Hallowed by thy name. Thy kingdom come. Thy will by done in earth, as it is in heaven!" (Matt. 6:9-10).

God's Terribleness and Gentleness

Joseph Parker (1830-1902) was one of England's
most popular preachers. Largely self-educated, Parker
had pulpit gifts that soon moved him into leadership
among the congregationalists. He was a fearless and
imaginative preacher who attracted both common
people and the aristocracy, and he was particularly a
"man's preacher." His *People's Bible* is a collection of
the short-hand reports of the sermons and prayers
Parker delivered as he preached through the entire
Bible in seven years (1884-91). He pastored the Poultry Church, London, later called The City Temple,
from 1869 until his death. This sermon is taken from
Volume 15 of *The People's Bible* (London: Hazell,
Watson and Viney; 1900).

Joseph Parker

6

GOD'S TERRIBLENESS
AND GENTLENESS

I will destroy and devour at once. I will make waste mountains and hills, and dry up all their herbs; and I will make the rivers islands, and I will dry up the pools. And I will bring the blind by a way that they knew not; I will lead them in paths that they have not known: I will make darkness light before them, and crooked things straight (Isaiah 42:14-16).

IT IS A fearful thing to fall into the hands of the living God. It is better to fall into the hands of men. Our God is a consuming fire—God is love. These are great, yet contradicting truths about our God.

The combination of great power and great restraint—indeed, the combination of opposite qualities and uses generally—is well-known in civilized life and in the laws of nature. The fire that warms the room when properly regulated, will, if abused, reduce the proudest palaces to ashes. The river, which softens and refreshes the landscape, if allowed to escape its banks, can devastate the most fruitful fields.

The engine, which swiftly bears the laughing child to his longed-for home, will, if mismanaged, wreak the most terrible havoc. The lightning, which may be caught and utilized by genius and skill, can burn the forest and strike armies blind.

We are familiar with such illustrations of united opposites. Our knowledge of them inspires our enterprise and makes cautious the noble audacity of practical science.

In our text in Isaiah we are confronted with the highest expression of the same truth: The mighty God is the everlasting Father; the terrible One is more gentle than the gentlest friend; He who rides in the chariot of thunder stoops to lead the blind by a way that they know not and to gather the lambs in His bosom.

In pointing out the terribleness of God, I do not appeal to fear. I do so to support and encourage the most loving confidence in His government. We do not say, "Be good, or God will crush you." That is not virtue, that is not liberty—it is vice put on its good behavior. It is iniquity with a sword suspended over its head. It is not even negative goodness, but mischief put *hors de combat*.

The great truth to be learned is that all the terribleness of God is the good man's security. When the good man sees God wasting the mountains and the hills, and drying up the rivers, he does not say, "I must worship Him or He will destroy me." He says, "The beneficent side of that power is all mine. Because of that power I am safe. The very lightning is my guardian, and in the whirlwind I hear a pledge of benediction."

The good man is delivered from the fear of power. Power has become to him an assurance of rest. He says, "My Father has infinite resources of judgment, and every one of them is to my trusting heart a signal of unsearchable riches of mercy."

Destruction and God

Look at the doctrine of the text in relation to bad men who pride themselves in their success and their strength. Daily life has always been a problem to devout wisdom.

Virtue has often been crushed out of the front rank as vice forced its way to preeminence. The praying man often has to kneel upon cold stones while the profane man walks on velvet. These are commonplace occurrences in the daily study of the affairs of men.

The doctrine of the text teaches that there is a power beyond man's and that nothing is held safely which is not held by consent of that power. Think of wealth as a mountain or of social position as a hill. God says, "I will make waste mountains and hills."

Our greatest is nothing to Him; our mountain smokes when He touches it, and our rock melts at His presence.

All our gain, our honor, our standing should be looked at in the light of this solemn doctrine.

We are not at liberty to exclude the destructive power of God from our practical theology. We have not to make a God, to fancy a God, or to propose a modification of a suggested God—God is before us in His might, His glory, and His love. Our portion is to acquaint ourselves with Him.

God is not to be described in parts; He is to be comprehended in the unity of His character. A child describing the lightning might say, "It was beautiful, so bright, and swifter than any flying bird, and so quiet that I could not hear it as it passed through the air." That description would be true.

A tree might say, "It was awful. It tore off branches that had been growing for a hundred years; it rent me in twain down to the very root, and no summer can ever recover me—I am left here to die." This also would be true.

So it is with Almighty God; He is terrible in power, making nothing of all that man counts strong, yet He will not break the bruised reed nor quench the smoking flax.

Building Houses; Building Character

Men are bound to be as commonsense in their theology as they are in the ordinary works of life. For example, in building character they are to use at least as much foresight and wisdom as they do in building their houses of stone. How do we conduct our arrangements in building a house?

Suppose it were possible for a man never to have seen any season but summer. Then suppose that this man was called upon to advise in the erection of a building. You can imagine his procedure; everything is to be light, because he never heard a high wind. Waterpipes may be exposed, for he never felt the severity of frost. The most flimsy roof will be sufficient, for he knows nothing of the great rains of winter and spring.

Tell such a man that the winds will become stormy, that the rivers will be chilled into ice, that his windows will be blinded with snow, and that floods will beat upon his roof. If he is a wise man, he will say, "I must not build for one season, but for all seasons. I must not build for fine days, but for days that will be tempestuous. I must, as far as possible, prepare for the most inclement and trying weather." That is simple common sense.

Why be less sensible in building a character than in building a house? We build our bricks for severity as well as for sunshine, so why build our character with less care? If in summer we think about the frost, why not in prosperity have some thought for adversity? If in July we prepare for December, why not in the flattering hour of exultation think of the judgment that is at once infallible and irresistible?

As he would be infinitely foolish who would build his house without thinking of the natural forces that will try its strength, so is he cursed with insanity who builds his character without thinking of the fire with which God will try every man's work.

Preparing for Rough Seas

Is not the same truth illustrated by every ship on the great seas? The child who has only sailed his paper boat on the edge of a placid lake might wonder why enormous beams and bars of iron, innumerable bolts and screws, and clasps and bars of metal are needed in making a ship.

Ask the sailor, and he will answer. He says we must be prepared for something more than calm days. We must look ahead. The breakers will try us, and the winds will put us to the test. We may come upon an unknown rock; we must be prepared for the worst as well as for the best.

We call this prudence. We condemn its omission. We applaud its observance. What happens to men who attempt the stormy and treacherous waters of life without any regard for the probable dangers of the voyage?

We prepare for the severe side of nature—why ignore the severe aspect of God? We think of fire in building our houses—why forget it in building our character? On one side of our life we are constantly on the outlook for danger—why forget it where the destiny of the soul is concerned?

When a man builds his house or his ship strongly, we do not say that he is the victim of fear. We never think of calling him a fanatic. Instead, we say that he is a cautious and even scientific man.

Likewise, when I make appeal to the severity of God—to His fire, His sword, His destroying tempests and floods—I am not preaching the mere terrors of the Lord to move people by alarm rather than by love. I am simply being faithful to facts—I am reminding you that God is not less complete than the seasons which He has made. And I am asking you in the summer of His mercies not to forget the winter of His judgments!

Winter Is Coming

The so-called success of the bad man has yet to stand the strain of divine trail. God will go through our money to see if it has been honestly obtained. He will search our reputation, and our hypocrisy will not be able to conceal the reality of the case from His all-seeing eye. He will examine our title-deeds, and if we have ill-gotten property, He will set the universe against us until we restore it with penitence or have it wrenched out of our keeping by retributive misfortune. Yes, though our strength be as a mountain, it shall be wasted; though it be as a hill, it shall be blown away, and the world will see how poorly they build who build only for the light and quietness of summer. Do not say the winter is long in coming; it will come, and that is the one fact that should move our concern and bring us to wisdom.

In these days when the world is in a constant panic when men are over-driving one another, when commerce has been turned into gambling, and thieves pass as honest men it is essential that we all remind ourselves that God will judge people righteously and try all men by the test of His own holiness.

Remember, we are not stronger than the weakest point in the walls of our character. And true wisdom requires that we watch even the smallest gate that is insufficient or insecure.

When the Least Have the Most

Look at the doctrine of the text as an encouragement to all men who work under the guidance of God. "I will bring the blind by a way that they knew not: I will lead them in paths that they have not known: I will make darkness light before them, and crooked things straight."

God thus declares himself gentle to those who truly need Him. He promises nothing to the self-sufficient; He promises much to the needy. The text shows the principle upon which divine help is given to men—the principle of conscious need and of willingness to be guided.

Let a man say, "I am rich and increased with goods and have need of nothing," and God will leave him to his proud sufficiency. Let this man, on the other hand, feel his weakness and insignificance, and God will bless him with all the help that he requires in the most difficult passages of life.

A true understanding of this doctrine will give us a new view of daily providences: Men who are apparently most destitute may in reality be most richly enjoying the blessings of God. Clearly, we are not to judge human life by outward conditions. We are not to overlook the beneficent law of compensation.

Those who apparently have least may in reality have most. Who can tell what visions of Himself God grants to men who cannot see His outward works? Blindness may not be merely so much defect, but another condition of happiness. Who can say that it does not bring the soul so much nearer God?

Be that as it may, it is plainly taught in the text that God undertakes to lead all men who will yield themselves to His guidance. And their defects, instead of being a hindrance, are in reality the express conditions on which offers of divine help are founded.

It is because we are blind that He will lead us. It is because we are weak that He will carry us. It is because we have nothing that He offers to give us all things. God, addressing Himself to human weakness, is the complement of God wasting mountains and hills. God, shedding the morning dew on awaking flowers, is the complement of God terrifying the earth with tempests and vexing the sea with storms.

There is an unsearchable depth of pathos in the doctrine that God is gentle to human weakness and that He will make up with His own hands what is wanting in human faculty. Strong men seldom care for the weak, the blind are put on one side, the incapable are dismissed with impatience; but here is God, the Lord, the Creator of the ends of the earth taking the blind man's hand and leading him like a specially loved child!

Meddling in God's Work

Therefore, it is clear that self-sufficiency on the part of man is an offense to God. What's more, it is a vexation to man himself. All efforts at completeness and independence of strength end in mortification.

Toward one another we are to be self-reliant; toward God we are to be humble, dependent, all-trustful. How infinite is our folly in seeking to remove by our own power the mountains and hills that bar our way! God says He will remove them for us; why should we turn away His mighty arm?

He claims such work as His own; why should we meddle with it as if we could do it better than He? But some of us will meddle. We persist in seeking omnipotence in our own hands and trying to reach the tone that the winds and the seas will obey. We will do it.

The devil urges us, and we yield. He says, "Be your own God," and we snatch at the suggestion as a prize. He says, "This little mountain you might surely manage to remove," and then we set to work with pickax and shovel. Yet behold, the mountain grows as we strike it!

Still the tempter says, "It stands to reason that you must be making some impression upon it. Try again." And we try again, and again we fail. The mountain does not know us, the rock resents our intrusion, and having wasted our strength, the devil laughs at our impotence. He tells us in bitter mockery that we will do better next time! Yes! Next time—next time—and then next time—and then hell!

God says to us, when we stand at the foot of great hills and mountains, "I will beat them into dust, I will scatter the dust to the winds; there shall be a level path for your feet, if you will but put your trust in Me." That is a sublime offer. No man who has heard it ought to assume he is free to act as if God had not made a proposition to him.

Such propositions should endear God to our hearts. Here He is beside us, before us, round about us, to help, to lead, to bless us in every way. He is not a figure in the distant clouds. He does not make occasional appearances under circumstances that dazzle and confound us.

Instead He is always at our right hand, always within reach of our prayer, always putting out His hand when we come to dangerous places. As a mere conception of God, this reaches the point of sublimity. The coarsest mind might dream of God's infinite majesty, but only the richest quality of heart could have discovered Him in the touch of gentleness and the service of condescension.

Let us make such use of this revelation of the divine character as will save us from turning our theology into the chief terror of our lives. To some men, their theology is, indeed, a frightful specter. They would be happier if they were atheists. They fitfully slumber on the slopes of a volcano, and to them heaven itself is but the lesser of two evils.

Behold! Behold! I call you to a God whose very terribleness may be turned into an assurance of security, and whose love is infinite, unchanging, eternal!

God Has the Right of Way

Men of business! You whose barns are full, whose rivers overflow, on whose estates the sun has written "prosperity," and into whose harvest fields autumn has forced the richest of her golden sheaves! These things are all gifts of God, and He who gave them can also withdraw them. "I will destroy and devour at once—I will dry up all their herbs."

He has the right of way through our fields and orchards. Our vineyards and oliveyards are His, and He can blow upon them till they wither. He can cause their blossom to go up like the dust. "I have seen the wicked in great power, and spreading himself like a green baytree. Yet he passed away, and, lo, he was not: yea, I sought him, but he could not be found" (Ps. 37:35, 36).

Not a fibre of his root could be discovered. Not so much as a withered leaf drifted into a ditch could be traced. All gone—the great branches gone—the bark gone—the trunk gone—the root gone—and the very name had perished from the recollection of men!

It is poor prosperity that is not held by God's favor. Gold goes a little way if it is not sanctified by prayer and giving of thanks. Bread cannot satisfy, unless it is broken by God's hands. Our fields may look well at night, but in the morning they may have been trampled by an invisible destroyer.

Do not say that I am urging you by fear; it is because of coming winter that I advise men to build strongly, and it is because of inevitable judgment that I call upon men to walk in the light of righteousness in all the transactions of life.

The Only One to Fear

Children of God, especially those who are called to suffering and weakness and great unrest because of manifold defect, God offers you His hand. Are you blind? He says, "I will lead the blind." Are you full of care? He says, "Let me carry your burden." Are you in sorrow? He says, "Call upon me in the day of trouble, and I will answer thee."

Is there a very steep road before you at this moment—in business, in your family, in your responsibilities? He says, "I will make waste mountains and hills, and the rough places shall be made plain."

So you are not alone—not alone, for the Father is with you. He is with you as a father—not to try your strength but to increase it; He is not with you to make experiments upon you but to magnify His grace in you by working out for you a wonderful redemption. Rest on God. His arm, not your own, must be your strength. Fear God, and no other fear will ever trouble you.

NOTES

The God of Comfort

Henry Ward Beecher (1813-1887) was known as "the American Spurgeon." He was born into a famous family: His father was Lyman Beecher, theologian and educator, and one of his sisters was Harriet Beecher Stowe, who wrote *Uncle Tom's Cabin*. Beecher pastored in Indiana (1837-47) before moving to the Plymouth Congregational Church in Brooklyn, NY. There were twenty-one members when he came and almost 2,500 when he died. In 1872 he delivered the first of the "Lyman Beecher Lectures on Preaching," which were established at Yale by a deacon of the Plymouth Church. The sermon "The God of Comfort" is taken from *The Sermons of Henry Ward Beecher in Plymouth Church* (New York: J. B. Ford & Co., 1869).

Henry Ward Beecher

7

THE GOD OF COMFORT

Blessed be God, even the Father of our Lord Jesus Christ, the Father of mercies, and the God of all comfort; who comforteth us in all our tribulation, that we may be able to comfort them which are in any trouble, by the comfort wherewith we ourselves are comforted of God (2 Corinthians 1:3-4).

I CALL THE New Testament the Book of Joy. There is nowhere in the world another book that is pervaded with such a spirit of exhilaration. Nowhere does it pour forth a melancholy strain. Often pathetic, it is never gloomy. Full of sorrows, it is full of victory over sorrow.

In all the round of literature, there is not another book that can cast such cheer and inspire such hope. Yet it eschews humor, and forgoes wit. It is intensely earnest, and yet full of quiet. It is profoundly solemn, yet there is not a strain of morbid feeling in it.

Some books have recognized the wretchedness of man's condition on earth, and in some sense have produced exhilaration; but it was done rather by amusing their readers. These books have turned life into a comedy. They have held up men's weakness to mirth. They have turned men's passions to ridicule, sharply puncturing their folly by wit. They have sought to redeem them from suffering by taking out all earnestness, all faith, all urgent convictions.

Not so the Christian Scriptures. They never jest; they never ridicule; they never deal in comic scenes. They disdain, in short, all those methods by which other writings have inspired cheer. Yet, by a method of their own, they produce in all who accept them a reasonable sympathy, elevation of mind, high hope, and cheerful resignation.

The New Testament recites the wicked deeds that pride and vanity and selfishness have evermore produced in mankind. It paints no paradise of innocent sufferers. It sweeps a circle around a guilty race, lost in trespasses and sins, and so given over to them that all strength for recovery is gone. Death, universal and final, towers and glooms over the race like a black storm that will soon burst forth unless some kind wind arises to bear it back and sweep it out of the hemisphere.

The New Testament: Full of Hope and Cheer

Strange as it is in statement, it is while dealing with such a scene that the New Testament writers suffuse their compositions with a transcendent joy; and not once, nor twice, but always, and all the way through, they flash with radiant hope and cheer. This is without a parallel.

What is the source of this strange cheer overhanging so strange a subject? What is the source of that joy which glances from every argument, from almost every line, while treating such tremendous realities of sadness? Why are the sacred writers so inspiring? As birds fly easier against the wind (if it is not too strong) does joy, too, rise more easily against the breath of this world's great sorrows? How is it?

The fountain and unfailing source of this sober exhilaration was found in the divine nature, as it had been revealed to the apostles. Our text is an admirable expression of this representation of the divine nature. I will attempt to open this passage so as to give some insight into those experiences, both of sorrow and of consolation, which have made the apostles the leaders of men for so many ages.

God: Father of Mercies

God is here styled *the Father of mercies, and the God of all comfort*. We are not to take our conceptions of God from human systems, for these systems have been built up out of mere selections from the Word of God. But God's Word is a vast forest. And just as a man can build either a hut or a common mansion or a palatial residence out of the timber that is growing in the forest, so out of the Word of God man can build a poor theology, a rich theology, or a glorious one, according as he is skillful in this selections.

Men had heard of the God who *created* all things, who *governed* all things, who weighed and measured all human thoughts and feelings, and who stamped with unchangeable lines the moral character of the race. This magisterial and juridical Deity, revealed to men through the types of civil government, was powerful to incite fear and to restrain from evil.

This vision of God must always remain, having certain purposes, and having in it the office of representing certain truths respecting the divine nature. But this view does not express God. To represent a being as perfectly holy and as sitting in the circle of holiness while holding the race to absolute purity, almost without sympathy, except that which is doled out on certain conditions—that is not to represent God, though it is to represent something about God.

Men had also heard of a God who was perfect in holiness. Their thoughts had ranged until weary through that vast circle inhabited by the ideal of perfect justice and truth.

It was the latest disclosure of the divine nature that, within that august power which had been revealed, and beating like a heart within that perfect holiness, there was a nature of exquisite sympathy and tenderness. It was also in the divine nature that the energies of that Almighty Being were exerted in the service of mercy and kindness; that the direction of God's nature was toward love; and that, although alternatively there were justice and judgment, they were but alternative. The length and breath, and the height and depth of God was in the sphere of love—potential, fruitful.

Consider what the nature must be which is here styled *the Father of mercies.* When a man begets children, they are in his own likeness. God groups all the mercies of the universe into a great family of children, of which He is the head. Mercies tell us what God is. They are His children. He is the father of them, in all their forms, combinations, multiplications, derivations, offices. Mercies in their length and breadth, in their multitudes infinite, uncountable—these are God's offspring, and they represent their Father.

Judgments are *effects* of God's power. Pains and penalties go forth from His hand. Mercies are God Himself. They are the issues of His heart. If He rears up a scheme of discipline and education that requires and justifies the application of pains and penalties for special purposes, the God who stands behind all special systems and all special administrations, in His own interior nature pronounces Himself *the Father of mercies, and the God of all comfort.* Of mercies it is said that they are *children.* They are part of God's *nature.* They are not what He *does* so much as what He *is.*

God of All Comfort

But even more strongly is it said that He is *the God of all comfort.* By *comfort,* we mean those influences which succor distress, which soothe suffering, which alleviate grief, and which convert the whole experience of sorrow to gladness.

Consider that God is declared, not *at times* and upon fit occasions, to produce comfort, but *always.* He is the very God of it. Imagine a kingdom wide and rich in all the elements of consolation, where every ill found its remedy, and every sorrow its cure—a celestial sanitarium, out of which issued winds bearing health everywhere. There, in its own center, and exalted to the highest place, is God, sovereign and active *in comforting.* For this He thinks; for this He plans; for this He executes; for this He waits; for this He lives.

Oh! What a realm of sorrow lies under this kingdom. Oh! What a need there has been in this world that there should be somebody to comfort. "The whole creation has groaned and travailed in pain until now" (Rom. 8:22).

Men have been born, it would seem, that they might be sufferers. Nations have been wrapped in darkness. Tribulation has come like the sheeted doom of storms—sweeping whole continents. Ages have been stained with blood. Tears have been so abundant that they have been too cheap to count. Weeping has had more work in this world then laughing. Trouble has ruled more than joy. Even yet, men high advanced in the causes of a better living and existing in the very midst of civilization, are scarcely creatures of joy, but more of care and trouble and sorrow.

Every household, every heart, in its turn, is pierced. Men go lonely, yearning, longing, unsatisfied. They are bereaved. They are filled with shocks of calamities. They are overturned. All their life is at times darkened. They are subverted. In midday, there walk ten thousand men in these cities, men who say, "Our life is done. We have sown to the wind, and reaped the whirlwind" (Hos. 8:7).

There are thousands of dying children, and thousands of mothers that would die. There are armies of men beguiling their leisure by destroying armies of men. There are nations organized so as to suppress manhood. The very laws of nature are employed as forces to curtail men's conveniences by impoverishing them. Commerce and manufacturing, and work itself, man's best friend— these are putting on chains and shackles.

The city makes suffering, and the town makes suffering. Man himself heaps up in himself, by his own work, ten thousand sources of misery. And it is true that "the whole creation groans and travails in pain." We march like so many soldiers, but we march to a requiem, not to a pean. The sounds that fill the world are sounds of mourning and of sorrow.

Divine Hope

Oh! What need there is that up out of this darkness and trouble and sadness, out of these calamities, there should be exalted, somewhere, an image that writes upon itself, "I am the God of comfort." That brings God right home to man's need. The world would die if it had no hope of finding such a God.

He penetrates and pervades the universe with His nature and with His disposition. My flagging faith has need of some such assurance. I have walked very much in thought with those old philosophers who believe that there was a God of evil, as well as one of good. I am more willingly a disciple, therefore, of that inspired teaching which declared that evil is not a personage. It is not even an empire.

Like the emery and sand with which we scour off rude surfaces, evil and trouble in this world are but instruments. And they are in the hands of God. If they bite with sharp attrition, it is because we need more scouring. It is because men's troubles need ruder handling and chiseling, that evils float in the air, swim in the sea, and spring up from out of the ground.

But all is under the control of *the God of consolation,* as it is said elsewhere; *the God of comfort, and the Father of mercies,* as it is said here. More are the tender thoughts, the inspired potential actions, in God, than in the stars in the heavens. Innumerable are the sweet influences that He sends down from His realm above. More and purer are His blessings than the drops of dew that night shakes down on the flowers and grass.

He penetrates and pervades the world with more saving mercies than does the sun with particles of light and heat. He declares that His nature in Himself is boundless—that this heart of mercy is inexhaustible—that His work of comfort is endless.

Comprehending God

Listen to this symphony and chant of Paul, wherewith he prays that "we might be able to comprehend with all saints." Stand back as he builds the statue, glowing at every touch with supernal brightness!

"That we might be able to comprehend" what? That wire-drawn, fine, finical character that too often theology has skeletonized; that filmy and silky substance abstracted almost beyond the grasp of the understanding, reduced, for the sake of a certain notion of perfection, to an abstraction that is absolutely unusable in practical life—is this God?

No. As Paul builds, listen: "That Christ may dwell in your hearts by faith; that ye, being rooted and grounded in *love*, may be able to comprehend" (Eph. 3:17). Ah! old hoary student, do you think because you can read Hebrew and Syriac and Arabic and Greek and Latin, that you can teach me about God? Ah! old grammarian, who comes fighting me on doctrines, who marshals sentences with exegesis, sharp both at the point and at the edge, cutting both ways. Do you think that because you are so wise in construction, you can teach me of God? He is not found by either.

"That ye, being rooted and grounded in *love*"—which is the only interpreter of the divine nature—"may be able to comprehend, with all saints, what is the breadth"—look from where the sun comes to where he sets; and look again from where he sets to where he comes, if you would gain any measure—"that ye may be able to comprehend, with all saints, what is the breadth, and length, and depth, and height; and to know the love of Christ which passeth knowledge, that ye might be filled with all the fullness of God" (Eph. 3:18, 19).

This is the true conception of God. This is that majestic and mighty Heart—rich, glowing, glorious, yearning and desiring good, and scattering it as through the spheres He scatters light and atmosphere. This is that vast, voluminous God that Paul saw riding triumphantly and spreading His bow over the storms that beat and afflicted Him in this lower mortal state.

This is the God that declares Himself to be, in this wicked, sin-smitten, ruined world, *the God of all comfort*. He is the great-breasted God, the mother-God into whose arms come those who weep, where He comforts them, even as a mother comforts her child. And the earth itself is rocked, as it were, by that same tending, nursing, loving God. If only its inhabitants knew the consolation that is offered to them!

Seeing Jesus as Comforter

This view of Christ was the peculiar manifestation. Would that we could have it again, as the first century Christians had it in their time. For, when the apostles lived, most of them had seen Him. Even Paul—in some respects better—had seen Him by celestial vision, and he lived in all the fresh remembrances of the whole lore of Christ's love, His words, and His actions.

It is very plain that Christians during the first hundred years lived in the presence of Christ, as a person near and dear to them. It was as if He had been born in their own household and had gone out from them as a child or a parent goes. The apostles saw Christ, but they did not see or think of Him as we do in modern times.

It is difficult for me to make you understand when I say that it is right to philosophize in respect to the nature of God, that indeed it must be done, and that yet this philosophy can never take hold of the soul and satisfy it. You may read all the writings of the apostles, and you will not find once that the nature of God in Christ Jesus arose to them as a question of mental philosophy.

Yet, handed from school to school, from theory to theory, almost our whole conception of God is one that has been philosophized. We are ranking Him; we are counting His attributes; we are telling how much makes God less than that which cannot be God; we are declaring His functions; we are philosophizing, analyzing, synthetizing; and our divinity is one that is largely made up from the standpoint of mental philosophy. For theology is nothing but mental philosophy applied to the divine mind and the divine government.

But the apostles looked upon God from a different point of view. They saw Him in respect to His practical relations to the wants of the individual heart and the wants of the world. They thought of Him in His adaptation to the needs of the human soul and to the world's need. They seemed to say in themselves, "Here are all the troubles of life; here is this beneficent Being who carries cure with Him." And to their view He was God, because He supplied the universal need; because He had that without which the world's life would die.

It was this practical adaptation of the divine nature to the wants of the suffering world that made Christ so unquestionably divine. The questions that are still discussed in the church respecting the divinity of Christ would long since have ceased as useless, and evaporated as worthless, if men had more habitually contemplated Christ as a life-power, as a Redeemer and a Savior.

The apostles held for certain that—in spite of nature, organization, the drift of things, kingdoms, powers, influences—this meridian mercy, this divine consolation, would yet regulate the world. The world was not, therefore, a pit of hopeless incurables. The matchless power of God would finally overcome all evil and sweep it out of the universe. And they lived in the anticipation of victory.

So, then, they were neither so disgusted as many are with the wrongdoing of men, nor were they so hopeless as others are who believe that a world so wicked, bound, and hereditated in wickedness, can never be changed nor repaired. The apostles looked up at the power that is above and said, "There is hope for the world. Men can be regenerated. Men can be transformed. A new heaven there will yet be, and a new earth in which righteousness dwells." Therefore their conception of the character of God, and of its relations to this world, filled them with a surprise of perpetual joy and with the inspiration of hope.

Sharing the Comfort

They were also inspired, by the example of Christ, to make their sorrows so many medicines for others. In other words, they learned that the business of sorrow was not simply to be comforted. The comfort that they received was to make itself the comforter of others.

> Blessed be God, even the Father of our Lord Jesus Christ, the Father of mercies, and the God of all comfort; who comforteth us in all our tribulation, that we may be able to comfort them which are in any trouble by the comfort wherewith we ourselves are comforted of God (2 Cor. 1:3-4).

This world is not an orb broken loose and snarled with incurable evils. If we would know what this world is coming to, we must not look too low.

Have you never noticed in summer when the sun stands at the very meridian height, how white and clear the light is; how the trees stand revealed; how all things are transparently clear? But let the sun sink and droop till it shoots level beams along the surface of the earth. Then those beams are caught and choked up with a thousand vapors, with dust, with all the day's breedings from swamp, river, and fen, and the sunlight grows thick and murky. We call it *roseate,* and *orange,* and what not, but it is the poisoned light of the sun, which, in its own nature, is white and pure.

Likewise, when men's eyes glance along the surface of the world, looking at moral questions, they look through the vapors that the world itself has generated. They cannot see clearly. That is why many men think this world is bound to wickedness, and that all philanthropic attempts are mere efforts of weakness and inexperience.

There are many men who ascribe to themselves great superiority and are proud of their cynical wisdom. They sit with a kind of impudent, pitying leer, looking upon men who instruct the ignorant, who clothe and feed the poor and the needy, who spend—*waste* as they say—their time in going out into the highways to do good. "What does it matter," say they, "whether this great beast of the world dies with its hair licked one way or another? What does it matter if all the wombs of time are generating wickedness, and if man is born to wickedness, whether anything is done for him or not? You might as well attempt to cure volcanoes with pills, as to attempt to cure the human heart by any of your poor medicine."

Men are wicked, and no one can be charitable with others who does not start with the belief that they are wicked in all parts of their nature. And then, no one can be charitable with others who does not believe that it is the essential nature of God to cure and not to condemn; that His first and latest thought is, "O Israel, thou hast destroyed thyself; but in me is thy remedy" (Hosea 13:9).

God the Remedy

God is Himself a vast medicine. God's soul and nature are the blood of the universe. Ask the physician what it is that he trusts to throw out deadly influences from the human system. If there are diseased organs, what cures them? Do you think pills do the work? They do but little except to say to the lazy organ, "Wake up and go to work, and throw out the enemy that is preying upon you." What is medicine? It is merely a coaxer. Its business is to say to the part affected, "Lazy dog! Wake up and get well."

If a man gets well, he cures himself—often, thanks to the doctor; more often, thanks to the nurse; always, thanks to nature. That does the work, if it is done at all. What is the stream that carries reparation to the wasted parts, that carries stimulation to the dormant parts, that carries nutrition to the exhausted parts? What is it that fights? It is the blood.

And throughout the vast heaven, throughout time and the universe, the blood of the world comes from the heart of God. The mercies of the loving God throb everywhere—above and below, within and without, endless in circuits, vast in distribution, infinitely potential. It is the heart of God that carries restoration, inspiration, aspiration, and final victory. And as long as God lives, and is what He is "the Father of mercies, and the God of all comfort"—this world will not go to rack and ruin.

The earth is to stand up. The earth is not forever to groan. There is to come a day when God will sound the note from the throne where He is. And when from afar off, catching that keynote and theme, this old earth, so long dismal and rolling and wailing the sad requiem of sin and death, shall surprise the spheres and fill all the universe with that chanting song of victory: "Christ hath redeemed us, and He reigns in every heart, and over all the earth." The time shall come.

Work on then, brother! Work on then, sister! Not a tear that you drop to wash away any person's trouble, not a blow that you strike in imitation of the strokes of the Almighty arm, will be forgotten. And when you stand in the presence of the Lord Jesus Christ, and He says to you, "Inasmuch as ye have done it unto one of the least of these my disciples, ye have done it unto me," it will mean more to you than if you wore the crowns of the Caesars and carried all the honors of the earth. The world will be redeemed; for our God's name is Mercy and Comfort. The Redeemer of Israel is His name.

Now, there is victory for each true Christian heart over its troubles, yet not by disowning them; not by discarding them. Every man runs that way. The first impact of pain and trouble leads every man to say, "Cast it out!" Every man's prayer to God is, "Lord, remove this thorn in the flesh." He has not a thought of anything but that. "Thrice," says the apostle Paul, the most heroic of mortal men, "I besought the Lord." And His answer was what? "My grace shall be sufficient for thee" (2 Cor. 12:9). He whose crown of thorns is now more illustrious and radiant than previous stones could make a crown, says to every one of His disciples who has thorns piercing him, "My grace shall be sufficient for you." Then bear, *bear,* BEAR!

Bear how? Resignedly? Oh! If you cannot do any better, be resigned. That is better than murmuring—only just, though. I hear persons in great trouble and affliction saying, "I strive to be resigned." Well, strive for that; strive for anything; strive for the lowest degree of Christian attainment rather than not strive at all.

But oh! Is the disciple better than the Master? Would you, if you could, reach forth your hand and take back one single sorrow, gloomy then, but gorgeous now, that made Christ to you what He is? Is it not the power of Jesus in heaven, and to all eternity will it not be His glory, that He was the Sufferer, and that He bore suffering in such a way that He vanquished suffering? And is He not the Lord over all by reason of that?

Now you are His followers; and will you follow Christ, and will you desire to be worthy of His leadership by slinking away from suffering? Do not seek it; but if it comes, remember that no sorrow comes but with His knowledge. If He does not draw the golden bow that sends the silver arrow to your heart, He knows it is sent, and sees it fall. You are never in trouble that He does not know it.

And what is trouble but that very influence that brings you nearer to the heart of God than prayers or hymns? I think sorrows usually bring us closer to God than joys do. But sorrows, to be of use, must be borne, as Christ's were, victoriously, carrying with them intimations and sacred prophecies to the heart of hope. This is not only so we will not be overcome by them, but also so we will be strengthened and ennobled and enlarged by them.

I ask you, brethren what has made you so versatile? What has made you so patient? What has made you so broad, so deep, and so rich? God put pickaxes into you, though you did not like it. He dug wells of salvation in you. He took you in His strong hand and shook you by His north wind. He rolled you in His snows and fed you with the coarsest food. He clothed you in the coarsest raiment and beat you as a flail beats grain till the straw is gone and the wheat is left.

And you are what you are by the grace of God's providence, many of you. By fire, by anvil-strokes, by the hammer that breaks the flinty rock, you are made what you are. You were gold in the rock, and God played miner, and blasted you out of the rock. Then He played stamper, and crushed you. Then He played smelter, and melted you.

Now you are gold, free from the rock by the grace of God's severity to you. As you look back upon those experiences of 5, 10, or 20 years ago and see what they have done for you, and what you are now, you say, "I would not exchange what I learned from these things for all the world."

What is the reason you have never learned to apply the same philosophy to the trouble of today? Why is that, when trouble comes on you today, your heart cannot rise up and say, "O God of darkness, I know thee; clouds are around about thee; but justice and judgment are the habitations of thy throne?" (Ps. 89:14).

When God comes to you wrapped and wreathed in clouds, and in storms, why should we not recognize Him, and say, "I know you, God; and I will not flee you; though you slay me, I will trust thee"? If a man could see God in his troubles and take sorrow to be the lore of inspiration, the light of interpretation, the sweet discipline of a bitter medicine that brings health, though the taste is not agreeable—if one could so look upon his God, how sorrows would make him strong!

Once more. No person is ordained until his sorrows put into his hands the power of comforting others. Did anybody but Paul ever think as Paul did? See what a genuine nobleness and benevolence there was in everything he did. Sorrow is apt to be very selfish and self-indulgent, but see how sorrow worked in the apostle. "Blessed be God," he said, "even the Father of our Lord Jesus Christ, the Father of mercies, and the God of all comfort; who comforteth us in all our tribulation, that we may be able to comfort them which are in any trouble by the comfort wherewith we ourselves are comforted of God."

Ministers of Comfort

There is a universal illustration of this truth. When the daughter is married and leaves home, much as she loves her chosen companion, how often her heart goes back to her father's house! Father and mother are never so dear as about 2 or 3 years after the child has been separated from them—just long enough to get over the novelty of being independent. At no other time—and this is a comfort to you, mothers, who cry when your daughters get married, and you think they love somebody else besides you—do they come back so often to their parents for counsel. And that is as it should be for father and mother are the true counselors of the child.

As time goes on, the daughter suffers from sickness; children are multiplied in the family; she does not know which way to turn; and the mother comes to her, journeying from afar. And oh, what a light there is in the dwelling! The mother's face is more than stars in the night, more than the sun in the daytime, to the homesick daughter.

The mother tarries in the family. The children are sick; there is trouble in the household; but the daughter says, "Mother is here." And when from her lips fall sweet words of consolation, and she says, "My dear child, nothing surprising has befallen you; I have gone through it all," and she narrates some of the inward history of her own life, of the troubles that she has experienced. While she is telling her story, strangely, as if exhaled, all these drops of trouble that have been sprinkled on the daughter's heart have gone, and she is comforted. Why? Because the consolations by which the mother's heart was comforted have gone over and rested on the daughter's mind. Now, the apostle says, "When Christ comforts your grief, He makes you mother to somebody else."

There are persons who, having had losses, go around with their hat in their hand begging a penny of comfort. Wherever they go, they want to have somebody talk about their griefs and ask about them. If people do not ask about them, they tell about them without being asked. They carry a tail to their griefs as long as a comet's tail. All the time, their omnivorous mouth is open to give forth something concerning their griefs. They want everybody to be interested in their griefs and sympathize with them on account of them. They make their griefs an occasion of begging.

And what does the apostle say? That when God comforts your griefs, he ordains you to be a minister of comfort to others who are in trouble. You are not to seek comfort for yourselves, but are, out of your experiences of heart, to pour comfort into other people's wounded hearts. That is the ministry of sorrow.

Christian brethren, does God so comfort you that you are able to bear the yoke and endure the piercing thorn? And when God enables you to bear it, is your first thought this, "I am now marked with the cross, as one that bears for others; I am lifted up among my fellowmen, not to be praised, but that I may go about as my Master did, and minister to them the consolations by which I myself have been comforted?"

Do not ever say, "The cup is too large and too bitter." Never. The hand that was pierced for you takes the cup and gives it to you, and Christ loves you too much to give you a cup that you cannot drink. Do not say, "The burden is too great; I cannot bear it." He that loves you, as you do not even love yourself, the Redeemer, "the God of all comfort," "the Father of mercies," lays every burden on you. And He who lays the burden on will give you strength to bear it.

Take up your cross. God gives everybody, I think, a cross, when He enters upon a Christian life. When it comes into the believer's hands, what is it? It is the rude oak, four-squared, full of splinters and slivers, and rudely tacked together. And after 40 years I see some men carrying their cross just as rude as it was at first.

Others, I perceive, begin to wind around about it faith, hope, and patience, and after a time, like Aaron's rod, it blossoms all over. At last their cross has been so covered with holy affections that it does not seem anymore to be a cross. They carry it so easily and are so much more strengthened than burdened by it, that men almost forget that it is a cross, by the triumph with which they carry it.

Carry *your* cross in such a way that there will be victory in it. Let every tear, as it drops from your eye, glance also, as the light strikes through it, with the consolations of the Holy Spirit.

There be many of you who are standing in dark hours now, and you need these consolations. My dear child, my daughter, my, son, do not be surprised—certainly not out of your faith. God is not angry with you. It is not necessarily for your sins that you are afflicted—though we are all sinful. For your *good* God afflicts you, and He says to you, "What father is he that chastiseth not his son? If ye endure chastisement, ye are my sons. Whom the Lord loveth he chasteneth." O glorious fact! O Blessed truth! These are God's love letters, written in dark ink. "Whom the Lord loveth he chasteneth, and scourgeth every son whom he receiveth. If ye endure chastening . . ." (Heb. 12:6, 7), you are *the sons* of God; if not, *bastards.*

Grant, O God, that we may be sons. Now speak, and see if You scare us. Now thunder, and see if we tremble. Now write, and see if we do not press your messages to our heart. Afflict us, only do not forget us. Comfort us, and we will bear to others *the comfort wherewith we are comforted.*

God's Greatness and Man's Greatness

Frederick W. Robertson (1816-1853) wanted to be a soldier, but he yielded to his father's decision that he take orders in the Anglican church. The courage that he would have shown on the battlefield, he displayed in the pulpit, where he fearlessly declared truth as he saw it. Never strong physically, he experienced deep depression; he questioned his faith, and he often wondered if his ministry was doing any good. He died a young man, in great pain, but in great faith and courage. He had ministered for only 6 years at Trinity Chapel, Brighton, but today his printed sermons have taken his brave message around the world. This one is from his *Sermons, Third Series,* published in 1900 in London by Kegan Paul, Trench, Trubner and Company.

Frederick W. Robertson

8

GOD'S GREATNESS AND MAN'S GREATNESS

For thus saith the high and lofty One that inhabiteth eternity, whose name is Holy; I dwell in the high and holy place, with him also that is of a contrite and humble spirit . . . (Isaiah 57:15).

THE ORIGIN OF this announcement from God to Israel seems to have been the state of contempt in which religion found itself in the days of Isaiah. One of the most profligate monarchs who ever disgraced the page of sacred history sat on the throne of Judah. His court was filled with men who recommended themselves chiefly by their licentiousness.

The altar was forsaken. Sacrilegious hands had placed the abominations of heathenism in the Holy Place. And piety—banished from the state, the church, and the royal court—was once more as she had been before, and will be again: a wanderer on the face of the earth.

Now, however easy it may be to contemplate such a state of things at a distance, it never takes place in a man's own day and time without suggesting painful perplexities of a twofold nature. In the first place, it raises suspicions respecting God's character, and, in the second place, misgivings as to one's own duty. For a faithless heart whispers, Is it worthwhile to suffer for a sinking cause? Honor, preferment, and grandeur follow in the train of unscrupulous conduct. To be strict in goodness is to be pointed at and shunned. To be no better than one's neighbors is the only way of being at peace.

It seems to have been to such a state as this that Isaiah was commissioned to bring light. He vindicated God's character by saying that He is "the high and lofty One that inhabiteth eternity." He encouraged those who were trodden down to persevere by reminding them that real dignity is something very different from present success. God dwells with him "that is of a contrite and humble spirit."

With that in mind, let us consider two points:

- God's greatness
- Man's greatness

God's Greatness Relating to Time

The first measurement, so to speak, that is given us of God's greatness, is in respect to time. He inhabits eternity. There are some subjects on which it would be good to dwell if only for the sake of the enlargement of mind that is produced by their contemplation. Eternity is one of these. You cannot steadily fix the thoughts upon it without being sensible of a peculiar kind of elevation at the same time you are humbled by a personal feeling of utter insignificance.

You have come in contact with something so immeasurable—beyond the narrow range of our common speculations—that you are exalted by the very conception of it. Now, the only way we have of forming any idea of eternity is by going, step by step, up to the largest measures of time we know of, and so ascending, on and on, till we are lost in wonder. We cannot grasp eternity, but we can learn something of it by perceiving that whatever portion of time we consider, eternity is vaster than the vastest.

We take up, for instance, the history of England. When we have spent months mastering the mere outline of those great events which, in the slow course of revolving centuries, have made England what she is, her earlier ages seem so far removed from our own times that they appear to belong to a hoary and most remote antiquity.

But then, when you compare those times with even the existing works of man, and when you remember that when England was yet young in civilization the pyramids of Egypt were already grey with 1500 years, you are impressed with a double amount of vastness. Double that period, and you come to the far distant moment when the present aspect of this world was called, by creation, out of the formless void.

Modern science has raised us to a pinnacle of thought beyond even this. It has commanded us to think of countless ages in which that formless void existed before it put on the aspect of its present creation.

The mind is lost in dwelling in such thoughts as these. When you have penetrated far, far back by successive approximations, and still see the illimitable distance receding before you as distant as before, imagination absolutely gives way, and you feel dizzy and bewildered with new strange thoughts that have not a name.

But this is only one aspect of the case. It looks only to time past. The same overpowering calculations wait us when we bend our eyes on that which is to come. Time stretches back immeasurable, but it also stretches on and on forever.

Now, it is by such a conception as this that the inspired prophet attempts to measure the immeasurable of God. All that eternity, magnificent as it is, never was without an Inhabitant. Eternity means nothing by itself. It merely expresses the existence of the High and Lofty One that inhabited it.

We make a fanciful distinction between eternity and time—there is no real distinction. We are in eternity at this moment (that has begun to be with us which never began with God). Our only measure of time is by the succession of ideas. If ideas flow fast, and many sights and many thoughts pass by us, time seems lengthened. If we have the simple routine of a few engagements, the same every day, with little variety, the years roll by us so fast that we cannot mark them.

It is not so with God. There is no succession of ideas with Him. Every possible idea is present with Him now. It was present with Him 10,000 years ago. God's dwelling place is that eternity which has neither past nor future. It is one vast, immeasurable present.

God's Greatness Relating to Space

There is a second measure of God given us in this verse. It is in the respect of space. He dwells in the high and lofty place. He dwells, moreover, in the most insignificant place—even the heart of man. And the idea by which the prophet would here exhibit to us the greatness of God, is that of His eternal omnipresence.

It is difficult to say which conception carries with it the greatest exaltation—that of boundless space or that of unbounded time. When we pass from the tame and narrow scenery of our own country, and stand on those spots of earth in which nature puts on her wilder and more awful forms, we are conscious of something of the grandeur that belongs to the thought of space.

Go where the strong foundations of the earth lie around you in their massive majesty, and mountain after mountain rears its snow to heaven in a giant chain. When this scene bursts upon you for the first time, there is that peculiar feeling which we call, in common language, an enlargement of ideas.

But then we are told that the sublimity of those dizzy heights is but a nameless speck in comparison with the globe of which they form the girdle. We think of that globe itself as a minute spot in the mighty system to which it belongs, so that if our world were annihilated, its loss would not be felt. And we are told that 80,000,000 of such systems roll in the world of space, to which our own system again is as nothing.

When we are again pressed with the recollection that beyond those furthest limits creative power is exerted immeasurably further that eye can reach or thought can penetrate; then, brethren, the awe that comes upon the heart is only, after all, a tribute to a *portion* of God's greatness.

Yet we do not need science to teach us this. It is a thought that oppresses very childhood—the overpowering thought of space. A child can put his head on his hands and think and think until he reaches in imagination some far distant barrier of the universe, and still the difficulty presents itself to his young mind,

"And what is beyond that barrier?" The only answer is "The high and lofty place."

And this, brethren, is the inward seal with which God has stamped Himself upon man's heart. If every other trace of Deity has been expunged by the fall, these two at least defy destruction—the thought of Eternal Time and the thought of Immeasurable Space.

God's Greatness Relating to Holiness

The third measure of God that is given us respects His character. His name is Holy. The chief idea that this would convey to us is separation from evil. Brethren, there is perhaps a time drawing near when those of us who will stand at His right hand, purified from all evil taint, will be able to comprehend absolutely what is meant by the holiness of God.

At present, with hearts cleaving to earth, and tossed by a thousand gusts of unholy passion, we can only form a dim conception *relatively* of what holiness implies. None but the pure can understand purity. The chief knowledge that we have of God's holiness comes from our acquaintance with unholiness. We know what impurity is—God is *not* that. We know what injustice is—God is *not* that.

We know what restlessness, guilt, and passion are. Deceitfulness, pride, waywardness—all these we know. God is none of these. And this is our chief acquaintance with His character. We know what God is *not*. We scarcely can be rightly said to know, that is to feel, what God *is*. Therefore, this is implied in the very name of holiness. Holiness in the Jewish sense means simply separateness. From all that is wrong and mean and base, our God is forever separate.

There is another way God gives us a conception of what this holiness implies. Tell us of His justice, His truth, His lovingkindness. All these are cold abstractions. They convey no distinct idea of themselves to our hearts. What we want was that these should be exhibited to us in tangible reality.

This is just what God has done. He has exhibited all these attributes, not in the light of *speculation,* but in the light of *facts.* He has given us His own character in all its delicacy of coloring in the history of Christ. Love, mercy, tenderness, purity—these are no mere names when we see them brought out in the human actions of our Master.

Holiness is only a shadow of our minds until it receives shape and substance in the life of Christ. All this character of holiness is intelligible to us in Christ. "No man hath seen God at any time, the only begotten Son . . . of the Father, he hath declared him" (John 1:18).

There is a third light in which God's holiness is shown to us, and that is in the sternness with which He recoils from guilt. Because Christ died for man, I know what God's love means. Because Jesus wept human tears over Jerusalem, I know what God's compassion means. Because the stern denunciations of Jesus rang in the Pharisees' ears, I can comprehend what God's indignation is. Because Jesus stood calm before His murderers, I have a conception of what serenity is.

Brethren, revelation opens to us a scene beyond the grave, when this will be exhibited in full operation. There will be an everlasting banishment from God's presence of that impurity on which the last efforts have been tried in vain. It will be a carrying out of this sentence by a law that cannot be reversed—"Depart from me, ye cursed" (Matt. 25:41).

But it is quite a mistake to suppose that this is only a matter of revelation. We have traces of it now on this side the sepulchre. Human life is full of God's recoil from sin. In the writings of a heart that has been made to possess its own iniquities—in the dark spot that guilt leaves upon the conscience, rising up at times in a man's happiest moments, as if it will not come out it is there. In the restlessness and the feverishness that follow the efforts of the man who has indulged habits of sin too long—in all these there is a law repelling wickedness from the presence of the Most High—which proclaims that God is holy.

Brethren, it is in these that the greatness of God consists—Eternal in Time—Unlimited in Space—Unchangeable and Pure in character. His serenity and His vastness arise from His own perfections.

Now let's consider, in the second place, the greatness of man.
- The nature of that greatness.
- The persons who are great.

Man's Greatness: Habitation of Deity

Our text brings before us, in this one fact, that man has been made a habitation of the Deity: "I dwell with him that is of a contrite and humble spirit." At the very outset, this is the distinction between what is great in God and what is great in man.

To be independent of everything in the universe is God's glory, and to be independent is man's shame. All that God has, He has from Himself—all that man has, he has from God. The moment man cuts himself off from God, he cuts himself off from all true grandeur.

There are two things implied when Scripture says that God dwells with man. The first is that peculiar presence that He has conferred on the members of His church.

Brethren, we do not presume to define what that presence is and how it dwells within us—we are content to leave it as a mystery. But this we know: Something of a very peculiar and supernatural character takes place in the heart of every man on whom the gospel has been brought to bear with power.

"Know ye not," said the apostle Paul, "that your bodies are the temples of the Holy Ghost" (cf. 1 Cor. 6:19). And again in the epistle to the Ephesians, "In Christ ye are builded for an habitation of God through the Spirit" (cf. 2:22). There is something in these expressions that refuses to be explained away. They leave us but one conclusion, that in all those who have become Christ's by faith, God personally and locally has taken up His dwelling place.

There is a second meaning attached in Scripture to the expression "God dwells in man." According to the first meaning, we understand this expression in the most plain and literal sense the words are capable of conveying. According to the second, we understand His dwelling in a figurative sense, implying that He gives an acquaintance with Himself to man.

For instance, when Judas asked, "Lord, how is it, that thou wilt manifest thyself unto us and not unto the world?" Our Redeemer's reply was this, "If a man love me, he will keep my words: and my Father will love him, and we will come unto him, and make our abode with him" (John 14:22, 23).

In the question it was asked *how* God would manifest Himself to His servants. In the answer it was shown *how* He would make His abode with them. And if the answer be any reply to the question at all, what follows is this—that God making His abode or dwelling in the heart is exactly the same thing as God's manifesting Himself to the heart.

Brethren, in these two things the greatness of man consists. One is to have God so dwelling in us as to impart His character to us; the other is to have God so dwelling in us that we recognize His presence and know that we are His and He is ours. They are two things perfectly distinct. To *have* God in us, this is salvation; to *know* that God is in us, this is assurance.

Man's Greatness: Examples

Lastly, we inquire as to the persons who are truly great. These the Holy Scripture has divided into two classes—those who are humble and those who are contrite in heart. Or rather, it will be observed that it is the same class of character under different circumstances. Humbleness is the frame of mind of those who are in a state of innocence; contrition, of those who are in a state of repentant guilt.

Brethren, do not let the expression "innocence" be misunderstood. Innocence, in its true and highest sense, never existed but once on this earth. Innocence cannot be the religion of man now.

Our text describes those with whom God dwells as the humble in heart. Two things are required for this state of mind. One is that a man should have a true estimate of God, and the other is that he should have a true estimate of himself.

Vain, blind man places himself on a little corner of this planet, a speck upon a speck of the universe, and begins to form conclusions from the small fraction of God's government he can perceive.

The astronomer looks at the laws of motion and forgets that there must have been a First Cause to commence that motion. The surgeon looks at the materialism of his own frame and forgets that matter cannot organize itself into exquisite beauty. The metaphysician buries himself in the laws of the mind and forgets that there may be spiritual influences producing all those laws.

All this, brethren, is the unhumbled spirit of philosophy—intellectual pride. Men look at nature, but they do not look through it up to nature's God. There is an awful ignorance of God, arising from indulged sin, which produces an unhumbled heart. God may be shut out from the soul by pride of intellect or by pride of heart.

Pharaoh is presented in Scripture as a type of pride. His pride arose from ignorance of God. "Who is the Lord, that I should obey His voice? I know not the Lord, neither will I let Israel go" (Ex. 5:2). This was not intellectual pride; it was a pride in a matter of duty.

Pharaoh had been immersing his whole heart in the narrow politics of Egypt. The great problem of his day was to aggrandize his own people and prevent an insurrection of the Israelites. That small kingdom of Egypt had been his universe.

Pharoah shut his heart to the voice of justice and the voice of humanity. In other words, he was great in pride of human majesty but small in the sight of the high and lofty One. He shut himself out from the knowledge of God.

The next ingredient of humbleness is that a man must have a right estimate of himself. There is a vast amount of self-deception on this point. We say of ourselves what others would not. A man truly humbled would take it only as his due when others treated him in the way that he says that he deserves.

But my brethren, we kneel in our closets in shame for what we are, and we tell our God that the lowest place is too good for us. Then we go into the world, and if we meet with slight or disrespect, or if our opinion is ignored, or if another is preferred before us, there is all the anguish of a galled and jealous spirit.

Half the bitterness of our lives comes from this, that we are smarting from what we call the wrongs and the neglect of men. Brethren, if we saw ourselves as God sees us, we would be willing to go anywhere, to be silent when others speak, to be passed by in the world's crowd, and thrust aside to make way for others.

We should be willing to give credit to others for what we might have received praise ourselves. This was the attitude of our Master— this is the meek and quiet spirit, and this is the attitude of the humble with whom the high and lofty One dwells.

The other class of those who are truly great are the contrite in spirit. At first sight it might be supposed that there must ever be a vast distinction between the innocent and the penitent. This is what the elder son in the parable thought when he saw his brother restored to his father's favor. He was surprised and hurt. He had served his father these many years—his brother had wasted his substance in riotous living.

In this passage God makes no distinction. He places the humble, consistent follower and the broken-hearted sinner on the same level. He dwells with both the one who is contrite *and* the one who is humble. He sheds around them both the grandeur of His own presence.

The annals of church history are full of examples of this marvel of God's grace. By the transforming grace of Christ, men who have done the very work of Satan have become as conspicuous in the service of heaven as they were once in the career of guilt.

So indisputably has this been so, that men have drawn from such instances the perverted conclusion that if a man is ever to be a great saint, he must first be a great sinner. God forbid, brethren, that we should ever make such an inference. But this we infer for our own encouragement: past sin does not necessarily preclude us from high attainments.

We must "forget the things that are behind." We must not mourn over past years of folly as if they made saintliness impossible. Deep as we may have been once in earthliness, so deep we may also be in penitence, and so high we may become in spirituality.

We have so few years to do our work! Let us try to do it so much faster. Christ can crowd the work of years into hours. He did it with the dying thief. If the man who has set out early may take his time, it certainly cannot be so with *us* who have lost our time.

If we, in the past, have lost God's bright and happy presence by our rebellion, what then? Unrelieved sadness? Nay, brethren. Calmness and purity, may have gone from our heart, but *all* is not gone yet. Just as sweetness comes from the bark of the cinnamon when it is bruised, so the spirit of the cross of Christ, bring beauty and holiness and peace out of the bruised and broken heart. God dwells with the contrite as much as with the humble.

Conclusion

To conclude, the first inference we collect from this subject is the danger of coming into collision with such a God as our God. Day by day we commit sins of thought and word which the dull eye of man takes no notice. Yet, He whose name is Holy cannot pass them by.

We may elude the vigilance of a human enemy and place ourselves beyond his reach. But God fills all space—there is not a spot in which His piercing eye is not on us and His uplifted hand cannot find us out.

Man must strike soon if he would strike at all, for opportunities pass away from him, and his victim may escape his vengeance by death. There is no passing of opportunity with God, and it is this which makes His longsuffering a solemn thing. God can wait, for He has a whole eternity before Him in which He may strike. "All things are naked and opened unto the eyes of Him with whom we have to do" (Heb. 4:13).

In the next place, we are taught the heavenly character of condescension. It is not from the insignificance of man that God's dwelling with him is so strange. It is as much the glory of God to bend His attention on an atom as to uphold the universe.

But the marvel is that the habitation He has chosen for Himself is an impure one. And when He came down from His magnificence to make this world His home, still the same character of condescension was shown through all the life of Christ. Our God selected the society of the outcasts of earth, those whom none else would speak to.

Brethren, if we would be Godlike, we must follow in the same steps. Our temptation is to do exactly the opposite. We are forever hoping to obtain the friendship and the intimacy of those above us in the world, to win over men of influence to truth—to associate with men of talent, station, and title. This is the world-chase, and this is too much the religious man's chase.

But if you look simply to the question of resemblance to God, then look to the man who makes it a habit to select that one in life to do good to or that one in a room to speak with, whom others pass by because there is nothing either of intellect or power or name to recommend him, but only humbleness. *That* man has stamped upon his heart more of heavenly similitude by condescension than the man who has made it his business to win this world's great ones, even for the sake of truth.

Lastly, we learn the guilt of two things of which this world is full—vanity and pride. There is a distinction between these two. But the distinction consists in this: The vain man looks for the admiration of others; the proud man requires nothing but his own.

Now, it is this distinction that makes vanity despicable to us all. We can easily find out the vain man—we soon discover what it is he wants to be observed, whether it be a gift of person, or a gift of mind, or a gift of character. If he is vain of his person, his attitudes will tell the tale. If he is vain of his judgment or his memory or his honesty, he cannot help an unnecessary parade. The world finds him out, and this is why vanity is ever looked on with contempt.

As soon as we let men see that we are suppliants for their admiration, we are at their mercy. We have given them the privilege of feeling that they are above us. We have invited them to spurn us. And therefore vanity is but a thing for scorn.

It is very different with pride. No man can look down on him that is proud, for he has asked no man for anything. They are forced to feel respect for pride, because it is thoroughly independent of them. It wraps itself up in the consequence of its own excellences, and it scorns to care whether others take note of them or not.

It is just here that the danger lies. We have exalted a sin into a virtue. No man will acknowledge that he is vain, but almost any man will acknowledge that he is proud. But tried by the balance of the sanctuary, there is little to choose between the two. If a man look for greatness outside of God, it matters little whether he seeks it in his own applause or in that of others.

The *proud* Pharisee, who trusted in himself that he was righteous, was condemned by Christ as severely, and even more, than the *vain* Jews who could not believe because they sought honor from one another, and not that honor which comes from God only.

It may be a more dazzling and splendid sin to be proud. It is not less hateful in God's sight. Let us speak God's word to our own unquiet, swelling, burning hearts. Pride may disguise itself as it will in its own majesty, but in the presence of the high and lofty One, it is but littleness after all.

God's Omnipresence

John Wesley (1703-1781), along with his brother
Charles, and George Whitefield, founded the
Methodist movement in Britain and America. On May
24, 1738, he had his great spiritual experience in a
meeting at Aldersgate Street, when his "heart was
strangely warmed" and he received assurance of
salvation. Encouraged by Whitefield to do open-air
preaching, Wesley soon was addressing thousands, in
spite of the fact that many churches were closed to
him. The Methodist "societies" he formed became local
churches that conserved the results of his evangelism.
He wrote many books and preached 40,000 sermons
during his long ministry. This one is taken from *Works
of John Wesley*, volume 3, published by the Wesleyan
Methodist Book Room, London, 1872 and was
preached in Portsmouth, August 12, 1788.

John Wesley

9

GOD'S OMNIPRESENCE

Do not I fill heaven and earth? saith the Lord (Jeremiah 23:24).

HOW STRONGLY AND beautifully these words express the omnipresence of God! And can there be, in the whole realm of nature, a more sublime subject? Can there be anything more worthy of the consideration of every rational creature? Is there anything more necessary to be considered and to be understood?

How many excellent purposes it fulfills! What deep instruction it conveys to all the children of men, and, more directly, to the children of God!

How is it then so little has been written on so sublime and useful a subject? It is true that some of our most eminent writers have occasionally touched upon it. They have several strong and beautiful reflections that were naturally suggested by it. But which of them has published a regular treatise, or so much as a sermon, upon the omnipresence of God?

Perhaps many were conscious of their inability to do justice to so vast a subject. And it is possible that there are many such messages hidden in the voluminous writings of the last century. But if they are hid, even in their own country, they are of no use. If we cannot read them, or if they are buried in oblivion, it is the same.

What seems to be needed for general use is a plain discourse on the omnipresence, or ubiquity, of God. First, it should explain and prove that glorious truth, "God is in this and every place." Second, it should apply to the consciences of all thinking men in a few practical inferences.

The Glorious Truth

I will endeavor, by the assistance of the Holy Spirit, to present that message. First, I should like to explain the omnipresence of God and to show how we are to understand the glorious truth: "God is in this and every place."

The psalmist, you may remember, speaks strongly and beautifully about it in Psalm 139. He observes, in the most exact order, first, "God is in this place;" and then, "God is in every place." He observes first, "Thou art about my bed, and about my path, and spiest out all my ways" (v. 3); "Thou hast fashioned me behind and before, and thine hand is upon me" (v. 5).

The *manner* of God's omnipresence he could not explain; *how* it was he could not tell. "Such knowledge," he says, "is too wonderful for me: I cannot attain unto it" (v. 6).

He next observes, in the most lively and affecting manner, that God is in every place. "Whither shall I go then from thy Spirit, or whither shall I go from thy presence? If I climb up into heaven, thou art there: If I go down to hell, thou art there also" (vv. 7, 8).

If I could ascend, he is saying after the manner of men, to the highest part of the universe, or if I could descend to the lowest point, God is alike present. He says, "If I should take the wings of the morning, and remain in the uttermost parts of the sea, even there thy hand would lead me" (vv. 9, 10)—thy power and thy presence would be before me,—"and thy right hand hold me."

God, he says, is equally in the length and breadth, and in the height and depth, of the universe. Indeed, God's presence and knowledge not only reach the utmost bounds of creation, but

> Thine omnipresent sight,
> Even to the pathless realms extends
> Of uncreated night.

In a word, there is no point of space, whether within or without the bounds of creation, where God is not.

Indeed, this subject is far too vast to be comprehended by the narrow limits of human understanding. We can only say, the great God, the eternal, the almighty Spirit, is as unbounded in His presence, as in His duration and power.

In condescension, indeed, to our weak understanding, He is said to dwell in heaven. But strictly speaking, the heaven of heavens cannot contain Him. He is in every part of His dominion. The universal God dwells in universal space, so that we may say,

> Hail, FATHER! whose creating call
> Unnumber'd worlds attend!
> JEHOVAH, comprehending all,
> Whom none can comprehend!

If we may dare attempt to illustrate this a little further: What is the space occupied by a grain of sand, compared to that space which is occupied by the starry heavens? It is as a cipher; it is nothing; it vanishes away in comparison.

What is this grain of sand compared to the whole expanse of space? The whole creation itself when seen in proportion with the universe, is infinitely less than a grain of sand! And yet this expanse of space, to which the whole creation bears no proportion at all, is infinitely less, in comparison to the great God, than a grain of sand, yes, even a millionth part of it.

The Supernatural God

This seems to be the plain meaning of those solemn words which God speaks of Himself: "Do not I fill heaven and earth?" And these sufficiently prove His omnipresence, which may be further established from this consideration: God acts everywhere and therefore is everywhere. It is an utter impossibility that any being, created or uncreated, should work where it is not. God acts in heaven, in earth, and under the earth, throughout the whole compass of His creation by sustaining all things. Without Him everything would in an instant sink into its primitive nothing.

He governs all, every moment superintending everything that He has made; strongly and sweetly influencing all, and yet not destroying the liberty of His rational creatures. Even the heathens acknowledged that the great God governs the large and conspicuous parts of the universe—that He regulated the motions of the heavenly bodies: the sun, moon, and stars; that He is

> The all-informing soul,
> That fills, pervades, and actuates the whole.

But the heathens had no conception of His concern for the least things as well as the greatest. They had no idea that He presides over all that He has made—that He governs atoms as well as worlds. This we could not have known, unless it had pleased God to reveal it to us Himself.

Had he not Himself told us so, we should not have dared to think that "not a sparrow falleth to the ground, without the will of our Father which is in heaven." We wouldn't have guessed that "even the very hairs of our head are all numbered!" (Matt. 10:29, 30).

This comfortable truth, that "God filleth heaven and earth," we have also seen in Psalm 139:5-8: "If I climb up into heaven, thou art there; if I go down to hell, thou art there also. If I take the wings of the morning, and remain in the uttermost parts of the sea, even there thy hand shall lead me."

The plain meaning is this: If I travel to any distance whatsoever, You are there. You still beset me, and lay your hand upon me. Let me flee to any conceivable or inconceivable distance; above, beneath, or on any side; it makes no difference. You are still equally there: In You I still "live, and move, and have my being" (Acts 17:28).

The Space-filling God

Where no creature is, God is still there. The presence or absence of any or all creatures makes no difference with regard to God's presence. He is equally in all, or without all.

Many have been the disputes among philosophers whether there is any such thing as empty space in the universe. It is now generally supposed that all space is full. Perhaps it cannot be proved that all space is filled with matter, but the heathen himself will bear us witness.

"All things are full of God." Yes, and whatever space exists beyond the bounds of creation (for creation must have bounds, since nothing is boundless—nothing can be, but the great Creator), even that space cannot exclude Him who fills the heaven and the earth.

Just equivalent to this is the expression of the apostle Paul, who said, "The fullness of him that filleth all in all" (Eph. 1:23). Literally translated, the words "all in all" mean *all things in all things*. This is the strongest expression of universality that can possibly be conceived. It necessarily includes the least and the greatest of all things that exist. If any expression could be stronger, it would be stronger than even the "filling of heaven and earth."

Indeed, this very expression, "Do not I fill heaven and earth?" (the question being equal to the strongest affirmation), implies the clearest assertion of God's being present everywhere and filling all space. It is well-known that the Hebrew phrase "heaven and earth" includes the whole universe—the whole extent of space, created or uncreated, and all that is therein.

We cannot believe the omnipotence of God unless we believe His omnipresence. We have already observed that nothing can act where it is not. If there were any space where God was not present, He would not be able to do anything there. Therefore, to deny the omnipresence of God implies, likewise, the denial of His omnipotence. To set bounds to the one is undoubtedly to set bounds to the other also.

Indeed, wherever we suppose Him not to be, there we suppose all His attributes to be in vain. He cannot exercise there either His justice or mercy, either His power or wisdom. In that extra-mundane space (so to speak), where we suppose God not to be present, we must, of course, suppose Him to have no duration. As it is supposed to be beyond the bounds of the creation, so it is also beyond the bounds of the Creator's power. Such is the blasphemous absurdity implied in this supposition!

The Invisible God

But to all that is or can be said of the omnipresence of God, the world has one grand objection: they cannot see Him. This is really at the root of all their other objections. Long ago our blessed Lord observed, "Whom the world cannot receive, because they see Him not" (John 14:17).

But is it not easy to reply, "Can you see the wind?" You cannot. But do you therefore deny its existence or its presence? You say, "No, for I can perceive it by my other senses." But by which of your senses do you perceive your soul? Surely you do not deny either the existence or the presence of this! And yet it is not the object of your sight or of any of your other senses. Suffice it then to consider that God is a Spirit, as is your soul. Consequently, "Him no man hath seen, or can see" (1 Tim. 6:16), with eyes of flesh and blood.

Drawing Some Conclusions

What inference should we draw from the fact that God is in every place; that He is "about our bed, and about our path" and that He "besets us behind and before, and lays His hand upon us?" What use should we make of this consideration?

Godly Fear. Is it not right to humble ourselves before the eyes of His Majesty? Should we not labor continually to acknowledge His presence "with reverence and godly fear"? (Heb. 12:28). This, of course, is not like the fear of devils, who believe and tremble, but with the fear of angels—with something similar to that which is felt by the inhabitants of heaven, when

Dark with excessive bright his skirts appear,
Yet dazzle heaven, that brightest seraphim
Approach not, but with both wings veil their eyes.

Right Living. If you believe that God is about your bed and about your path and spies out all your ways, then take care not to do the least thing, not to speak the least word, not to indulge the least thought that you think would offend Him. Suppose a messenger of God, an angel, were now standing at your right hand and fixing his eyes upon you. Would you not take care to abstain from every word or action that you knew would offend him?

Yes, suppose one of your mortal fellowmen, suppose only a holy man, were to stand by you. Would you not be extremely cautious how you conducted yourself, both in word and action? How much more cautious ought you to be when you know that not a holy man, not an angel of God, but God Himself, the Holy One "that inhabiteth eternity," is inspecting your heart, your tongue, your hand, every moment. He Himself will surely bring you into judgment for all you think and speak and act under the sun!

In particular, if there is not a word in your tongue nor a syllable you speak, but he "knoweth it altogether," how exact you should be in "setting a watch before your mouth, and in keeping the door of your lips"! (Ps. 141:3). How it behoves you to be wary in all your conversations, being forewarned by your Judge, that "by your words you shall be justified, or by your words you shall be condemned"! (Matt. 12:37).

How cautious you should be, lest "any corrupt communication" or any uncharitable or unprofitable discourse should "proceed out of your mouth" instead of "that which is good to the use of edifying, and meet to minister grace to the hearer"! (Eph. 4:29).

If God sees our hearts as well as our hands in all places; if He understands our thoughts long before they are clothed with words, how earnestly we should urge that petition, "Search me, O Lord, and prove me; try out my reins and my heart; look well if there be any way of wickedness in me, and lead me in the way everlasting!" (Ps. 26:2; 139:23, 24).

How needful it is to work together with him in "keeping our hearts with all diligence" (Pr. 4:23), until He has "cast down imaginations," evil reasonings, "and everything that exalteth itself against the knowledge of God, and brought into captivity every thought to the obedience of Christ"! (2 Cor. 10:5).

Faithfully Serving. On the other hand, if you are already enlisted under the great Captain of your salvation, and you see yourself continually under the eye of your Captain, how zealous and active you should be to "fight the good fight of faith, and lay hold on eternal life" (1 Tim. 6:12); "to endure hardship, as good soldiers of Jesus Christ" (2 Tim. 2:3); to use all diligence, to "war a good warfare," and to do whatever is acceptable in His sight!

How studious you should be to approve all your ways to His all-seeing eyes, so that He may say to your hearts what He will proclaim aloud in the great assembly of men and angels, "Well done, good and faithful servant!" (Matt. 25:21).

In order to attain these glorious ends, spare no pains to preserve always a deep, continual, lively, and joyful sense of His gracious presence. Never forget His comprehensive word to the great father of the faithful: "I am the Almighty [rather, the all-sufficient] God; walk before me, and be thou perfect"! (Gen. 17:1).

Cheerfully expect that He, before whom you stand, will ever guide you with His eye; will support you by His guardian hand; will keep you from all evil; and "when you have suffered a while, will make you perfect, will stablish, strengthen, and settle you" (1 Peter 5:10), and then "preserve you unblamable unto the coming of our Lord Jesus Christ"! (1 Thess. 5:23).

NOTES

God's Omniscience

Charles Haddon Spurgeon (1834-1892) is undoubtedly the most famous minister of modern times. Converted in 1850, he united with the Baptists and very soon began to preach in various places. He became pastor of the Baptist church in Waterbeach in 1851, and three years later he was called to the decaying Park Street Church, London. Within a short time, the work began to prosper, a new church was built and dedicated in 1861, and Spurgeon became London's most popular preacher. In 1855, he began to publish his sermons weekly; and today they make up the fifty-seven volumes of *The Metropolitan Tabernacle Pulpit.* He founded a pastor's college and several orphanages. This sermon is taken from *The New Park Street Pulpit,* volume II, published in 1857, and was preached on June 15, 1856, in Exeter Hall, London.

Charles Haddon Spurgeon

10

GOD'S OMNISCIENCE

Thou God seest me (Genesis 16:13).

THERE ARE MORE eyes fixed on man than he realizes:
He sees not as he is seen. He thinks himself obscure
and unobserved, but let him remember that a cloud of
witnesses holds him in full view. Wherever he is, at
every instant, there are beings whose attention is
riveted on his doings, and whose gaze is constantly
fixed on his actions.

Within this hall, there are myriads of spirits unseen
to us—spirits good and spirits evil; upon us tonight the
eyes of angels rest. Attentively those perfect spirits
regard our order, they hear our songs, they observe
our prayers. It may be that they fly to heaven to convey
to their companions news of any sinners who are born
of God, for there is joy in the presence of the angels of
God over one sinner who repents.

Millions of spiritual creatures walk this earth, both
when we wake and when we sleep. Midnight is peopled
with shadows unseen, and daylight has its spirits too.
The prince of the power of the air, attended by his
squadron of evil spirits, often flits through the ether.
His evil spirits watch our halting every instant.

Meanwhile, good spirits, battling for the salvation of
God's elect, keep us in all our ways and watch over our
feet, lest at any time we dash them against a stone.
Hosts of invisible beings watch over every one of us at
different periods of our lives.

We must remember, also, that not only do the spirits of angels, elect or fallen, look on us, but "the spirits
of the just made perfect" continually observe our conversations. We are taught by the apostle Paul that the
noble army of martyrs and the glorious company of

confessors are "witnesses" of our race to heaven. He said, "seeing, then, that we are compassed about with so great a cloud of witnesses, let us lay aside every weight and the sin which doth so easily beset us."

From beyond the blue heaven the eyes of the glorified look down on us. There the children of God sit on their starry thrones, observing how well we uphold the banner around which they fought. They behold our valor, or they detect our cowardice. And they are intent to witness our valiant deeds of noble daring, or they observe our ignominious retreat in the day of battle.

Remember, you sons of men, you are not unregarded. You do not pass through this world in unseen obscurity. In darkest shades of night, eyes glare on you through the gloom. And in the brightness of the day angels are spectators of your labors. From heaven there look down upon you spirits who see everything that finite beings are capable of beholding.

But if we think this thought worth treasuring, there is another which sums it up and drowns it, even as a drop is lost in the ocean. It is the thought, "Thou God seest me." It is nothing that angels see me, it is nothing that devils watch me, it is nothing that the glorified spirits observe me—compared with the overwhelming truth that God at all times sees me. Let us dwell on that now, and may God the Spirit make use of it to our spiritual profit!

In the first place, I will notice the *general* doctrine, that God observes all men. In the second place, I will notice the *particular* doctrine, "Thou God seest *me.*" And in the third place I will draw from it some *practical and comforting inferences* for different persons in different situations.

The General Doctrine: God Sees All Men

This may be easily proved, even from the nature of God. It is hard to imagine a God who could not see His own creatures; it is difficult in the extremes to imagine a divinity who could not behold the actions of the works of His hands.

The word the Greeks applied to God implied that He was a God who could see. They called Him *Theos*, and they derived that word, if I read rightly, from the root *Theisthai,* to see, because they regarded God as being the all-seeing one. His eye took in the whole universe at a glance, and His knowledge extended far beyond that of mortals.

God Almighty, from His very essence and nature, must be an omniscient God. Strike out the thought that He sees me, and you extinguish Deity by a single stroke. There would be no God if that God had no eyes, for a blind God is no God at all. We could not conceive Him.

Stupid as idolators may be, it is very hard to think that even they had fashioned a blind god. Even they have given eyes to their gods, though they do not see. Juggernaut has eyes stained with blood. Also, the gods of the ancient Romans had eyes, and some of them were called far-seeing gods.

Even the heathen can scarcely conceive of a god who had no eyes to see, and certainly we are not so mad as to imagine for a single second that there can be a Deity who lacks the knowledge of everything that is done by man beneath the sun.

I say it is as impossible to conceive of a God who did not observe everything, as it is to conceive of a round square. When we say, *"Thou God,"* we do, in fact, comprise in the word "God" the idea of a God who sees everything. "Thou God seest me."

We can be sure that God must see us, for we are taught in the Scriptures that God is everywhere. If God is everywhere, what hinders Him from seeing all that is done in every part of His universe? God is here: I do not simply live near him, but *"in* him I live, and move, and have my being" (Acts 17:28). There is not a particle of this mighty space that is not filled with God. Go out into the pure air, and there is not a particle of it where God is not. In every portion of this earth where I tread and the spot where I move, there is God.

Within thy circling power I stand;
On every side I find thy hand:
Awake, asleep, at home, abroad,
I am surrounded still with God.

Take the wings of the morning and fly beyond the most distant star, but God is there. God is not a being confined to one place, but He is everywhere. He is there, and there, and there: in the deepest mine man ever bored; in the unfathomable caverns of the ocean; in the heights, towering and lofty; in the gulfs that are deep, which fathom can never reach. Yes, God is everywhere.

I know from His own words that He is a God who fills immensity; the heavens are not wide enough for Him; He grasps the sun with one hand and the moon with the other. Where the solemnity of silence has never been broken by the song of an angel, there is God. God is everywhere. Conceive space, and God and space are equal.

Well, then, if God is everywhere, how can I refrain from believing that God sees me wherever I am? He does not look upon me from a distance. If He did, I might screen myself beneath the shades of night. But He is here, close by my side—and not *by* me only—but *in* me. He is within this heart, where these lungs breath, or where my blood gushes through my veins, or where this pulse is beating, like a muffled drum, my march to death.

God is here: within this mouth, in this tongue, in these eyes, in each of you God dwells. He is within you, and around you; He is beside you, and behind, and before.

Is not such knowledge too wonderful for you? Is it not high, and you cannot attain unto it? I say, how can you resist the doctrine, which comes upon you like a flash of lightning, that if God is everywhere He must see everything, and that therefore it is truth: "Thou God seest me."

Lest anyone suppose that God may be in a place, and perhaps slumbering, let me remind him that in every spot to which a person can travel, there is not simply God, but also *God's activity*.

Wherever I go, I will find a God who is busy about the affairs of this world. Take me to the pleasant pasture. Why, every little blade of grass there has God's hand in it, making it grow. And every tiny daisy, which a child likes to pluck, looks up with its little eye, and says, "God is in me, circulating my sap, and opening my little flower."

Go where you will through this earth. Where vegetation is scarcely to be found, look up and see those rolling stars; God is active there. It is His hand that wheels along the stars and moves the moon in her nightly course.

But if there be neither stars nor moon, there are those clouds, heavy with darkness. Who steers them across the sea of azure? Does not the breath of God blowing upon them drive them along the heavens? God is everywhere, not as a slumbering God, but as an active God.

I am upon the sea, and there I see God making the everlasting pulse of nature beat in constant ebbs and flows. I am in the pathless desert, but above me screams the vulture; I see God winging the wild bird's flight. I am shut up in a hideaway, but an insect drops from its leaf, and I see in that insect life God preserves and sustains.

Yes, shut me out from the animate creation and put me on the barren rock where moss itself cannot find a footing and there will I discern my God bearing up the pillars of the universe and sustaining that bare rock as a part of the colossal foundation upon which He has built the world.

Wher'er we turn our gazing eyes,
Thy radiant footsteps shine;
Ten Thousand pleasing wonders rise,
And speak their source divine.

The living tribes of countless forms,
In earth, and sea, and air,
The meanest flies, the smallest worms,
Almighty power declare.

You can see God everywhere. If you do not see Him around you, look within you. Is He not there? Is not your blood now flowing through every portion of your body, to and from your heart? Is God not active there?

Do you not know that every pulse of your heart needs a volition of Deity as its permit, and yet more, needs an exertion of divine power as its cause?

Do you not know that every breath you breathe needs Deity for its inspiration and expiration, and that you would die if God were to withdraw that power? If we could look within us, we would see mighty works going on in this mortal fabric—the garment of the soul— which would astonish us and make us see that God is not asleep, but active and busy.

There is a working God everywhere, a God with His eyes open everywhere, a God with His hands at work everywhere. He is a God doing something—not a slumbering God, but a laboring God.

Oh! Does not this conviction flash upon your mind with a brightness against which you cannot shut your eyes: since God is everywhere and everywhere active, it follows as a necessary and unavoidable consequence that He must see us and know all our actions and our deeds.

I have one more proof to offer, which I think is conclusive. When we remember that *God can see a thing before it happens* we may be sure He sees us. If He beholds an event before it transpires, surely He must see a thing that is happening now.

Read the ancient prophecies about what God said should be at the end of Babylon and of Nineveh. Just turn to the chapter where you read of Edom's doom or where you are told that Tyre would be desolate. Then walk through the lands of the East and see Nineveh and Babylon cast to the ground, the cities ruined.

Then answer this question, "Is not God a God of foreknowledge? Can He not see the things that are to come?" Indeed, not a single event will transpire in the next cycle of a thousand years that is not already past to the infinite mind of God. Not a deed will be transacted tomorrow or the next day or the next, through eternity, if days can be eternal, but God knows it altogether.

If He knows the future, does He not know the present? If His eyes look through the dim haze that veils us from the things of futurity, can He not see that which is standing in the brightness of the present? If he can see a great distance, can he not see near at hand?

Surely that Divine being who discerns the end from the beginning must know the things that occur now. And it must be true that "Thou God seest us," even the whole of us, the entire race of man.

The Particular Doctrine: God Sees Me

"Thou God seest *me*." There is a disadvantage in having too many hearers, as there is always in speaking to more than one at a time, because persons are apt to think, "He is not speaking to me."

Jesus Christ preached a very successful sermon once when he had but one hearer. He had the woman sitting on the well, and she could not say that Christ was preaching to her neighbor. He said to her, "Go, call thy husband, and come hither" (John 4:16). Something He said struck her heart; she could not evade the confession of her guilt.

In regard to our congregations, the old orator might soon see his prayer answered. "Friends, Romans, countrymen, lend me your ears," for when the gospel is preached, we lend our ears to everybody.

We are accustomed to hear for our neighbors and not for ourselves. Now, I have no objection to your lending anything else you like, but I have a strong objection to you lending your ears. I would be glad if you kept them at home for a minute or two, for I want to make you hear for yourselves this truth. "Thou God seest *me*."

God sees you as much as if there were nobody else in the world for Him to look at. If I have as many people as there are here to look at, of course my attention must be divided. But the infinite mind of God is able to grasp a million objects at once and yet to focus as much on one as if there were nothing else but that one.

Therefore you, tonight, are looked at by God as much as if throughout space there were not another creature but yourself. Can you conceive that? Suppose the stars were all blotted out in darkness, suppose the angels were dead; imagine the glorified spirits above are all gone, and you are left alone, the last man, and there is God looking at you. What an idea it would be for you to think of—that there was only you to be looked at! How steadily He could observe you! How well He would discern you! But hear this: God does really look at you this night as much, as entirely, as absolutely without division of sight, as if you were the only being His hands had ever made. Can you grasp that?

God sees you with all His eyes, with the whole of His sight—you—*you*—You—YOU! are the particular object of His attention at this very moment. God's eyes are looking down upon you. Remember that!

God sees you entirely. He does not merely note your actions; He does not simply notice what the appearance of your countenance is; He does not merely observe what your posture may be. Remember, God sees what you are thinking of; He looks within.

In every man's heart God has a window through which He looks. He does not want you to tell Him what you are thinking about—He can see that. He can read right through you.

Do you not know that God can read what is written on the rocks at the bottom of the ocean, even though ten thousand fathoms of water roll above? And I tell you He can read every word that is in your heart; He knows every thought, every imagination, every conception. He even knows unformed imagination—the thought scarcely shot from the bow, reserved in the quiver of the mind. He sees it all, every particle, every atom of it.

> My thoughts, scarce struggling into birth,
> Great God! are known to Thee:

Abroad, at home, still I'm enclosed
With Thine immensity.

Behind I glance, and Thou art there:
Before me, shines Thy name;
And 'tis Thy strong almighty hand
Sustains my tender frame.

Can you appropriate that thought? From the crown of your head to the sole of your foot, God is examining you now. His scalpel is in your heart, his lancet in your breast. He is searching your heart and trying your reins; He knows you behind and before. "Thou God seest me;" Thou seest me entirely.

God sees you constantly. You are sometimes watched by man, and then your conversation becomes tolerably correct. At other times you seek retirement, and you indulge yourselves in things you would not dare to do before the gaze of your fellow creatures. But wherever you are, God sees you.

You may lay yourselves down by the side of the hidden brook where the willows shelter you, where all is still without a sound—God is there looking at you! You may retire to your chamber, and draw the curtains of your couch, then throw yourself down for repose in midnight's gloomiest shade—God sees you there.

I remember going into a castle sometime ago, down many a winding stair, round and round and round and round, where light never penetrated. At last I came to a narrow space about the length of a man.

"There," said the keeper, "so-and-so was shut up for so many years. No ray of light ever penetrated his cell. Sometimes they tortured him, but his shrieks never reached through the thickness of these walls, and never ascended that winding staircase. Here he died, and there, sir, he was buried," pointing to the ground. Though that man had none on earth to see him, God saw him.

Yes, you may shut me up forever, where ear will never hear my prayer, where eye will never see my misery, but one eye will look on me, and one contenance will smile on me, if I suffer for righteousness' sake. If for Christ's sake I am in prison, one hand will be on me, and one voice will say, "Fear not; I will help thee."

At all times, in all places, in all your thoughts, in all your acts, in all your privacy, in all your public doings, at every season, this is true, "Thou God seest me."

God sees you supreme! I can see myself, but not as well as either my friends or foes can. Men can see me better than I see myself, but man cannot see me as God sees me. A man skilled in the human heart might interpret my deeds and translate their motives, but he could not read my heart as God can read it.

No one can tell another as God can tell us all. We do not know ourselves as God knows us. With all your self knowledge, with all you have been told by others, God knows you more fully than you know yourself. No eye can see you as God sees you.

You may act in daylight, you may not be ashamed of your actions, you may stand up before men and say, "I am a public man, I wish to be observed and noticed." And you may have all your deeds chronicled, and all men may hear of them, but men will never know you as God knows you.

If you could be chained, as Paul was, with a soldier at your arm; if he were with you night and day sleeping with you, rising with you; if he could hear all your thoughts, he could not know you as God knows you, for God sees your superlatively and supremely.

Let me now apply that to you: "Thou God seest *me*." This is true of each of you. Try and think of it for a moment. Even as my eye rests on *you,* so in a far greater sense God's eye rests on *you.* Standing, sitting, wherever you are, this is true, "Thou God seest *me*."

It is said that when anyone heard Rowland Hill— whether stuck in a window or farther away at the door—he always had the conviction that Hill was preaching at him. Oh! I wish I could preach like that! If I could make you feel that I was preaching at you in particular—that I singled you out, and shot every word at you—then I should hope for some effect. Try and think, then, "Thou God seest me."

Different Inferences for Different Persons for Different Purposes

To the prayerful. Prayerful man, prayerful woman, here is a consolation—God sees you. And if He can see you, surely He can hear you. Why, we can often hear people when we cannot see them. If God is so near to us, and if His voice is like the thunder, He will be sure to answer us.

Perhaps you cannot say a word when you pray. Never mind. God does not want to hear; He can tell what you mean even by seeing you. "There," says the Lord, " is a child of mine in prayer. He says not a word; but do you see that tear rolling down his cheek? Do you hear that sigh?"

Oh, mighty God! You can see both tear and sigh; you can read desire before desire has clothed itself in words. God can interpret the naked wish. He does not need us to light the candle of our desires with language; He can see the candle before it is lit.

He knows the desire, when words stagger under the weight of it. He knows the wish when language fails to express it. "Thou God seest me." Ah, God, when I cannot pray with words, I will throw myself flat on my face, and I will groan my prayer. If I cannot groan it I will sigh it. And if I cannot sigh it I will wish it.

When these eye-strings break, and when death has sealed these lips, I will enter heaven with a prayer that you will not hear but which you will see—the prayer of my inmost spirit, that God may be the strength of my life and portion forever.

There is comfort for you, you praying ones, that God sees you. That is enough; if you cannot speak He can see you.

To the anxious. Some here are very full of care and doubts, anxieties and fears.

"Oh, sir!" you say, "if you could come to my poor house, you would understand why I feel anxious. I have had to part with much of my furniture to provide myself with a living. I am brought very low. I do not have a friend in London. I am alone, alone in the wide world."

Stop, stop, Sir! You are not alone in the world; there is at least one eye seeing you; there is one hand that is ready to relieve you. Don't give up in despair. If your case is so bad, God can see your care, your troubles, and your anxieties.

For a good man, it is enough to *see* destitution to relieve it, and for God it is enough to see the distresses of His family at once to supply their wants. If you were lying wounded on the battlefield, and if you could not speak, you still believe your comrades, who are coming by with an ambulance, will pick you up, if they but see you; and that is enough for you.

So, if you are lying on the battlefield of life, God sees you. Let that cheer you! He will relieve you, for He only needs to see the woes of His children at once to relieve them. Go on then; hope yet; in night's darkest hour, hope for a brighter morrow. God sees you, whatever you are doing.

To the slandered. There are some of us who receive a large share of slander. It is seldom that the slander market is much below par; it usually runs up at a very mighty rate. There are persons who will take shares to any amount. If men could dispose of railway stock as they can of slander, those who happen to have money here would be rich by tomorrow at 12 o'clock.

There are some who have a superabundance of that matter; they are continually hearing rumors of this, that, and the other. There are fools who do not have brains enough to write sense, nor honesty sufficient to keep them truthful, who, therefore, writes the most infamous libels concerning some of God's servants.

Well, what does it matter? Suppose you are slandered; here is a comfort: "Thou *God* seest me." They say that such-and-such is your motive, but you need not answer them. You can say, "God knows that matter."

Suppose you are charged with such-and-such a thing and you are innocent. Your heart is right concerning the deed because you didn't do it. Well, you have no need to battle for your reputation. You need only point your finger to the sky, and say, "There is a witness there who will right me at last—there is a Judge of all the earth, for whose decision I am content to wait. This answer will be a complete exoneration of me, and I will come out of the furnace, like gold seven times purified."

Young men, are you striving to do good, and are others imputing wrong motives to you? Do not be particular about answering them. Just go straight on and your life will be the best refutation of the charges.

David's brothers said that in his pride and the naughtiness of his heart he had come to see the battle. "Ah!" thought David, "I will answer you soon enough." Off he went across the plain to fight Goliath. He cut off his head and then came back to his brothers with a glorious answer in his conquering hand.

If any man desires to reply to the false assertions of his enemies, let him go and do good; he does not need to say a word—his actions will be his answer. I am the object of detraction, but I can point to hundreds of souls that have been saved on earth by feeble instrumentality.

My reply to all my enemies is this, "You may say what you like, but seeing these lame men are healed, can you say anything against them? You may find fault with the style or manner, but God saves souls, and we will hold up that fact, like giant Goliath's head, to show you that although it was nothing but a sling or stone, so much the better, for God has gotten the victory."

Go straight on and you will live down your slandered. Remember, when you are most distressed, "Thou God seest me."

To some of you who are ungodly and know not Christ, what shall I say to you but this. How heinous are your sins when they are put in the light of this doctrine! Remember, sinner, whenever you sin, you sin in the teeth of God. It is bad enough to steal in darkness, but he is a very thief who steals in daylight.

It is vile, it is fearfully vile, to commit a sin that you desire to cover, but to do my sin when man is looking at me shows much hardness of heart. Ah, sinner, remember, you sin with God's eyes looking on you. How black must be your heart! How awful your sin, for you sin in the very face of justice when God's eye is fixed on you.

I was looking the other day at a glass beehive, and it was very interesting to observe the motions of the creatures inside. But this world is nothing but a huge glass beehive. God looks down on you, and He sees all. You go into your little cells in the streets of this huge city. You do to your business, your pleasure, your habits, and your sins.

But remember, wherever you go, you are like the bees under a great glass shade—you can never get away from God's observation. When children disobey before the eyes of their parents, it shows that they are hardened. If they do it behind their parents' back, it proves that there is some shame left. But you sin when God is present with you; you sin while God's eyes are searching you through and through.

Even now you are thinking hard thoughts of God while God is hearing all those silent utterances of your evil hearts. Does not that render your sin extremely heinous? Therefore, I beseech you, think of it, and repent of your wickedness, that your sins may be blotted out through Jesus Christ.

And one more thought. If God sees you, O sinner, *how easy it will be to condemn you.* What will you think, O sinner, when you are brought before God, and God shall say, "Thou didst so-and-so." What will you do when he mentions what you did in the darkness of the night when no eye was there?

You will start back amazed and say, "Oh, heavens! How does God know? Is there knowledge in the Most High?" He will say, "Stop, sinner; I have more to startle you with yet." And He will begin to unfold the records of the past; leaf after leaf He will read of the diary He has kept of your existence.

Oh! I can see you as He reads page after page: your knees are knocking together, your hair is standing on end, your blood is frozen in your veins, congealed for fright, and you stand like a second Niobe, a rock bedewed with tears.

You are thunder struck to find your thoughts read out before the sun, while men and angels hear. You are amazed beyond degree to hear your imaginations read, to see your deeds photographed on the great white throne, and to hear a voice saying, "Rebellion at such a time; uncleanness at such a time; evil thoughts at such an hour; blasphemy at such a time; theft at such an hour; hard thoughts of God at such a period; rejection of His grace on such a day; stiflings of conscience at another time" and so on to the end of the chapter.

Then there comes the awful final doom: "Sinner, depart accursed! I saw you sin; it needs no witnesses. I heard your oath; I heard your blasphemy; I saw your theft; I read your thought. Depart! depart! I am clear when I judge you. I am justified when I condemn you: for you have done this evil in My sight."

You ask me what you must do to be saved. I will never let a congregation go, I hope, until I have told them that. Hear, then, in a few words, is the way of salvation. Christ said to the apostles, "Preach the gospel to every creature. He that believeth and is baptized shall be saved; but he that believeth not shall be damned" (Mark 16:15, 16).

Or, to give you Paul's version, when he spoke to the jailor, he said, "Believe on the Lord Jesus Christ, and thou shalt be saved."

You ask what you are to believe. Why, this: That Christ died and rose again; that by His death He bore the punishment of all believers; and that by His resurrection He wiped out the faults of all His children.

If God gives you faith, you will believe that Christ died for you, and will be washed in His blood, and you will trust His mercy and His love to be your everlasting redemption when the world ends.

The Boundless Love of God

John Henry Jowett (1864-1923) was known as "the greatest preacher in the English-speaking world." Born in Yorkshire, England, he was ordained into the Congregational ministry. His second pastorate was at the famous Carr's Lane Church, Birmingham, where he followed the eminent Dr. Robert W. Dale. From 1911-18, he pastored the Fifth Avenue Presbyterian Church, New York City, and from 1918-23, he ministered at Westminister Chapel, London, succeeding G. Campbell Morgan. He wrote many books of devotional messages and sermons. This message comes from *Things That Matter Most,* published in 1913 by Fleming H. Revell Co.

John Henry Jowett

11

THE BOUNDLESS LOVE OF GOD

I have loved thee with an everlasting love (Jeremiah 31:3).

WHAT IS THE biggest thing on which the human mind can reflect? In what can we most easily lose ourselves in the overwhelming sense of the immeasurable?

There are the vast lone spaces of the stellar fields, peopled with countless worlds, crossed by mysterious highways, with stars as the pilgrims, ever moving on their unknown journeyings. We can lose ourselves there.

There is "the dark backward and abysm of time," opening door after door of ever-receding epochs, back though twilight and dawn into the primeval darkness, where the inquisitive mind falters and faints. And we can lose ourselves there.

There is the appalling wilderness of human need, beginning from my own life, with its taint of blood, its defect of faculty, its dreary gap in circumstance and condition, and repeated in every other life in every street, in every city and village and country through out the inhabited world. And we can lose ourselves there.

And then there is the deadly, ubiquitous presence of human sin, in all its chameleon forms—well-dresses, ill-dresses, blazing in passion, mincing in vanity, and freezing in moral indifference and unbelief. All these are stupendous themes, and the mind that ventures upon them is like the dove that ventured upon the waste of waters, and, soon growing weary of flight, returned to the place of its rest.

But there is something more majestic than the heavens, more wonderful than the far, mysterious vistas of time, more pervasive than human need, and more abounding than human sin. *The biggest thing with which the mind can cope is the infinite love of God.* All our sanctified powers and all the ministries of holy fellowship, and all the explorations of eternity, will never reach a limit in its unsearchable wealth.

The biggest thing you and I will ever know is the love of God in Jesus Christ our Lord. There will always be "a region beyond," and for the already wondering eyes there will always be a new surprise: "The height, and depth, and length, and breadth, and to know the love of God, which passeth knowledge" (Eph. 2:18, 19).

Its Height

Let us reverently gaze into the *height* of the love of God. In love the scale of height is measured by the degree of purity. The height in the scale of diamonds is determined by an analogous standard. A diamond is of the "first water" when it is without flaw or tint of any kind. And love is lofty in proportion to its brilliance.

Love can be deteriorated and degraded by the tint of jealousy. It can be debased by the tint of envy. It can be vulgarized by a strain of carnal passion. These earthly elements may be mixed with the heavenly substance, and its spiritual value is reduced.

So the first test to apply to any love is the test of purity. This is the test of height, the test of how far it is sublimated and separated from selfish and fleshly ingredients that dim and spoil its luster.

Now, it is here Scriptures begin in their revelation of the love of God. They begin with its brilliance, its holiness. "In him is no darkness at all!" How would that be as a description of a diamond? "No darkness at all!" Nothing sinful in His love! But more than that. Nothing shady in it, nothing questionable, nothing compromising or morally indifferent! No darkness at all; no blackness of faithlessness; no twilight of forgetfulness; "no night there!"

And thus it is that when the Book guides us in the contemplation of the eternal love, it first leads us into the contemplation of the eternal light. Always and everywhere this is where we begin.

If I listen to the psalmist, he leads me into the holy place: "Exalt the Lord our God, and worship at his holy hill; for the Lord our God is holy" (Ps. 99:9). If I listen to the prophet, I am led into the same sacred precincts: "The high and lofty One whose name is holy" (Isa. 57:15).

If I listen to the mystic seraphim of the Old Testament, I hear them cry one to another, "Holy, holy, holy is the Lord of hosts" (Isa. 6:3). If I listen to the songs of the Apocalypse, I find them burdened with the same theme: "They rest not day and night saying, Holy, holy, holy, Lord God Almighty" (Rev. 4:8).

If I reverently listen to the Master in His secret communion with the Unseen, I hear Him say, "Holy Father" (John 17:11). And if I listen to the prayer which He Himself teaches me to pray, I am led immediately to the holy glory of the Lord: "Our Father, . . . hallowed by thy name" (Matt. 6:9).

Always and everywhere this is the beginning of our contemplation. We are led away into the light, into the unshadowed brilliance, into the holiness of God. If, therefore, God's love is symbolized by a mountain, its heights will be clothed in the dazzling whiteness of the everlasting snow.

Love's heights are found in love's holiness. "God is light," "God is truth," "God is love."

From this primary teaching I wish to adduce *two inferences.* The first is this: *The force of love always depends upon its height.* We find the analogy in water. The force of falling water is determined by its height. It is even so with love. There is a type of love that has no vigor because it has no height. It is a weak, sickly sentiment that just crawls about you. It is low and, therefore, it has no enlivening force. It is mixed with earthly elements and, therefore, it has no heavenly quickening. It enervates, it does not invigorate. The more holy love is, the higher it is, and the more fraught it is with vitality.

How, then, must it be with the love of God? Born in holiness, it has power enough to waken the dead. Have you seen an Alpine river, born amid the snows, and rolling gloriously though the valley?

That is the figure we need: "And I saw a river of water of life, clear as crystal," proceeding from "the great white throne" (Rev. 22:1), out of the unshadowed depths of eternal holiness. "There is a river the streams whereof shall make glad the city of God" (Ps. 46:4), and the holy power of that river is determined by the holy heights in which it is born.

The second inference is that *the ultimate ministry and goal of love are also determined by the height of its holiness.* Once again seek your analogy in water. Water rises no higher than its source. Water can lift no higher than its source. It is even so with love. Our love can never raise a loved one higher than the love itself.

There are aspects of that law which are altogether staggering. Take the love of a parent for his child. Our own tainted love will not lift our child into purity. Our own jealous love will not lift our child into an unembittered disposition. Our own envious love will not lift our child on to moral serenity.

Our love will not lift above its own level. That is the solemn responsibility of a lover: That if his love is low, it will scarcely lift the beloved one above the plains. If we want to lift higher, we must heighten our love.

How, then, is it with the love of God? His love, so glorious in holiness, can raise to its own level, and lift us into "heavenly places in Christ Jesus" (Eph. 2:6). "They shall sit with me on my throne." "*God so loved* the world that he gave his only begotten Son, that whosoever believeth on him should not perish, but have *everlasting life*" (John 3:16). God's love imparts its own loveliness, until one day we too shall be "altogether lovely."

From the supreme height of the highland plateaus on the island of Arran, there comes rolling down the granite slopes a gloriously alive and vitalizing stream. They call it "The White Water," and it is well named. It gleams on the slopes like the whitest foam. From a distance out at sea, when everything else was obscure,

I could see the white water running on its ceaseless errand.

Oh, the loveliness of its bequests, and the unutterable beauty of its dells and glens! It feeds the bracken, it nourishes the stalwart heather, it moistens the retiring fern. The White Water endows its haunts with its own loveliness.

And the white water of the eternal love, ceaselessly flowing from the holy heart of God, brings with it power to make everything lovely, and at last to present everything spotless before the throne.

Its Depth

Let us gaze into its *depths*. Let me link together detached sentences from the Word, that in their associations we may discern what is meant by the depth of the love of God. "The high and lofty One whose name is holy." "He is gone to be guest with a man that is a sinner!" "Jesus, knowing that the Father had given all things into his hands, and that he was come from God, and went to God . . . began to wash the disciples' feet." "And one cried with another, saying, Holy, holy, holy is the Lord!" "Neither do I condemn thee: go, and sin no more!"

All these are suggestive of what is meant by the love-depths of our God. And on these I want to build this teaching, that it is only the really lofty that can truly reach the really deep. The arm that can reach far upward is the only arm that can reach far downward.

It is only holy love that can deal with humanity's deepest needs. A low love has no depths of service. Low love is a thing of compromise and has no dealings with extremes, whether of holiness or of sin.

Pharisaic love had no height. "I thank thee I am not as other men are." That is not loftiness. It is superciliousness; it is not vision from the snow-white hills. And because Pharisaic love had no height, it had no corresponding depth. When the Pharisee saw One descending into the deep pits of human need, he cried in self-respecting amazement, "He eateth and drinketh with publicans and sinners!" (Mark 2:16).

Holy love, crystalline love, goes down and down into human necessity, and it is not afraid of the taint. Sunbeams can move among sewage and catch no defilement. The brilliant, holy love of God ministers in the deepest depths of human need.

God's love is *deeper than human sorrow*. My appointed lot gives me daily and deepening experience of how deep that is. But drop your plum line into the deepest sea of sorrow, and at the end of all your soundings, "underneath are the everlasting arms." God's love is deeper that death, and there are multitudes who know how deep grim death can be.

"Just twelve months ago," said a near friend of mine a week or two ago, "I dug a deep grave!" Yes, and I know it was deep enough. But the grave-digger's spade cannot get beneath our Father's love. God's love is deeper than the deepest grave you ever dug! "And entering into the sepulcher they saw an angel" (Mk. 16:5), and you can never dig into any dreary, dreary dwelling of death that is beyond the reach of those white-robed messengers of eternal love.

Yes, God's love is *deeper than death*. "O death, where is thy sting? O grave, where is thy victory?" (1 Cor. 15:55).

And God's love is *deeper than sin*. One night, when I was crossing the Atlantic, an officer of our boat told me that we had just passed over the spot where the *Titantic* went down. I thought of all that life and wreckage beyond the power of man to recover and redeem. I thought of the great bed of the deep sea, with all its held treasure, too far down for man to reach and restore.

"Too far down!" And then I thought of all the human wreckage engulfed and sunk in oceanic depths of nameless sin. Too far gone! For what? Not too far down for the love of God!

Listen to this: "He descended into hell" (Eph. 4:9) and He will descend again if you are there. "If I make my bed in hell, thou art there" (Ps. 139:8). "Where sin abounded, grace did much more abound" (Rom. 5:20). "He *bore* our sin" (1 Peter 2:24); then He got beneath it, down to it and beneath it. There is no human wreckage, lying in the ooze of the deepest sea in iniquity, that His deep love cannot reach and redeem.

What a gospel! However far down, God's love can get beneath it!

> Stronger His love than death of hell,
> Its riches are unsearchable:
> The first-born sons of light
> Desire in vain its depths to see,
> They cannot tell the mystery,
> The length, and breadth, and height!

Its Breadth

Let us gaze into its *breadth*. Here again I want to say that the breadth of love is determined by its height. Low love is always very confined and exclusive. Lofty love is liberal and expansive.

Low love is like a lake; lofty love is like a river. We can imprison a lake within our own estate; we cannot imprison a river. It will be out, and about, and on! Sometimes we foolishly try to imprison the love of God. We make His love too narrow by false limits of our own. Men have tried to appoint social limits, national limits, ecclesiastical limits, and credal limits. We may as well try to break up the sea into allotments as to "peg out" the love of God.

The love of God is as broad as the race, and nowhere is there a single man in any climate, or of any color; in congested city, in tropical jungle, or in a lonely frontier line where a pioneer has built a primitive home— nowhere is there a single man, woman, or child who is orphaned of a place in the eternal Father's heart. O Love of God, how broad!

Its Length

And what of its *length?* There is no end to it. To what length will it not go? "Greater love hath no man than this, that a man lay down his life for his friends" (John 15:13). To that length! "Becoming obedient unto death, even the death of the cross!" (Phil. 2:8). To that length! "Goeth after that which is lost until he find it" (Luke 15:4). To that length!

God's love is as long as the longest road. God's love is as long as the longest day. God's love is as long as the longest night. God's love is as long as life. God's love is as long as eternity.

"I have loved thee with an everlasting love" (Jer. 31:3).

"I will never leave thee *nor* forsake thee" (Heb. 13:5).

"Love never faileth" (1 Cor. 13:8).

NOTES

Immutability: God's Crowning Attribute

Arthur John Gossip (1873-1954) pastored churches in
England and Scotland before becoming Professor of
Practical Theology at Trinity College, Glasgow. He gave
the Warrack Lectures on Preaching in 1925, published
under the title *In Christ's Stead,* and he published several
books of sermons. He was not a dramatic preacher, but
the intensity of his delivery and the depth of his message
and character attracted and held the listeners. Perhaps
his most famous sermon is "But When Life Tumbles In,
What Then?" which he preached the Sunday after his
wife suddenly died after what was supposed to be minor
surgery. This sermon taken from his book, *From the Edge
of the Crowd,* published in 1924 by T. & T. Clark,
Edinburgh, Scotland.

Arthur John Gossip

12

IMMUTABILITY: GOD'S CROWNING ATTRIBUTE

If we disown Him, He also will disown us; and even if our faith fails, He remains true—He cannot prove false to Himself (2 Timothy 2:12-13, Weymouth).

WE OFTEN ACT more or less out of character, in a way that on the stage would strike playgoers as extremely improbable. But in real life anything may happen, and these natures of ours have no fixed geography as yet. They are like a world still only half-solidified, subject to unexpected cataclysms and upheavals.

A quiet countryside that has dozed drowsily for centuries may reel under an earthquake shock. Amid the snows and thick-ribbed ice of Arctic lands there may appear, incongruously, a wide lava torrent, boiling and seething. And in the most unlikely people, ugly sins may suddenly show through. Hot passions that have never been suspected blaze up in hungry flames, leaving us gaping at an incredible thing.

To our bitter cost we all know how, when we are tired and rushed and put about, we are not ourselves. As people put it charitably, we are peevish and crabby. We do not know why we are so cross and touchy, yet we cannot get back into the accustomed smooth ruts in which we normally travel. Instead, we go bumping and jolting through a horrid day till we come to ourselves again.

Surely we sympathize with the person who plaintively exclaims with much self-pity, "Really I am a decent, kindly, likeable soul, only there is another horrid fellow with repulsive ways, who will come at times and sit in my clothes, use my name, and get mistaken for me."

In all of us there is a queer element of unexpectedness, the erratic eccentricities of which can never be predicted. The pattern of our character does not run through the web from end to end, but breaks off suddenly and in the oddest ways into some other, here and there, that clashes with it noisily.

We never can be quite sure of ourselves. At any moment we may act out of harmony with the whole architecture of our nature, like that strange breakaway-from-plan in Ripon Cathedral, or like a river that has burst its banks and goes roaring, not in its real bed at all.

God's Character Never Changes

But, say the Scriptures, the crowning glory of God is that He never acts out of character. He never falls below His best, He cannot be false to His own blessed nature. This means that if even once you come upon Him with no clouds and darkness around Him to confuse your mind, blur your vision, and tempt you to imagine things that are not there; if even once you meet Him face to face, then you know what He always is. You can depend upon that absolutely and forever.

The wonderful thing about Christ is that as people looked at Him, followed Him, and watched Him, it became apparent to them that this is what God must be like. They concluded that if there is a God at all, then He must have Christ's eyes, Christ's ways, Christ's ever-helpful hands, Christ's character. We can safely argue this fact, for the creature cannot morally out-top the Creator; a greater cannot be formed from a least.

Do not forget, says Scripture, that what God is, He always is. Stand upon Calvary and know that if today He loves like that, He always loves like that. Yes, even when our hearts become hot and suspicious of Him or soured and bad-tempered toward Him for His ordering of our lives and crossing our wishes, He still loves us.

Christ knew that it is not easy to believe that. What was it in Him that first drew you to the Master? "God," said Emerson, "enters by a private door into each individual." And what, I think, attracted me to Him at the beginning was not even His compassion, nor His generosity in judgment, nor His odd faith in hopeless-looking folk. It was His winning honesty—the daring way in which He states the case against Himself and the tenets most dear to Him—that drew me to Christ. He puts into words, quite staggering in their boldness, the doubts that hover in the background of our minds, but which we ourselves would hesitate to express.

I know, He says, that days will come when this gospel of Mine will seem a mere exasperation, disproved by the hard facts of your life. Sometimes your tried hearts will be tempted to hurl it from you impatiently as a thing visibly untrue.

Love, love! Where is there any trace of loving-kindness of God's way toward me? Is He not rather like a grouchy neighbor who will not bother to give what cost him nothing, and would make all the difference to me? A Father! Or an unjust Judge, who callously refuses what are my bare dues? We can always trust Christ to have thought things through and to have seen the other side of them. He is the Christ whose own life was so difficult and whose own faith was so tremendous. And His happy creed was no fairweather thing that a drop or two of rain would smudge and crumple and make run.

Carlyle, at times of trial, could not stand what he estimated to be the cheap and easy and dishonest optimism of Emerson's mind. Carlyle thought of him irritably as one standing well up on the beach, out of the spray, chattily throwing a cheery word or two to poor souls wrestling for their very lives in great dark deeps, with thunderous billows knocking the breath out of them. Emerson's view of God was naïve, according to Carlyle.

God Is Always Love

But it was from the darkness round the cross that there rings out a voice so sure that God is love. Stand there for a moment, and surely you feel that, there and then at least, beyond all doubting, God was love. But in Him there are no moods, no caprice, no changeableness.

Do what you will to Him. However you may hurt and disappoint and break His heart, you cannot alter His essential nature. After all, in spite of all, through it all, He is still love toward you. Look, cries Christ, pointing to a cluster of farmer's huts, high on a sunny slope, there is a man openly irreligious, impudently immoral, yet God's sunshine does not skip his fields!

If you have really been at Calvary, have really seen it all with your own eyes—if you know it and are sure of it—then, remember, that is not a mood from which He might pass, but His mind is settled toward you.

His love for you is not something outside of God's ordinary life to which He once turned aside, one supreme effort to which He braced Himself, and then fell back upon a lower and more selfish mode of being. It is a sudden revelation of what His divine existence always is.

Always to be God means to stoop lower by far than any man could stoop, to bear what never a human heart would dream of bearing, to give oneself with an abandon of unselfishness that leaves us staring at something almost unbelievable.

God's wisdom is not wisdom, but omniscience. His power is not power as we know it, but omnipotence. Likewise, His love is a hugeness beyond all human reckoning. It is an everlasting Calvary.

Our mood changes, our emotions cool; for us there come dreary seasons of gray skies and dripping spiritual weather, but God does not change. What we saw Him to be, He still is.

As James put it very grandly, think of the glory of a midsummer day, in that hushed hour of noon when everything is still, and the sun blazes down in its meridian splendor until every nook and cranny lies saturated and soaked through and through with warmth and light. Ah! but the sun dips, and the shadows lengthen, and the chill of evening comes, and then the dark.

But God's love is a sun that never sets. It is always, always, at its full noonday glory! He can never fall below His best, He cannot be untrue to His own nature.

If we could only be quite sure of that, and always certain of God's Christlikeness, would not a mass of difficulties be as good as over! Plato, you remember, likened this life of ours to a wild tumbling sea. He said that the best we can do is to knock together, as best we can with our poor numbed fingers, some makeshift raft of speculation. On that raft perched precariously, we may make our slow way, wet and miserable and in constant danger, to some kind of land. Yet there is some surer Word of God on which we can ride safely. There is. But having found it, fools that we are, in rough weather, just when we need it most, we let the blasts and heavy seas sweep us away from it again, and once more we are struggling in stormy waters.

Sometimes we are quite sure that God is love, and then one of the grim facts of life knocks at our door, wilting and withering our faith like a wild flower suddenly touched by the scythe's sharpness. Or perhaps the web of our days grows sad—colored and grey. We doubtingly ask, "Can it be hands that were pierced for us that weaves this for us?" Clouds rise from our own frightened minds, and we cry desperately that the sun has been extinguished.

If only we could understand that whenever and wherever God meets us we are dealing with the heart we see on Calvary. If only we would see that whatever comes to us, it is He who gave His Son, His best, His all, who sends it to us. Then, if facing trouble, we could say with Fraser of Brea, "this is a harsh-featured messenger, yet he comes to me from God; what kindness does he bring me?"

If, like Dante (whose sour mind waded intrepidly down to the lowest deeps of hell because on the gates he had read the tremendous words, "Eternal love made me"), we had grasped, in a richer way than he did, that wherever we come upon God, He is the same God still—still love, still eagerness to help, still thrilled to spend Himself for any confused, blinded, blundering lost soul that will accept it.

If, like Festus in Browning, immersed in life's perplexities, we could take our stand on this as a fixed fact, "God, Thou art Love, I build my faith on that," we could tolerate whatever life may send us. Then we would pull ourselves together, saying, "But I did climb Calvary, did see with my own eyes. I know in whom I have believed and am persuaded that He, who loved me there like that cannot have grown harsh to me now. Would we not then face whatever was coming unafraid, meeting it with gallantry and calm?

God Is Always Holy

Yet it is desperately hard not to fall back at times into the foolish notion that God is like ourselves; sometimes better, sometimes worse, kind yesterday no doubt, but strangely forgetful now, inconsistent and incalculable as we are.

For one thing, the God we see on Calvary is a Holy God—One who loathes evil and to whom it is horrible that stately creatures like us should be soiled by it. God will make no compromise with it, but cost Him what it may, He will hunt it down and chase it from His universe, and grind it into annihilation.

That we know. That is our hope—that the power behind things is stubbornly set on righteousness; that the original make-up of the world is opposed to evil: that this is no haphazard place, a mere chaos and welter of moral confusion, where anything may or may not happen. We know that to sin is to fling ourselves against the powers that be; that evil is insanity, leading one straight, sooner or later, to inevitable punishment. That is the settled basis upon which we build our thinking.

A great nation wrongs the world, and we appeal to God with confidence, living through dark days unafraid, because He is on the throne. Much is amiss in the earth, so when nothing happens and reform is slow to come, we boldly lay hands upon immortality, claim all eternity, argue that if things do not right themselves here, then there must be something more where evil does go down and where good does come to its own. It must be, we say. God must be holy or the ground gives beneath our feet, and human life is a mere gibbering madhouse.

Yet, although so sure of that in theory, nonetheless we are apt instinctively to deny it when life seems to contradict it. To assume that God is inconsistent and self-contradictory, that He makes exceptions and will surely do so in our favor; and that His laws are not laws, strictly speaking, with tremendous sanctions at their back, rather mere good advice, which we can take or leave; and that at times He lets go His holiness, stoops to unblushing favoritism, if it can be given such a name.

At a funeral we are all apt to take it for granted, in the face of very tremendous and outspoken Scriptures, that whatever the dead man may have been, all is now made somehow well for him. And, in truth, seeing that we have all failed and come short of God's glory, what can we frail blunderers do but leave our erring fellow and ourselves to God's illimitable mercy, and that hopefully.

Yet we carry it far. I once stood looking down at a dead scoundrel who had left a sinister trail of misery behind him though the years. His character had been a kind of upas tree, the deadly drip of which had poisoned and killed every fair thing upon which its shadow fell. "Ah, well!" said his wife softly, "he is at rest now."

One wondered if he were: if all the vivid warnings of the grim consequences of deliberate sin are only nursery tales, with no substance behind them. And then there came a memory of that day when Christ was preaching and was interrupted by the rending of rafters overhead, the falling dust, and then the sudden sky broke through. Eager, heated faces peered down as they lowered a poor object, too far gone to have a touch of faith himself, before the Master's feet. He looked up gratefully, smiled at these hot, resourceful, desperate friends, "Your faith has saved him," He said happily; and it did.

God's love is very wonderful, and He seizes upon any loophole so perhaps, that woman's faith and sturdy affection that years of ill-usage had not killed, might somehow have pulled him through.

Yet, where it touches us and our dear ones, we just do not believe that God is holy. We feel that His moral laws will swerve, will bend aside on our behalf. We think He is much too good-natured to mean what He says, or really to stand by it.

We are well aware that there are many things in our character that ought to be put right, yet we are not alarmed, and leave them there, feeling that God will find some way to evade His own solemn words and let us off. It is the vainest of vain dreams! He cannot, and do we wish it? That is a fearsome prayer of Luther, "O Lord God, punish us, we pray Thee, punish us, but be not silent toward us!" Yet sometimes we can pray it.

In any case, whether we like it or not, there is a dreadful truth in the great fact of Karma that lies, like a shadow, over so much of the East. "Sow an act, and you reap a habit; sow a habit, and you reap a character; sow a character, and you reap a destiny," as Thackeray put it in words long ago grown trite, and they seed themselves so inevitably.

God Is Always Calling the Lost

It is not that God changes. Always His hands keep seeking, always His voice is calling, calling, calling our name like a mother calls her lost child's, desperate until He finds us. Only, there is the fearsome mystery of the human will. We think that we can set ourselves against the Almighty, can resist Him, can look Him impudently in the face and openly defy Him. Sometimes it is the rebel soul that has its way!

There came a time when even the tenderest of the prophets, rejected, broken-hearted, and beaten, cried out in despair, "Ephraim is joined to his idols, let him alone" (Hos. 4:17). There was a day when Jesus Christ, with His eyes full of tears, could only cry, "O Jerusalem, how often would I have gathered thee; and ye would not! Behold, your house is left unto you desolate" (Matt. 23:37, 38).

John Donne, whom some rank as perhaps the noblest of all English preachers, had a tremendous passage that some critics put among the best of English prose. It is appalling in its terrible, slow, accumulating coldness of horror, until the heart is not far from screaming. "It is a fearful thing to fall into the hands of the living God: but to fall out of the hands of the living God, is a horror beyond our expression, beyond our imagination."

Then, after musing upon His inexplicable patience toward us—how time after time, thwarted and denied, He begins again as hopefully as ever in some yet other way—he ends, "that this God at last, should let this soule goe away as a smoake, as a vapour, as a bubble; and that this soule cannot be a smoake, a vapour, nor a bubble, but must lie in darknesse, as long as the lord of light itselfe, and never sparke of that light reach to my soule—to be excluded eternally, eternally, eternally from the sight of God!"

That is great English, but the words are not well-chosen. No one is excluded from God's presence; but one can shut himself out. God cannot be false to His own nature; "if we deny Him He will deny us." We cannot have both sin and Him; it must be one or other. Sin is always a madman's choice. Let us beware lest, like miserable Judas throwing down his accursed pieces and hating himself for his incredible folly, we too stand one day looking down bewildered at the poor little nothings, faded and rotted, that lie in our hand, trying to take it in, to beat it into our stunned brain, "For this, for this, for this, I have lost God!"

But to end there would mean there would be no gospel, but one of those half-truths which can be, of all things, the most cruelly untrue. Ben Jonson held the opinion that even Shakespeare would have been a greater writer, if he had not "forgot that last and greatest art, the art to blot." Few things in the New Testament are so interesting and illuminating as its corrections and its emendations. "That you may know the love of Christ," writes Paul. Then he pauses, turns back, and puts his pen through that. He writes above it, "that is silly, you can never know it, for it passes knowledge." Or, to the Galatians, "Now that ye know God," and then he strokes that out, and substitutes, "or, rather, are known of Him."

So here in 2 Timothy Paul also paused, looking back, and read what he had quoted, the ink not yet dry: "If we deny Him, He will deny us." He did feel that is true, and yet it might mislead. So he added the glorious parallel fact which is even more foundational: "if we are faithless, He remains faithful—for He cannot be untrue to Himself!" That is the teaching of Christ.

Moses, in his day, had a high moment when God was so real and near to him that he seemed to see and hear Him proclaiming Himself as "the Lord God, merciful and gracious, long-suffering, and forgiving transgression and sin." His people never forgot that. Though they failed, they came back to God each time at last. They took His promise in their hands, and boldly held it before Him, pleading, "You have told us that You would be gracious and forgiving always. You put no limit to it; You gave no conditions. Therefore, have pity on us, who need You so, and pardon us out of pure grace.

God Keeps His Promises

You too have had high moments when God was very close: the day your mother died, the first day in a home of your own, or when a little one was born to you. Your heart was touched and tender, and you swore you would be faithful. You made a convenant with God and He with you. Oh, it is long ago now, and you had quite forgotten, have grown and dusty, and quite ordinary after all! But God remembers. He still stands by His covenant. His promises still hold and are open to you. He faithfully abides, even if we fail.

That is the dominant note of Scripture—the amazing, persistent loyalty of God. You hear it everywhere. "Turn ye, turn ye, for why will ye die, O house of Israel?" (Ezek. 18:31). "All day long I have stretched out imploring hands to you" (Rom. 10:21). God, says Paul, haunts us like a begger not to be repulsed. He keeps following us and breaking in on us again whenever He sees any chance of gaining our attention. He pleads with us to be reconciled to Him, who has nothing but love in His heart for us.

The son in a far country, says Christ, forgot all about the father, but the father all the time remembered him. He saw him far off because his eyes were always searching the road by which he must come, and he always was slipping out to look for him. "That's him," he cried, when he at last saw a far-off, shabby, hesitating, limping figure. "That is surely him," and he ran to him.

It is a wonderful reading of God's heart, and oh, the splendor of the fact that it is true! We sin, and God's answer is love; we heap up more sin, and He gives more love; we make our sin an inexcusable thing, and His answer is Calvary. Though we are faithless, He abides faithful to His own essential nature. He cannot be untrue to Himself.

When Oliver Cromwell, the Protector, died, it was a wild September day with the winds howling, and his soul had to wade through a deep patch of darkness. He asked his minister, "Tell me, is it possible to fall from grace?" "No, it is not possible." "Then I am safe, for I know that I was once in grace." And again, "I think I am the poorest wretch that lives, but I love God; or rather am beloved of God." Again that same correction! Again that clinging to the thought that, though we fail, God will stand to His convenant! It is our only hope.

I think that minister was too audacious. I have fallen from grace a thousand times. I have grown cold and hard and torpid—sick of the whole business. But it is strangely difficult to escape from God. He follows us, haunts us, hems us in, will not be repulsed nor take refusal! Once in the flock of the Good Shepherd, we have at our back an immensity of sleepless skill and patience that, however often we may spill through each inviting gap in every hedge, finds us again.

It is slow work, herding sheep—slow tiring work! They are so apt to stray and to follow one another. They are so stupid and so easily tired. They are flustered into yet another stampede by just nothing at all. Yet it is a poor shepherd who loses even one.

And the most comfortable passage in the Bible is that in which Christ tells us that His own good name and honor and obedience to God are bound up in His getting us home safely: "I came down, not to do Mine own will, but the will of Him that sent Me: and this is the will of Him that sent Me, that of them that He hath given Me, I should lose—not one" (John 6:38, 39). If you are not there at the last, Christ's glory will be dimmed. "But," God will say to Him, "did I not tell you I must have that soul of Mine? Where is it?"

That is what the Calvinists meant by their doctrines. They were not proud, but very humble. They could find no standing ground within themselves, so they flung themselves on God. They built, not upon their faith, but on God's faithfulness; not on their love to Him so fickle and uncertain, but on His love to them, steady and sure. They did not build on their puny ineffectual efforts, but upon His eternal thoughts and plans. And so must you and I.

"One of the most convenient hieroglyphics of God," says Donne in a more Christian place, "is a circle; and a circle is endless; whom God loves, He loves to the end; and not only to their own end, to their death, but to His end; and His end is that He might love them still."

"Often and often," says Samuel Rutherford, "I have in my folly torn up my copy of God's convenant with me. But, blessed be His name, He keeps the principal in heaven safe; and He stands by it always."

SCRIPTURE TEXT INDEX

The reading of these sermons will enrich your life, and enhance your skills as an interpreter, teacher, and communicator of God's truth.

CLASSIC SERMONS ON CHRISTIAN SERVICE

Dynamic principles for Christian service will be found in these classic sermons by highly acclaimed pulpit masters. The Christian preacher or teacher will find many exciting insights to instruct and motivate participation in serving others.

CLASSIC SERMONS ON FAITH AND DOUBT

Twelve pulpit giants give you inspiration and devotional challenge for your faith in this book of sermons. Preachers and lay persons alike will be encouraged and find great blessing in these forceful messages.

CLASSIC SERMONS ON PRAYER

Pulpit giants present the need, the how-to, and the results of a life that is permeated with prayer. These classic sermons will energize your prayer life.

CLASSIC SERMONS ON SUFFERING

These pulpit giants provide you with resource material for comfort and solace and offer perspective, understanding, and encouragement for the depressed and brokenhearted.

CLASSIC SERMONS ON THE CROSS OF CHRIST

Inspiring sermons on perhaps the most significant event the world ever experienced—the Cross of Christ. The reader will gain a greater understanding of the theological, devotional, and practical importance of the Cross of Christ.

CLASSIC SERMONS ON THE PRODIGAL SON

These sermons offer unique insights into perhaps the most famous of Christ's parables and provide new understanding of the relationships between the son, father and other son. Believers will also be challenged to apply the wonderful truth of the Father's love to their own lives.

CLASSIC SERMONS ON WORSHIP

Rediscover the beauty of worship! A positive tool for understanding what the Bible says about worship and applying these vital truths to our lives and churches.